London

www.baedeker.com

Verlag Karl Baedeker

SIGHTSEEING HIGHLIGHTS ✶✶

The British Museum, Buckingham Palace, Big Ben – everyone knows these and other highlights of London. But some other sights, not quite so well known, are equally worth seeing.

Greenwich
Figurehead of the Cutty Sark, once the fastest tea-clipper

Buckingham Palace
Guards in bearskin hats

National Gallery
John Constable's »Hay Wain«

Westminster Abbey
Chapel of Henry VII

Tower of London
St Edward's Crown is part of the Crown Jewels.

BAEDEKER'S BEST TIPS

To enjoy your stay in London, you ought to know about the highlights. But for the city to be revealed in all its fascination, you need a little bit more than that: Baedeker's best tips on London.

■ Hear Samuel Pepys
An eye-witness report on the Great Fire of 1666. ▶ **page 29**

Samuel Pepys
witnessed the Great Fire and kept a diary.

■ Save money
Find out online about events that don't cost the earth and museums with free admission. ▶ **page 103**

■ Queens Market
An exotic market off the beaten track – immerse yourself in another world.
▶ **page 109**

■ Tour in a double-decker
On the top deck – but not necessarily in a tourist bus. ▶ **page 139**

■ www.royal.gov.uk
The royal family online – the Windsors present themselves. ▶ **page 156**

■ Bar with a view
Look out over the roofs of London from the terrace up on the second-to-top floor of the Royal Opera House.
▶ **page 163**

■ Rail & River Rover
When you go to Greenwich, make the trip a treat. ▶ **page 175**

■ Trafalgar Tavern
This pub on the Thames in Greenwich has hardly changed since it opened in 1837.
▶ **page 179**

Trafalgar Tavern
At high tide the Thames almost floods the bar.

■ From Hampstead to Highgate
A walk across London's high places.
▶ **page 183**

■ Souvenirs of London
Attractive gifts from Liberty department store. ▶ **page 202**

Tower of London
He makes sure that every visitor has a ticket.

Chinatown
A cultural and gastronomic experience

Always welcoming:
London pubs
▶ **page 67**

BACKGROUND

The griffin, heraldic animal of the City
▶ **page 18**

PRACTICALITIES FROM A to Z

Sightseeing by bus
► page 119

TOURS

The Great Court of the British Museum
► page 148

London Eye – the world's largest observation wheel
► page 251

SIGHTS
FROM A to Z

Houses of Parliament
▶ **page 187**

London police – wearing the famous helmet
▶ **page 290**

Background

LONDON IS QUITE SIMPLY
FASCINATING: A GLOBAL
FINANCIAL CENTRE AND
A MULTICULTURAL CITY
WITH IMPERIAL HERITAGE –
BACKGROUND INFORMATION
ON ONE OF THE WORLD'S LEADING CITIES.

A TRULY COSMOPOLITAN CITY

What is London? There is more than one way to look at it: for some »London« means only the City, the historic site of Roman and medieval London known as »the square mile« which is now the financial district. The City has no more than 5,200 residents, but during the day they have to share the square mile with almost 400,000 commuters who work there.

In official terms London is the Metropolitan County of Greater London and is more or less identical to the built-up area. However, its 7.3 million inhabitants live in areas so diverse that many of them think of themselves not as Londoners but as residents of, for example, Richmond. A third definition of London is the »capital region«

inhabited by more than 12 million people. There is one point on which everyone can agree: London is the capital of the United Kingdom, seat of the monarchy, parliament and the government, capital of the Commonwealth and above all a truly cosmopolitan city. Even first-time visitors to London cannot escape the feeling that they are seeing familiar sights – with well-known names on all sides, this is not surprising. Who hasn't heard of Buckingham Palace, Piccadilly Circus, Carnaby Street and Hyde Park? Is there anyone who doesn't know what Big Ben and Tower Bridge look like?

Monarchy
Buckingham Palace is the Queen's London residence. When she is at home, her standard flies from the roof.

Must-See Places and Other Sights

The fame of the city and its landmarks help visitors to London to enjoy their stay. What is the best way of getting to know the city? There are enough must-see places to fill a long trip: monuments to the imperial past, on Whitehall for example, historical landmarks like the Tower and Westminster Abbey, architectural gems such as St Paul's Cathedral and the Lloyd's Building, the fantastic theatre scene and the superb museums. A measure put through by Mayor Ken Livingstone which was initially highly controversial has made London a more pleasant place to visit: he introduced the congestion charge, a toll for every vehicle that enters inner London. The results speak for

Democracy
The heart of English democracy beats in Parliament. Big Ben stands guard.

Anachronisms
guard in a bearskin hat with modern equipment: one of many anachronisms that give London its charm.

Shopping heaven
It would not be hard to believe that shopping was invented in London. There are countless opportunities to spend money – in the food halls at Harrods, for example.

Multicultural

All the peoples of the earth meet in London – more than that, they live there, and celebrate festivals. The most spectacular is Notting Hill Carnival.

Inviting

No-one can claim to know the city without going inside a London pub.

Souvenirs

A policeman's helmet for the kids? A pocket-sized Tower Bridge? Union Jack underwear? There is no lack of souvenirs, and who wants to argue about taste

themselves: a 38% fall in road traffic, an increase in the number of cyclists and sales of bicycles, a clear run for buses on roads that used to be chronically jammed – London has changed visibly as a result. Not only that: the city treasurer is counting the financial blessings of the congestion charge and the fines for contravening it.

London is more than its essential sights: the life of the city is waiting to be discovered. Try taking a quiet walk through Hyde Park – in the morning, when the first joggers and horse-riders are out; in the afternoon, when nannies are wheeling babies through the park; or in early evening, when its grassy spaces are used for games of football and family picnics. Or watch London life in a pub – after work in the City, when noisy groups of bankers enjoy their free time; in a peaceful place like Greenwich on a sunny afternoon; or with the butchers of Smithfield market, when early risers sink the first pint of the day. Get to know London from the top of a double-decker bus, stroll through Chinatown or the Caribbean market in Brixton, take high tea in the Ritz – there is no more varied or multicultural way to spend a day.

The message to all those who have heard about British cooking but not yet tried it is: fear not! It is nowhere near as bad as its reputation; but if steak and kidney pie or Yorkshire pudding really are more than you can stomach, take consolation in such delights as Chinese dim sum, Indian lentil soup or Caribbean shark steak. The choice is unlimited – at least, for diners with an unlimited budget. London is, in truth, the most expensive city in Europe. Londoners feel this most of all in the exorbitant costs of buying or renting accommodation (a family of five can expect to pay £1000 per week in a perfectly normal residential area), tourists can easily pay £40 for an evening meal for two in a basic restaurant, and the price of a pint of beer in a pub is approaching £3.

All of this seems to have little effect on the drawing power of this fascinating city, which attracts 11.5 million visitors every year. Forty years after the invention of the mini-skirt, London is still swinging!

Modern

A pine cone? A gherkin? Whatever it resembles, Sir Norman Foster's Tower is an added attraction on the City skyline.

Facts

London is a colourful melting pot for all the peoples of the world and a centre of the global economy. The powerhouse that generates employment is the City. And anyone who is dissatisfied or wants to change the world only has to go to Speakers' Corner in Hyde Park.

Population · Politics · Economy

As early as the 17th century, when the city had a population of 500,000, London's importance as a place of manufacturing and trade attracted immigrants from all over the world. Huguenots in the 17th century were followed by the Irish in the 18th century. In the early 19th century African and Chinese immigrants settled in the dock areas, and after 1880 the main newcomers to the East End were Jews from eastern Europe. After the Second World War immigrants came from the West Indies, Africa, Cyprus, India and Pakistan, in the 1980s many Arabs. The number of residents in the City decreased steadily from the mid-19th century (1851: 130,000, today about 5,200), whereas the population of Greater London rose from 2.2 million in 1841 to more than 7.3 million today.

Ethnic diversity

Many parts of London are dominated by a particular ethnic group: Jamaicans in Brixton, Trinidadians in Notting Hill, Bangladeshis in the East End, Indians in Southall, Chinese in one part of the West End and rich Arabs in Kensington. The resulting rich mixture of peoples produces a unique cultural diversity expressed in restaurants, shops, festivals and traditions.

On the other hand this concentration of different cultures causes conflicts over issues of local autonomy, educational and cultural institutions, equal career opportunities – there are hardly any persons from ethnic minorities in top political and business positions – and religion. On top of this there are social problems that particularly affect Londoners from ethnic minorities: 23% of all employed persons and no less than 41% of all children (the highest percentage in Great Britain) live below the poverty line according to the official definition – in Europe's most expensive city.

Poverty in the most expensive city in Europe

Inner and Outer London

Twelve of the 33 London boroughs are grouped together to form Inner London. The others are known as Outer London. After the dissolution of the Greater London Council (GLC) in 1986 by the Thatcher government – the city council was too left-wing for Margaret Thatcher – the city administration was an unworkable, chaotic mix of responsibilities exercised by local authorities and government bodies. In May 2000 under the Blair government, the citizens of London elected a mayor for the whole city for the first time – they chose a left-wing critic of Blair, Ken Livingstone, and re-elected him in 2004 – and a 25-strong city council, the Greater London Assembly, which replaced the boroughs as the highest administrative au-

← *Democracy at its best: everyone can express an opinion at Speakers' Corner. However, there is no guarantee that anyone will listen.*

The griffin guards the boundary of the City.

THE CORPORATION OF LONDON

The constitution of the City of London, the so-called Corporation of London, is based on rights established in the Middle Ages and still operates according to age-old practices.

The Corporation of London has the same rights as the other, less ancient boroughs, but in addition exercises other powers such as that of policing the City. The Court of Common Council, which roughly corresponds to a city council, holds its meetings in Guildhall. It consists of the **Lord Mayor**, 24 **aldermen** and 131 **common councilmen**, the representatives of the 25 wards of the City who are elected each December; the aldermen, who are elected for life, and the Lord Mayor, himself an alderman, also represent the wards. The Common Council emerged in the 12th century from informal meetings of the Lord Mayor with the aldermen and was officially elected for the first time in 1384.

The Lord Mayor ...

The Lord Mayor is elected on Michaelmas Day for a one-year term. For this purpose a meeting of the liverymen, the representatives of the livery companies, is held. The list of candidates is read out and two are chosen by show of hands. The aldermen then elect one of these two to be Lord Mayor. On the Friday before the second Saturday in November the Lord Mayor elect is sworn in by his predecessor in the Silent

The city guard awaits the new Lord Mayor.

Ceremony, during which hardly a word is spoken. As part of a splendid procession on the following day, the Lord Mayor's Show, he goes to the Lord Chief Justice in a golden coach and takes his vows of office. On the following Monday the Lord Mayor's Banquet, which the prime minister and members of the royal family attend, is held in honour of the outgoing Lord Mayor.

... and his Assistants

The position of Sheriff is one of the traditional offices of the City. It has existed since the 7th century. The liverymen elect an Aldermanic Sheriff, who must be an alderman, and a Lay Sheriff, who does not have to be an alderman. They are charged with carrying out the orders of the High Court of Justice, and they accompany and assist the Lord Mayor, who is required to have served a term as Sheriff. Further important offices are

those of the Town Clerk (responsible for administration), the Chamberlain of London (responsible for finances), the Comptroller and Solicitor (responsible for law and order), the Remembrancer (master of ceremonies) and the Secondary Sheriff and High Bailiff of Southwark.

The Livery Companies

The livery companies developed from medieval guilds, and their name derives from the robes worn by members, known as **liveries**. Nowadays they act mainly as charitable organizations. Of the 97 livery companies that exist today, the following, known as the **Great Twelve**, are the oldest: the grocers, fishmongers, skinners, haberdashers, ironmongers, clothworkers, vintners, salters, tailors, goldsmiths, drapers and mercers. Only the goldsmiths, fishmongers and vintners still have responsibilities for regulating their trade.

London Boroughs

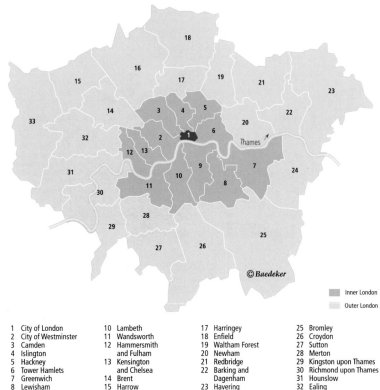

Inner London
Outer London

1 City of London	10 Lambeth	17 Harringey	25 Bromley
2 City of Westminster	11 Wandsworth	18 Enfield	26 Croydon
3 Camden	12 Hammersmith	19 Waltham Forest	27 Sutton
4 Islington	and Fulham	20 Newham	28 Merton
5 Hackney	13 Kensington	21 Redbridge	29 Kingston upon Thames
6 Tower Hamlets	and Chelsea	22 Barking and	30 Richmond upon Thames
7 Greenwich	14 Brent	Dagenham	31 Hounslow
8 Lewisham	15 Harrow	23 Havering	32 Ealing
9 Southwark	16 Barnet	24 Bexley	33 Hillingdon

thority. The government of the City of London (▶ Baedeker special p.18), by contrast, goes back to the Middle Ages.

Global Financial Capital

London as a place of business means the City, the world's leading financial centre: 324,000 are employed in the »square mile« alone. The pre-eminent event in recent business history was the **Big Bang** on 27 October 1986, when the London Stock Exchange abolished a host of restrictions and became an open market for transactions in stocks. A larger number of stocks are traded on the London Stock Exchange today than on any other exchange; London is the place where the most banking transactions (over £300 billion, close to US$600 bil-

Facts and Figures London

© Baedeker

Location
► in south-east England
► latitude: 51° 31' north
► longitude 0 (Greenwich meridian)
► 75km/47mi west of the mouth of the Thames

Area
► 1579 sq km/610 sq mi (Metropolitan County of Greater London)
► 2.6 sq km/1 sq mi (City of London)

Population
► 7.3 million (Metropolitan County of Greater London)
► 2.8 million (Inner London)
► 5,200 (City of London)

In comparison
► Berlin 3.4 million
► Paris 2.1 million
► New York 8.1 million

Government
► 33 boroughs
► head of government: Mayor of London

Economy
► leading stock exchange in the world measured by number of stocks quoted
► world's largest insurance market
► world's largest banking centre (daily turnover £300 billion, almost US$600 billion)
► centre of the British press

Transport
► principal airport: Heathrow, fourth-largest in the world with over 60 million passengers per year
► main system of transport: underground railway (tube); network 405km/252mi long, 3 million passengers per day

Addresses
► London's postal districts are designated by an alphanumeric code. The first part of the postcode gives a broad indication of where the address is located: the letters show the compass direction, and the number stands for a district, e.g. SW 3 is Brixton.

DOWNING STREET SW1
CITY OF WESTMINSTER

► E   = east
► EC   = east central
► N   = north
► NW   = north-west
► SE   = south-east
► SW   = south-west
► W   = west
► WC   = west central

lion, per day) are carried out. The consequence of this is that more American banks have a branch in London than in New York. The London Metal Exchange is one of the leading markets for raw mate-

rials and precious metals, and Lloyd's, the world's largest and oldest insurance exchange, is also based in London. It almost goes without saying that the Baltic Exchange is one of the principal global markets for container shipping – over half of the world volume is transacted here. Thanks to Sotheby's and Christie's auction houses the city is the global centre for the art business, and 11.5 million visitors annually make London the number one city as a tourist destination.

Heart of the British economy 220 of the 500 largest British companies, including Shell, BP and BAT, have their headquarters in London. As the importance OF trade and services has increased to a level (97% of total employment, in-

cluding low-paid jobs) which can hardly rise further, so manufacturing production has fallen. New factories in high-tech industries have mainly been established in the south-east region, to profit from the London market and the infrastructure of the capital, which includes Heathrow airport, the fourth-largest in the world, and the port of London, which remains one of the world's leading ports. Here, however, the centre of activity has shifted. Whereas ocean-going vessels unloaded at the 19th-century docks in the east of London until the 1960s, the container port is now about 25km/16mi east of Tower Bridge in Tilbury. The oil terminals Shellhaven, Thameshaven, Canvey Island and Coryton are even further downstream.

Good for the economy: the pomp and circumstance of the British Empire draw the tourists.

← *Rush hour on London Bridge: every morning tens of thousands pour across the bridge from London Bridge Station to their offices in the City.*

City History

From the »fortress on a pool« – this is thought to be the meaning of the Celtic name for London – to the capital city of an empire: the history of London is also the history of the British Empire. The empire no longer exists, but its traditions live on.

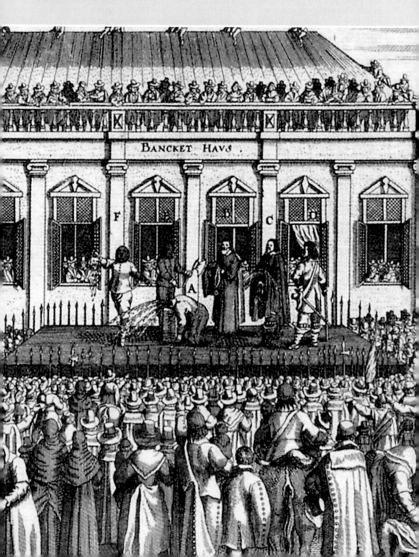

From Roman Times to the Middle Ages

Roman Londinium

AD 43	Start of Roman rule in Britannia
61	Rebellion of Celtic tribes led by Boudica
449	End of Roman rule

In AD 43 the army of Emperor Claudius conquered Britannia, a land occupied by Celts. The Romans established a »colonia« and built a trading-place, Londinium, on the north bank of the Thames. The resistance of the Celts was unsuccessful: in AD 61 the tribal queen **Boudica** burned the Roman settlement to the ground, but it was quickly rebuilt. The buildings of Roman London included a forum, a temple to Mithras and the first bridge across the Thames, made of wood. Londinium became a prosperous Roman city, even though Eboracum (York) and Verulamium (St Albans) were more important. From the year 200 the city was enclosed by a wall, the course of which still approximately marks the boundary of the City. Emperor Diocletian made Londinium the capital of one of the four late Roman provinces of Britannia. However, from 410 the Britannic legions were transferred to Germany, and Roman rule in Britannia came to a final end in 449. Londinium fell into decay.

Saxon Lundenwic

796	Lundenwic becomes capital of the kingdom of Essex
From 1016	Capital of England

Before long the island of Britain was occupied by Jutes, Angles and Saxons. It was the Saxons who established the port of **Lundenwic** outside the Roman walls. In 796 this settlement became capital of the Anglo-Saxon kingdom of Essex. In 851 Lundenwic was destroyed by the Danes, and old Londinium was not resettled until 35 years later, under Alfred the Great. It then grew to be the largest and wealthiest town in England by the 10th century. This period was followed between 1016 and 1066 by a Danish interlude that had far-reaching consequences for the city: London replaced Winchester as capital city of the kingdom under Canute I, and Canute's successor Edward the Confessor moved his residence from what is now the City to the

← *An inglorious end: the death of Charles I on the scaffold in front of Banqueting House on Whitehall.*

new monastery of St Peter in Westminster – a move between the two centres from which London developed.

Norman Period

1066	Battle of Hastings
1176	First stone bridge across the Thames
1189	First election of a Lord Mayor
1215	Magna Carta: right to elect the Lord Mayor
1381	Wat Tyler' s rebellion

In 1066 the Normans invaded England and defeated King Harold at the Battle of Hastings. Duke William of Normandy (William the Conqueror) was crowned in Westminster Abbey as King William I

The shrine of Edward the Confessor in Westminster Abbey

and confirmed the traditional rights of the city of London. The first demonstration of his power was the erection of the White Tower. The following centuries were a period of economic growth, manifested both in buildings – in 1176 Peter de Colechurch built the first stone bridge across the Thames – and in the pride of the London merchants, who established their own governmental institutions: as early as 1189 the guilds elected **Henry Fitzailwyn** as the first Lord Mayor of London. The Crown was repeatedly forced to recognize the citizens' rights: in the reign of Henry I, when London became the capital of England once and for all, it retained its independence as a self-governing city responsible only to the king; Richard the Lionheart signed a charter guaranteeing the rights of London citizens on the river Thames. The independence of the city was sealed in 1215 by the signing of **Magna Carta**, in which King John recognized the right of the guilds to elect the Lord Mayor each year. Regular meetings of the Common Council, an assembly of the Lord Mayor and aldermen that had existed informally since the 13th century, began in 1376. It became an official institution in the late 14th century. Peasants and the poor had no rights; their discontent was expressed in protests such as Wat Tyler's rebellion against poll tax in 1381 and Jack Cade's rebellion of 1450.

Tudors and Stuarts

1485	Start of Tudor rule
1509–1547	Reign of Henry VIII
1565	Foundation of the Exchange
1605	Gunpowder Plot
1649	Execution of Charles I
1665	Plague in London
1666	Great Fire

Tudor period

The rule of the house of Tudor began in 1485 with the accession of **Henry VII** and is traditionally taken to mark the end of the Middle Ages in England. The 16th century was a period of accelerated economic growth for London, thanks to the foundation of trade companies and the establishment of the Exchange by **Thomas Gresham** in 1565. By the end of the century London was the leading trading centre in the western world with a population of 200,000. The political events of this period include the establishment of the Anglican church by **Henry VIII**, who initiated a major building programme – most of it outside the city, for example in Greenwich und at Hampton Court – and brought well-known artists such as Hans Holbein to London.

Stuart period

The 17th century was one of the most turbulent periods in the history of London. The ill-fated attempt of **Guy Fawkes** to blow up Parliament in 1605, the Gunpowder Plot, was a prelude to the struggle for power between the Puritan Parliament and the Catholicizing tendencies of the Stuarts, who held the throne from 1603. London was a focal point of the conflict, which led to civil war in 1642 and culminated in the victory of **Cromwell** and his party and the execution of **Charles I** at Banqueting House in 1649. Eleven years of republican rule (the Commonwealth) were followed in 1660 by the restoration of the Stuart dynasty under Charles II. Hardly had the situation settled down when an outbreak of the plague in 1665 claimed the lives of almost 100,000 Londoners. A second catastrophe occurred just a year later: on the morning of 2 September 1666 the **Great Fire** broke out and raged for four days and nights, reducing four fifths of the City to ashes and destroying 13,200 houses and 84

The City in flames, seen from the south bank of the Thames

THE GREAT FIRE: AN EYE-WITNESS ACCOUNT

The most vivid account of the Great Fire was written by Samuel Pepys (1633–1703), First Secretary to the Admiralty, who described the catastrophe in his diary, one of the most interesting sources on 17th-century London:

2 September 1666

… Jane comes and tells me that she hears that above 300 houses have been burned down tonight by the fire we saw, and that it was now burning down all Fishstreet by London Bridge.

Samuel Pepys, First Secretary to the Admiralty and eye-witness to the Great Fire

So I made myself ready presently, and walked to the Tower and there got up upon one of the high places … and there I did see the houses at that end of the bridge all on fire, and an infinite great fire on this and the other side the end of the bridge …. So down, with my heart full of trouble, to the Lieutenant of the Tower, who tells me that it begun this morning in the King's bakers house in Pudding lane, and that it hath burned down St. Magnes Church and most part of Fishstreete already. So I down to the waterside and there got a boat and through the bridge, and there saw a lamentable fire …. Everybody endeavouring to remove their goods, and flinging into the River or bringing them into lighters that lay off. Poor people staying in their houses as long as till the very fire touched them, and then running into boats or clambering from one pair of stair by the waterside to another. Having stayed, and in

A hopeless struggle

an hour's time seen the fire rage every way, and nobody to my sight endeavouring to quench it, but to remove their goods and leave all to the fire … and the wind mighty high, and driving it into the city, and everything, after so long a drought, proving combustible, even the very stones of churches … We … stayed till it was dark almost and saw the fire grow … and in Corners and upon steeples and between churches and houses, as far as we could see up the hill of the City, in a most horrid malicious bloody flame, not like the flame of an ordinary fire … We stayed till, it being darkish, we saw the fire as only one entire arch of fire from this to the other side of the bridge, and in a bow up the hill, for an arch of above a mile long. It made me weep to see it.

4 September 1666

This night Mrs. Turner and her husband supped with my wife and I at night in the office, upon a shoulder of mutton from the cook's, without any

It made me weep to see it.

napkin or anything in a sad manner but were merry. Only, now and then walking into the garden and saw how horridly the sky looks, all on a fire in the night, was enough to put us out of our wits; and endeed it was extremely

dreadfull – for it looks just as if it were at us, and the whole heaven on fire. I after supper walked in the dark down to Tower street, and there saw it all on fire … and the fire with extraordinary vehemence. Now be-

> !   *Baedeker* TIP

Hear Samuel Pepys

To hear Samuel Pepys, go to the Museum of London, where an audio-visual show presents extracts from the diary about the Great Fire.

gins the practice of blowing up of houses in Tower street, those next to the Tower, which at first did frighten people more than anything; bit it stopped the fire where it was done … And [St] Pauls is burned and all Cheapside.

7 September 1666

Up by 5 a-clock and, blessed be God, find all well, and by water to Paul's wharfe. Walked thence and saw all the town burned, and a miserable sight of Pauls church, with all the roofs fallen and the body of the Quire fallen into St Fayths – Paul's school also – Ludgate – Fleet street – my father's house, and the church, and a good part of the Temple the like.

churches. 100,000 people were made homeless. The First Secretary to the Admiralty, Samuel Pepys, recorded the events in his diary (► p.28).

Sir Christopher Wren was the principal architect entrusted with the task of rebuilding the city. In addition to his greatest work, St Paul's Cathedral, he had built a further 52 churches by the time of his death in 1711. In spite of all disasters, London consolidated its position as a centre of world trade and had a population of 500,000 by the end of the 17th century.

Imperial Capital

In the 18th century Britain began to conquer an empire that spanned the globe and established its position as the leading maritime power. London benefited greatly from this. Magnificent buildings, wide paved streets and a flowering of the theatre reflected its wealth. The industrial revolution brought more and more people to the city. The first official census in 1801 recorded a total population of 860,035, which made London the world's largest city. Social problems grew in step with the population; the foundation of the London Metropolitan Police in 1829 can be seen as an indicator of the growing conflicts. In 1845 Friedrich Engels (1820–1895) described the contradictions of this period in *The Condition of the Working Class in England*:

I know nothing more imposing than the view which the Thames offers during the ascent from the sea to London Bridge. The masses of buildings, the wharves on both sides, especially from Woolwich upwards, the countless ships along both shores, crowding ever closer and closer together, until, at last, only a narrow passage remains in the middle of the river, a passage through which hundreds of steamers shoot by one another; all this is so vast, so impressive, that a man cannot collect himself, but is lost in the marvel of England's greatness before he sets foot upon English soil. But the sacrifices which all this has cost become apparent later. ... The most extensive working-people's district lies east of the Tower in Whitechapel and Bethnal Green, where the greatest masses of London working-people live. Let us hear Mr. G. Alston, preacher of St. Philip's, Bethnal Green, on the condition of his parish. He says:

»It contains 1,400 houses, inhabited by 2,795 families, comprising a population of 12,000. The space within which this large amount of population are living is less than 400 yards square (1,200 feet), and it is no uncommon thing for a man and his wife, with four or five children, and sometimes the grandfather and grandmother, to be found living in a room from ten to twelve feet square, and which serves them for eating and working in.«

Victorian London

1837–1901	Reign of Queen Victoria
1851	Great Exhibition
1863	The first underground railway goes into operation

London developed by leaps and bounds in the reign of Queen Victoria, which began in 1837. The first train ran from London Bridge to Greenwich in 1836. In 1863 the underground railway started operation on the Metropolitan Line between Paddington and Farringdon. A broad belt of suburbs arose around the city. Steam power enabled the docks and factories to grow rapidly, and the demand for workers drew people from the surrounding regions, and increasingly also from the European continent, to London. The Crystal Palace, which was built for the **Great Exhibition** of 1851 can be regarded as a symbol of the period. It no longer exists, but other buildings and streets bear witness to the wave of change that swept over the city: the Houses of Parliament, Trafalgar Square, Victoria Embankment and Regent Street. When Victoria died in 1901, London had a population of 4.5 million and was undisputedly the world's leading city.

Construction of a tunnel for the first underground line

The 20th and 21st Centuries

1940–1945	German air raids
1948	Olympic Games
1952	Coronation of Queen Elizabeth in Westminster Abbey
1986	Big Bang
1997	Funeral of Princess Diana
2000	Greater London has a mayor again
2002	Funeral of the Queen Mother
2005	On 7 July, a day after London was chosen as the venue for the 2012 Olympic Games, a terrorist attack on the underground railway claims 56 lives.

Life in the Underground: the tube tunnels protected Londoners from the »Blitz« in the Second World War. Entertainment was provided, too.

In London, as elsewhere, the two world wars were the dominant events of the first half of the 20th century. In the First World War – the first attack by a Zeppelin airship was in 1915 – the number of casualties of German air raids, approximately 700 killed and 2,000 injured, was relatively small. In the Second World War, however, the German bomber raids of 1940–41 (»The Blitz«) and attacks by the V1 and V2 flying bombs in 1944–45 killed more than 30,000 people. In the City hardly any buildings remained undamaged.

Swinging London and Big Bang Nevertheless, the 1948 Olympic Games were held in London. The mood of optimism lasted: in the 1960s the world of music and fashion revolved around »Swinging« London. However, the end of the British Empire meant a decline in the political and economic importance of London. The demise of the London docks and the associated wave of strikes in 1968 were perhaps the most dramatic illustration of this. The creation of the Greater London Council in 1965 to direct the government of the city was an attempt to solve London's growing problems, but this Labour-dominated body was dissolved in 1986 by Margaret Thatcher. In one other respect, too, 1986 marked a break with the past: the deregulation and reform of the stock exchange, the so-called **Big Bang**, helped London to become a major global financial centre. A city of docks and manufacturing became a centre for the service sector – a development visible from 1982 in the transformation of the Docklands to an office district and an up-market residential area. In May 2000 New Labour gave Greater London not only a new representative assembly and its first mayor – of all people, Tony Blair's old enemy **Ken Livingstone** (»Red Ken«) – but also spectacular new buildings for the new millennium (see p.42). Livingstone's congestion charge for the inner city has resulted in a noticeable reduction of road traffic. In 2005 London was chosen to hold the 2012 Olympic Games. The celebrations were short-lived, as four Muslim suicide bombers caused explosions on three underground trains and a bus, killing 52 people, on the following day.

2006 was the end of the road for a much-loved sight on the streets of the capital: the last Routemaster double-decker buses with their open platform at the back were withdrawn from service. In consolation they will continue to run as a tourist attraction on two routes.

? DID YOU KNOW …?

- … that the government of London is a bastion of the Labour Party? Since 1973 Labour has held the majority in the city council or provided the council leader or mayor.

Arts and Culture

What remains of Roman London? Where is the finest Norman and Gothic architecture in London? What did Sir Christopher Wren build after the Great Fire? Which monuments to their periods in government were left by Margaret Thatcher and Tony Blair?

Remains of the Roman Period

Following the establishment of Roman rule under Emperor Claudius after AD 43, Londinium became a centre of trade. The construction of a wooden bridge near today's London Bridge, where many coins from the Roman period have been found, encouraged the prosperity of the city, which had become the largest in Roman Britannia by the last quarter of the first century AD. Where Leadenhall Market now stands, an imposing basilica was erected with a huge forum next to it. The city had a drainage system and many bath-houses. The harbour, warehouses and the governor's palace were on the banks of the Thames. In 1954 a Temple of Mithras was excavated. The city wall built in the 2nd century was 6m/20ft high and up to 2.5m/8ft thick. It enclosed an area between the Tower and Ludgate Hill, where the Fleet River flows into the Thames. Many exhibits in the Museum of London, behind which a stretch of the city wall has been preserved, demonstrate the quality of life in Londinium.

Basilica and forum

Temple of Mithras

City wall

Norman London

The Normans were responsible for an enormous increase in building activity from the 11th century. The characteristics of Norman architecture are round arches, doorways with archivolts, rectangular and, in the later period, round or clustered piers, arcades and plain wooden roofs, which later evolved into barrel vaults or groin vaults. Decorative elements consisted of simple geometric forms and capitals with human or animal figures. From 1078 to 1097 William the Conqueror had the massive White Tower built within the Roman city wall using limestone from Caen. It marked the beginning of Norman building in the city. St John's Chapel, the apse of which can be seen in the south-east corner of the Tower, is one of the most significant works of early Norman architecture in London. It consists of a nave and two aisles, which continue around the choir. A passage in the form of a gallery runs all around the upper storey, an architectural feature typical of the south of France.

White Tower

A further impressive example of Norman architecture is the choir of St Bartholomew-the-Great. The massive masonry, the narrowness of the bays, the sturdy piers and the moulded blind arcades of the upper storey from the Norman period contrast with the late Gothic windows in the Perpendicular style.

St Bartholomew-the-Great

The first stone bridge across the Thames was the 20-arched London Bridge, built from 1176 by **Peter de Colechurch**. Immediately after its completion houses, shops and a chapel were built on the bridge on both sides of the roadway.

London Bridge

← *This portrait of Charles II by his court painter Anthony van Dyck is unfortunately not on show in London – it hangs in the Louvre in Paris.*

The High Middle Ages: The Gothic Period

Architecture
Early English
style ►

Many elements of Norman architecture are evident in the early Gothic period in England. However, there was a trend for walls to be pierced more, columns to become more slender and windows to take on the form of lancets. This first phase of English Gothic style, Early English, can be seen in exemplary form in **Westminster Abbey**. The proportions of the church, with its nave and two aisles, choir, sanctuary and radiating chapels are those of a French cathedral. The clear and simple tracery shows the influence of Amiens and Reims, while the round-arched trefoils in the arcades above the sedilia are characteristic of the very early Gothic period.

Decorated style ►

The Decorated style which follows breaks open the walls even more and adorns windows and openings with lively forms of tracery and arch. Doorways are decorated with strongly pierced gables, capitals freer in style and more ornamental, and rib vaulting evolves. An excellent example of this style is the late 13th-century Chapel of **St Etheldreda** near Smithfield Market.

Perpendicular
style ►

The Perpendicular style was the dominant style in English architecture until the 16th century. The characteristics of this speciically English version of late Gothic are greater complexity of detail in walls and vaulting, a reduction of flexibility and spontaneity of form, stylized ornamentation and more clearly structured design. Arches and

Gothic architecture of the highest order: Westminster Abbey

windows, which become even larger, gain a stronger horizontal ac-
centuation. In addition to lierne and stellar vaults, the fan vault, a
form unique to England, came into favour. Here the ribs radiate in
the shape of a fan from a single point. The **Chapel of Henry VII** with
its remarkable fan vault adorned with cone-like pendants is an ex-
ceptionally fine example of the Perpendicular style. The outstanding   ◀ Secular
secular building among the few that have survived from the Gothic   architecture
period is **Westminster Hall**, now part of the Houses of Parliament,
with its hammer-beam roof and window tracery. The crypt, assembly hall and main doorway of **Guildhall** date back to the period 1411
to 1439.

Developments in the art of sculpture can be seen by studying funer-   **Sculpture**
ary monuments. Recumbent figures on stone tombs such as the effigies in the **Temple Church** are characteristic of the 13th century. In
Westminster Abbey the tomb of Edmund Crouchback († 1296) represents a new departure. Its lavish architectural framework is derived from the shrines of saints. The sinuous pose of the mourning
figure on the tomb of John of Eltham displays the tendency to create
flowing forms that is apparent by 1250 and was to be a defining
characteristic of English sculpture.

In the 12th century the art of book illustration flowered in England   **Painting**
as at no other time. The native tradition of linearity combined with
influences from the European continent in a lively interchange most
conspicuous in motifs of the Angevin dynasty. **Matthew Paris**, the
most important English painter of miniatures, decorated the manu-
script of Historia Anglorum with illustrations in a manner that appears somewhat archaic and under the influence of the classical style,
but is nevertheless of its time in its naturalism and the emphasis on
emotions. The panels of an altarpiece in Westminster Abbey that has
been dated to the last quarter of the 13th century depict elegant,
elongated figures with light, soft drapery standing close together, one
behind the other. An impression of the secular painting of the period
is given by the frescoes commissioned by Henry III in the mid-
1230s in the so-called Painted Chamber of Westminster Palace. These
works by the court painter **Walter of Durham** have survived only as
18th-century copies.

Renaissance London

The Perpendicular style kept its importance throughout the Renaiss-   **Architecture**
ance period. The Tudor style (approx. 1485–1558) marks a time of
upheaval and transition. Tudor buildings in London include the   ◀ Tudor style
gatehouse, audience chamber and chapel of **St James's Palace**, and
Staple Inn in Chancery Lane. At **Hampton Court Palace** (1514–1540)
Italian decoration in the shape of terracotta medallions showing the
heads of Roman emperors adorns a Gothic building that is typical of

Elizabethan ▶ the Tudor period in its brickwork and especially in the slender chimneys with their geometrical decoration. The Elizabethan style (approx. 1558–1603) is the expression of a magnificent courtly culture that has, however, left few architectural traces in London. New theatres, in particular Shakespeare's Globe Theatre, are the principal

Jacobean ▶ evidence of the flowering of culture in this period. In the Jacobean period (1603–1625) Gothic elements are increasingly replaced by classical forms: classical columns, classical entablatures and symmetry take centre stage, and decoration becomes considerably more lav-

Palladianism ▶ ish. In the period after 1625 the Palladian style gained influence. Its leading exponent was **Inigo Jones** (1573–1652), whose buildings for royal and aristocratic patrons charted a course that was to be followed in later centuries. Sparing, refined decoration and solidity are characteristics of his work, as the severely Palladian **Queen's House** in Greenwich (1616–1635) superbly exemplifies. Jones's principal work, however, was Whitehall Palace, of which the **Banqueting House** (1619–1622) still stands today.

Painting and sculpture The Hornebolte family, invited to England from the Netherlands in about 1530 by Henry VIII, provided a stimulus to miniature painting. **Nicholas Hilliard** (1537/1538?–1618) specialized in portraits limited to the head and shoulders. **Hans Holbein** (1497–1543) played a pioneering role in the development of painting. At first he worked mainly for the merchants of the Steelyard, and later became court painter to Henry VIII. Rational observation and the precise rendering of physiognomy are the basis of his portraiture. Renaissance sculpture in London begins with the commission awarded to **Pietro Torrigiano** (1472–1528) from Florence to create the tomb of Henry VII and Elizabeth of York (1512–1518) in Westminster Abbey. It shows the couple in the traditional manner as separate recumbent figures, richly robed with hands folded. The individual physiognomy and the representation of the bodies, which can be discerned even under the drapery, was much imitated in London.

Sir Christopher Wren's Century

17th century – a period of architectural achievement The 17th century was a golden age for English architecture. Initially, Inigo Jones's style led the way, but the enormously productive figure of the second half of the century was Sir Christopher Wren (1632–1723), particularly through his rebuilding work after the Great Fire of 1666. His church building, including St Paul's Cathedral and a further 52 city churches, demonstrates a diverse and eclectic range. In many instances, however, he continued local tradition. To begin with he collaborated with Jones in Greenwich to extend the Royal Naval Hospital, Queen's House and Observatory. Wren's masterpiece is **St Paul's Cathedral** (1675–1711): the façade with its twin towers and the dome broke new ground. For the two colonnades he was indebted to the Parisian architecture of Perrault, while the upper storeys of the towers are influenced by Borromini's Roman Baroque and reappear in similar form on other towers by Wren. The interior represents a compromise between the basilica plan with a spacious choir, as the Anglican church demanded, and the architect's favoured design of a central plan with dome. As a trial run for St Paul's Wren built **St Stephen Walbrook**, where in the choir a large area with a square ground plan was crowned with a dome as an experiment in central-plan architecture. Wren designed fewer secular buildings; one of them is the somewhat monotonous cuboid east wing of Hampton Court Palace (1689–1692). Along with Sir John Vanbrugh and Nicholas Hawksmoor, Wren evolved around the year 1700 a strangely heterogeneous style of English late Baroque.

18th Century

Richard Boyle, Earl of Burlington, the main proponent of the classical and Palladian ideology, regarded Baroque as an unenlightened Roman Catholic style and brought together a small group of architects who chiefly took their inspiration from Italy. **William Chambers** (1723–1796), for example, drew on French and Roman influences for his classical design of Somerset House. At Kenwood House **Robert Adam** (1728–1792) emphasized the façade with aediculae and a classical portico, but attached more importance to elegant and refined neo-Roman interior decoration.

In 1630 with Covent Garden Piazza, Inigo Jones had been the first to implement the idea of a uniform row of buildings on the model of the Place des Vosges in Paris. However, rebuilding work after the Great Fire was not initially carried out in a uniform manner. Not until the construction of the east side of Gros-

A moral portrait of London: Hogarth's Beer Street (above) and Gin Lane (below)

venor Square was the concept of a standardized façade elevated to the status of an aesthetic principle, expressed in the design of residential buildings on several storeys as a harmonious ensemble in the form of a square, crescent or circus. Grey and yellow brick, light-coloured stucco and, as rhythmic elements, columns, pediments and doorways are the typical features of this restrained style. One of its leading practitioners was **John Nash** (1752–1835), whose major legacy is Regent Street and Regent's Park. At the time of construction from 1811 this was Europe's largest town planning project.

Painting   Until the early 18th century painters from continental Europe were at the forefront in England. The German artist **Sir Godfrey Kneller** (1646–1723), for example, produced elegant portraits, while Italians established the genre of historical painting. The only outstanding English painter was **Sir James Thornhill** (1675–1734) with decorative work such as the dome of St Paul's and ceilings at Hampton Court Palace. The generation that followed re-established the international reputation of English painting: **William Hogarth** (1697–1764) used popular narrative paintings to treat moral issues. He is also famous for his prolific production of copperplate engravings, in which his satirical scenes are based on close observation. **Sir Joshua Reynolds** (1723–1792), taking up the tradition of van Dyck and Rembrandt's manner of chiaroscuro colouring, was a major influence on the development of portraiture. He depicted his subjects, who were taken from polite society, in the poses of well-known antique statues or recreated famous compositions of the Renaissance period. The election of Reynolds as the first president of the Royal Academy in 1768 reinforced his pre-eminent position in the artistic life of London. **Thomas Gainsborough** (1727–1788) provided fresh impulses in the field of landscape painting and established an English Arcadian tradition with carefully composed scenes in which harmonious light colouring is prevalent.

The 19th Century

Architecture   The most significant architectural commission of the 19th century was the rebuilding of the Houses of Parliament, for which the Gothic or Elizabethan style was specified. In 1836 a design proposed by Sir **Charles Barry** (1795–1860) was chosen. It was not until 1860 that the neo-Gothic style achieved complete dominance for secular as well as religious architecture, as at the Royal Courts of Justice. **Sir John Soane** (1753–1837) was appointed as architect of the Bank of England in 1788.

Industrialization created a demand for housing, docks, markets and railway stations. Robert Stephenson and Philip Hardwick built Euston Station between 1835 and 1839 with a monumental entrance in the form of a wrought-iron Doric portico (demolished in 1963); Lewis Cubitt's design for King's Cross Station (1851–1852) had platforms with 24m/

> ! *Baedeker* TIP
>
> **Remains**
> Nothing remains of the wonderful Crystal Palace from the Great Exhibition of 1851. However, visitors to the Museum of London can admire a model of it. And one of the principal attractions of the exhibition survives in part: life-size plaster models of prehistoric animals in Crystal Palace Park.

80ft-wide barrel vaults and a glass façade. The greatest achievement of iron-and-glass architecture was the **Crystal Palace** for the Great Exhibition of 1851. In 1860 work began on the first underground railway. Not long after its opening advertising space could be rented in underground stations, and colourful posters soon added to the charm of the new transport system. Market halls and arcades such as Covent Garden, Burlington Arcade, Smithfield Market and Leadenhall Market bear witness to the prosperity of a city which gained a new landmark of the Victorian Gothic style with the construction of **Tower Bridge** from 1886 to 1894.

In landscape painting **John Constable** (1776–1837) developed his own way of handling colour and light: he captured nuances of light and air, aiming to put atmospheric moods on canvas by painting with free, concise brush-strokes that lent his works the character of sketches in oil rather than of paintings. **J.M.W. Turner** (1775–1851), was a self-taught painter who later attended Reynolds's master-classes and was influenced by his studies of Poussin and Lorrain. He became famous for impressionistic landscapes flooded with light, for scenes of hazy atmosphere and scintillating reflections which he painted without tangible contours, thus creating visionary images that sometimes have symbolic character. The fantastical and mystic art of William Blake (1757–1827) has caused him to be seen as a precursor of the **Pre-Raphaelites**. They took a romantic view of the past, concentrating on the period before Raphael, to which they were attracted by its expression of emotions and moods.

Painting

The 20th Century

The dominant mode of architecture until just after the end of the First World War was a tradition of monumentalism derived from the 18th century. The Piccadilly Hotel and Reginald Blomfield's Regent Street Quadrant are examples of this. A task that became increasingly urgent was the building of suburbs; the »Tecton« group designed the residential blocks Highpoint One and Highpoint Two with incomparable elegance and artistry. After the Second World War the **Festival Hall** represented a new style: concrete, horizontal lines and an impression of built landscape with platforms and bridges are the trademarks of this complex designed by Denys Lasdun. The 1980s saw the emergence of post-modern architecture: **James Stirling** was the architect of the Tate Gallery extension, and in 1986 **Richard Rogers** was responsible for the spectacular new Lloyd's building. The Docklands became a laboratory for modern architecture, bringing forth interesting work such as Cesar Pelli's office tower One Canada Square and Piers Gough's residential building The Cascades.

Architecture

At the start of the new millennium the face of London once again changed significantly. The erection of the world's largest observation wheel, the 131m/430ft-high **British Airways London Eye** on the bank

◄ Millennium architecture

The tilt is intentional: the new City Hall.

of the Thames opposite Parliament, is more interesting in technical than architectural terms. In a further contribution to the world of superlatives, **Richard Rogers** built the **Millennium Dome** in Greenwich, a tent 320m/350yd in diameter and 50m/165ft in height enclosing the world's biggest venue for events. The other British star architect, **Sir Norman Foster**, did not remain idle. His was the intricate design of the Millennium Bridge, a pedestrian link between St Paul's Cathedral and the new Tate Modern in the former Bankside Power Station. He also remodelled the Great Court of the British Museum, covering it with a glass dome. Two of the newest London landmarks are also Foster's work: City Hall close to Tower Bridge and the 180m/590ft-high tower, which has been nicknamed the »erotic gherkin«.

Painting and sculpture

There were three main currents in modern art before the Second World War: the presence of a number of artists from continental Europe such as Hans Arp, Laszlo Moholy-Nagy and Piet Mondrian reinforced the trend to Constructivism, harmonies of pure geometric forms and the rejection of representational art. The most popular avant-garde school was Surrealism, which met with a response in England through, among other influences, Roland Penrose's manifesto. These two currents came together in »Unit One«. The third trend drew on the Impressionist origins of Modernism and took as its subject matter the First World War, but also sexuality, as the sculpture of Jacob Epstein shows.

Post-war art was characterized by a revival of figurative work and the addition of new media: Richard Hamilton and Eduard Paolozzi employed the imagery of the consumer and media society in computer collages. Pop Art became the art form of the Sixties. In the early 1950s **Henry Moore** stood for moderately figurative sculpture, which Anthony Caro developed towards abstraction. In the 1960s the principles of Constructivism were widened to permit a greater degree of expression and emotion. Artists who went their own way were **Francis Bacon**, who took cruelty, violence and suffering as the themes of large-scale works; Frank Auerbach, who practised a wild

Eye-catching, for most people at least: the works of Gilbert & George

and seemingly spontaneous style of painting; and **Lucian Freud**, who unashamedly captured the voluptuousness of his models on canvas. The preferred medium of **Gilbert & George** and Bruce McLean was initially performance art. Later they expressed their ideas as permanent solutions. In the early 1990s artists such as Rachel Whiteread and **Damien Hirst**, who are now established figures, made waves in the art world. The provocative works of these YBAs (Young British Artists) are inseparably associated with the name of Charles Saatchi, patron of the movement.

The prestigious **Turner Prize** is the highest honour for young artists who are out to shock. One winner of the prize, Chris Ofili, caused outrage by his use of elephant dung and pornographic collages in images of the Virgin Mary. A more recent prize-winner, the transvestite potter Grayson Perry (2003), combines traditional ceramics with subversive motifs. Simon Starling, the 2005 prize winner, makes objects and installations. His themes include environmental issues and the transformation of one object or substance into another.

Famous People

What had Henry VIII's divorce to do with the foundation of the Anglican church? How much did Charles Dickens know about the life of the London poor? Who was William Booth? Short tributes to some people who were connected with London.

William Booth (1829–1912)

The soldiers of the Salvation Army command respect in their tireless work to spread the word of God and provide much-needed help in red-light districts and shelters for the homeless. The founder and first general of the organization was William Booth, born on 10 April 1829 in Nottingham. After serving his apprenticeship as a pawn-broker and many years as a preacher, he arrived in London in 1864 and founded the Christian Mission in Whitechapel in 1878. It was the basis of the Salvation Army, which Booth structured along the lines of the British army. Despite the hostility and derision which they attracted, General Booth and his soldiers succeeded in establishing their organization all over the world and gaining widespread recognition by the end of the 19th century. Booth died on 20 August 1912.

Founder of the Salvation Army

Charlie Chaplin (1889–1977)

Oversized shoes, moustache, bowler hat and walking stick: Charlie Chaplin's »Tramp« is one of the immortal figures in film history. Chaplin was born in Lambeth on 16 April 1889, as the son of a music-hall artist, and performed on stage as a child. In 1915 he played the tramp for the first time in the film of the same name. He kept faith with this role, which made him world-famous as early as the 1920s, in such films as *The Kid* and *The Gold Rush* in the United Artists film company, which he founded in 1919 in collaboration with Mary Pickford, Douglas Fairbanks and D.W. Griffith. Chaplin's career continued after the advent of sound films with *Modern Times* and, above all, *The Great Dictator*, a satire on Nazi Germany that, for all its comic side, was a profoundly moving appeal to resist barbarity. After the Second World War his political activity earned him a summons to the Committee for Un-American Activities, and the US government took the opportunity of a trip that Chaplin made to Britain to deny him re-entry to the country. Chaplin then settled in Switzerland. He took on a different type of role in later films such as *Monsieur Verdoux*, in which he played a confidence trickster who married and murdered widows. He died on Christmas Day 1977 in Vevey on Lake Geneva. Although he came to fame in the USA, he always retained his British citizenship.

Actor

Diana, Princess of Wales (1961–1997)

There is no adequate rational explanation for what happened on 6 September 1997 between Kensington Palace and Westminster Abbey. Over 1.5 million people lined the route of the funeral procession of Diana, Princess of Wales, and London drowned in a sea of flowers.

Princess

← Dr Samuel Johnson, a man who never tired of London

Diana,
Queen of Hearts

Diana Spencer became a legend in her own lifetime and the most public personality of the 1990s. When she married the future monarch of the United Kingdom on 29 July 1981 in St Paul's Cathedral, she perhaps did not realize what she had taken on. Her husband knew all too well what was at stake: »Love, whatever that means«. The nation needed an heir to the throne. It was not long before the heir was born, and he soon had a brother, but by then the marriage had already broken down. The images and headlines are familiar: personal coldness shown in public, bulimia, Charles and Camilla Parker Bowles, Diana and her riding-teacher. Separation followed in December 1992, divorce in 1996. But the pursuit of Diana by the paparazzi had only just begun, and it ended on a concrete pillar in Paris on 30 August 1997. The public gave Diana what family life failed to provide: warmth and affection. Diana had clearly succeeded in bridging the gulf between herself and the »common people«. Her own personal fate lent credibility to her sympathy for Aids sufferers, the victims of mine accidents and sick children. Even the royal family now showed signs of human emotions: against all court protocol Elizabeth II ordered that the Union Jack should fly at half mast over Buckingham Palace, and on the evening before the funeral she even made a TV broadcast to her people. Diana's grave in Althorp (125km/80mi north of London) has become a place of pilgrimage.

Charles Dickens (1812–1870)

Author The works of Charles Dickens, who was born on 7 February 1812, provide an outstanding and sympathetic portrait of the life of the poor in London. Dickens had, after all, experienced this life of poverty in his early years in the dockland districts when his father was in prison. Despite this Dickens worked his way up to become a law clerk, parliamentary stenographer, journalist and, in the end, the most successful author of his time and publisher of the *Daily News*. He made his name in 1837 with *The Pickwick Papers*; in such novels as *Oliver Twist*, *Nicholas Nickleby* and *David Copperfield* he created characters with a place in world literature. London was often the scene of his stories, which deal with the plight of the poor and the injustice done to them. Dickens's social campaigning never took place at the expense of his humour, and he was also capable of writing touching pieces such as his Christmas stories. Charles Dickens died on 9 June 1870.

Henry VIII (1491–1547)

King of England Henry VIII of the house of Tudor ruled England from 1509 to 1547. He is remembered as the founder of the Anglican church, for his immoderate life and because he had six wives. Henry, born on 28 June 1491 in Greenwich, was prepared for the throne from his eleventh year onwards. He had a humanist and theological education, was a

Henry VIII, notorious for his succession of wives

model of courtesy, a good dancer and huntsman and a physically imposing figure. Thanks to his chancellor, Thomas Wolsey, the first years of his reign seemed to confirm the high expectations placed in him. In recognition of a polemic that he wrote against Luther (in fact its main arguments came from Thomas More), Pope Leo X even awarded him the title »Defender of the Faith«. When his marriage to Catherine of Aragon failed to produce the desired male heir, Henry resolved to divorce his queen, but the pope refused. The resulting conflict ended in 1533 with the separation of the English church from Rome and the establishment of the Anglican church. Henry then married Anne Boleyn, who bore him a girl, the later Elizabeth I. However, he executed her in 1536 and married Jane Seymour, who died in 1537; then Anne of Cleves, whom he quickly divorced; Catherine Howard, whom he executed in 1542; and finally Catherine Parr, who survived him. In the last years of his life – he died on 28 January 1547 – after he had sent his chancellors Sir Thomas More and Thomas Cromwell to the scaffold, Henry VIII was a mistrustful tyrant.

Alfred Hitchcock (1899–1980)

Film director

»Suspense« was the key concept in the work of Alfred Hitchcock, who was born in London on 13 August 1889. By this he meant not the usual excitement of wondering »who dunnit?«, but a state of tension in the film-goer arising from the fact that the heroes seen on the screen, who are usually perfectly normal people, are caught up in completely irrational situations which either leave the viewer wholly in the dark (e.g. in *North by Northwest* and *Rear Window*) or on the contrary let the viewer know more than the film characters (e.g. in *Psycho*). Hitchcock, who was educated at a Jesuit college, is regarded as one of the greatest film directors. He worked with the leading

Hollywood stars and often appeared in his own films in fleeting roles. He died on 29 April 1980 in Los Angeles.

William Hogarth (1697–1764)

Painter   William Hogarth, the son of a schoolteacher, was born in London on 10 November 1697. He trained as an engraver, and his early employment was to produce copper engravings of book illustrations, but in his spare time he studied painting, and was to become equally distinguished as a painter and engraver. Hogarth was a talented portraitist, as his *Shrimp Girl* in the National Gallery shows, but his forthright nature and unwillingness to flatter were obstacles to success in this field. He is best known for his depiction of the high and low society of the time in narrative series such as *The Rake's Progress* and *The Harlot's Progress*, which he painted with a moral and satirical intent. Two works that highlighted social problems in 18th-century London were *Gin Lane* and *Beer Street*, contrasting the happy residents of Beer Street, where moderation and hard work ruled, with the drunken and impoverished inhabitants of Gin Lane. Hogarth regarded beer as a healthy, truly British beverage and cultivated a patriotism that verged on xenophobia, as in *The Gate of Calais*, showing the arrival of English roast beef in France, and *Taste in High Life*, a defence of English tradition against the perceived foppery of the French and Italians. Indeed Hogarth had a liberating effect on English art, which had previously been dominated by Italian influences. The moralizing narrative series of paintings were conceived as the basis for engravings, which were widely sold. Hogarth died on 26 October 1764 and was buried in the churchyard of St Nicholas in Chiswick in the west of London.

Who was Jack the Ripper?

Jack the Ripper

The most notorious murderer in the criminal history of London was Jack the Ripper. To this day the identity of the man behind the name remains a mystery. He (or she) bestially murdered five prostitutes in Whitechapel in the dark East End of London between August and November 1888: all victims had their throats cut, and from most he removed organs and arranged them around the body. The murderer taunted the police in several letters signed »Jack the Ripper« and announced further murders, but the killing of the 25-year-old Mary Kelly on 9 November 1888 was the last. Panic gripped the East End and the police made enormous, but unsuccessful, efforts –

! Baedeker TIP

The Ripper: Read All About It

... at www.casebook.org: the victims, the suspects, the theories, the witnesses, the newspaper reports. Even the Ripper's letters are reproduced in facsimile.

they even photographed the eyes of one victim in the hope that the face of the killer had been captured on the retina. Today the identity of Jack the Ripper is still the subject of wild speculation; the suspects have included the grandson of Queen Victoria and heir to the throne, the Duke of Clarence, the artist Walter Sickert, a Russian secret agent and a cousin of the writer Virginia Woolf.

Samuel Johnson (1707–1784)

Samuel Johnson, generally known as Dr Johnson, was born in Lichfield on 18 September 1709 as the son of a bookseller. His first visit to London was at the age of three, when he suffered from scrofula, then known as the king's evil, and was brought by his parents to be touched by Queen Anne as a cure. After studies at Oxford and an unsuccessful venture as a schoolmaster, a task in which his scarred face, nervous tics and melancholia were a handicap, Johnson came to London in 1737. His early years in the city were marked by poverty. He worked hard as a journalist and parliamentary reporter, and in 1746 began to produce the first dictionary of the English language, for which he wrote definitions of over 40,000 words and illustrated them with about 114,000 quotations drawn from all fields of knowledge. He also wrote *The Lives of the English Poets* and edited the works of Shakespeare. His fame as the pre-eminent man of letters of the 18th century rests not only on his prolific literary output but also on the brilliance of his conversation, as recorded in the biography written by his Scottish friend James Boswell. He expressed trenchant and much-quoted opinions about Scotland, foreigners, women and many other subjects, but could also be humorous at his own expense, as in his famous definition of a lexicographer: »A maker of dictionaries, a harmless drudge.« He went abroad only once: London, particularly the area around Fleet Street, and its inns and coffee-houses, was his world. He died on 13 December 1784 at his home in Bolt Court. His legacy of quotable remarks includes one of the greatest tributes that could be paid to the city he loved: »A man who is tired of London is tired of life.«

Author

Karl Marx (1818–1883)

Philosopher

After the failure of the revolution of 1848 in Germany Karl Marx, born on 5 May 1818 in Trier on the Moselle and publisher of the newspaper Neue Rheinische Zeitung in Cologne, was expelled from the state of Prussia. Via Brussels he came to London, where after a period living in Dean Street in Soho he settled at 41 Maitland Park Road with his wife Jenny. He struggled to support his family with journalism, often helped by his wealthy friend and collaborator Friedrich Engels. In London – mainly in the Reading Room of the British Library – he wrote his major work, *Das Kapital*. Karl Marx died in London on 14 March 1883; his much-visited grave is in Highgate Cemetery in north London.

Sir Thomas More (1477–1535)

Philosopher and Lord Chancellor

Sir Thomas More, born on 7 February 1477 as the son of a lawyer, attended the best school in London, St Anthony's, and the University of Oxford, and studied law at Lincoln's Inn. In December 1516 he published Utopia, the first-ever work of fiction about an ideal society. It describes a state ruled – in complete contrast to contemporary England or France – by reason and equality where there was no place for exploitation and envy. More had a career at court as adviser to Henry VIII. In 1523 he was elected speaker of the House of Commons and succeeded Wolsey as Lord Chancellor in 1529. His disagreement with Henry came when the king divorced Catherine of Aragon. After the break from the Catholic church, More declined to have any part in Henry's wedding to Anne Boleyn. He finally refused to recognize the king as head of the Anglican church and was thrown into the Tower in April 1534. A sentence of death was passed in July 1535, but More was given five days time to reconsider. He still refused to take the oath and was beheaded on 6 July 1535. His head was placed on a spike at the south end of London Bridge as a warning. Pope Pius XI canonized him in 1935.

Florence Nightingale (1820–1910)

Even as a young woman Florence Nightingale, who was born on 12 May 1820 in Florence, had the reputation of being an expert on health. After managing a hospital during the Crimean War she devoted herself to organizing medical care for the British army and became inspector general of nursing in military hospitals. In 1860 she founded the Nightingale School for Nurses in London, the world's first nursing college. Until her death on 13 August 1910 Florence Nightingale mainly lived in London and pursued her cause with great energy, but not without ruthlessness towards others. From 1857 she was an invalid, although no illness was ever diagnosed, and in addition she was blind from 1901.

The founder of modern nursing

Virginia Woolf (1882–1941)

Virginia Woolf's house in the Bloomsbury district of London was **Writer** the meeting place of the Bloomsbury Group, an association of friends which included E.M. Forster, Vita Sackville-West and John Maynard Keynes. Woolf, born on 25 January 1882 and married to the publisher Leonard Woolf, founded the Hogarth Press with her husband and wrote literary criticism for *The Times*. Through her work as an essayist, diarist and novelist she became the most celebrated female author in England in the 1920s. She suffered from severe depression and committed suicide on 28 March 1941.

Sir Christopher Wren (1632–1723)

Sir Christopher Wren, born on 20 October 1632, became Professor **Architect** of Astronomy at Gresham College in London in 1657 and in Oxford in 1661. At Oxford he began to study architecture and eventually found his vocation in this field after the Great Fire of 1666. He was appointed surveyor general and directed the rebuilding of London. He designed a total of 53 London churches, the Greenwich Hospital and the Chelsea Royal Hospital. His great work, however, was the new building of St Paul's Cathedral, in which he was buried after his death on 25 February 1723 beneath the following inscription: »Lector, si monumentum requiris, circumspice« – »Reader, if you seek a monument, look around you.«

The man who built London

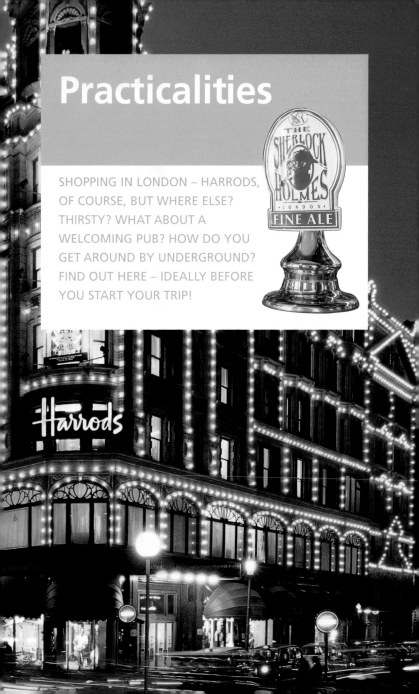

Practicalities

SHOPPING IN LONDON – HARRODS, OF COURSE, BUT WHERE ELSE? THIRSTY? WHAT ABOUT A WELCOMING PUB? HOW DO YOU GET AROUND BY UNDERGROUND? FIND OUT HERE – IDEALLY BEFORE YOU START YOUR TRIP!

Accommodation

Hotels

Book early! Hotel prices reflect the fact that London is one of the world's most expensive cities. Even in the lower price category, a good double room cannot be had for much under £70. It is important to book in good time. Reservation through a travel agent is a way of making significant savings.

Prices The prices given below are average prices for a double room and vary considerably (in the luxury category they can be much higher). As a rule only continental breakfast is included; a supplement is charged for English breakfast. The prices quoted do not normally include the 17.5% VAT which will be added. It is worth asking about special group and weekend rates.

● RECOMMENDED HOTELS

▶ ① etc. see plan p. 84/85
Addresses without a number are outside the area shown.

▶ **Reservations**
Tel. (020) 7 932 2020
http://uk.visitlondon.com

LUXURY: OVER £200

▶ ⑤ **Athenaeum**
116 Piccadilly, W 1
Tel. 7 499 3464, fax 7 493 1860
www.athenaeumhotel.com
Tube: Green Park
155 rooms. For its refined elegance and excellent service the hotel justifiably bears the same name as the nearby club. Tea time in the Windsor Lounge is a treat.

▶ **Basil Street Hotel**
8 Basil Street, SW 3
Tel. 7 581 3311, fax 7 581 3693
www.thebasil.com
Tube: Knightsbridge
93 rooms. Family-run hotel with country-house style, convenient location near Harrods. A favourite address amongst the ladies, as men are not allowed in the hotel's Parrot Club.

▶ **The Beaufort**
33 Beaufort Gardens, SW 3
Tel. 7 584 5252, fax 7 589 2834
www.thebeaufort.co.uk
Tube: Knightsbridge
28 rooms. Extremely elegant and intimate hotel, a stone's throw from Harrods. Only the hotel cat Harry is permitted to disturb the personal service.

▶ ② **Claridge's**
Brook Street, W 1
Tel. 7 629 8860
Fax 7 499 2210
www.the-savoy-group.com/claridges
Tube: Bond Street
197 rooms. One of the most high-class addresses in London, genuinely aristocratic and above all discreet.

▶ ③ **The Connaught**
Carlos Place, W 1
Tel. 7 499 7070, fax 7 495 3262
www.the-savoy-group.com/
connaught
Tube: Bond Street
90 rooms. Old-style British hotel tradition with an interior carved in oak in 1897: discretion is the guiding principle and guests' wishes are treated like holy writ. The best chance of making a reservation is to write a courteous letter, but the hotel does not take everyone, and regular guests take precedence.

▶ ④ **The Dorchester**
53 Park Lane, W 1
Tel. 7 629 8888, fax 7 409 0114
www.dorchesterhotel.com
Tube: Hyde Park Corner
244 rooms. Marble was one of the principal materials used when the hotel was built in 1900. Wonderful view across Hyde Park.

▶ **Eleven Cadogan Gardens**
11 Cadogan Gardens, SW 3
Tel. 7 730 7000, fax 7 730 5217
www.number-eleven.co.uk
Tube: Sloane Square
55 rooms. A stylish, quiet Victorian house in Chelsea with excellent service.

▶ ⑦ **The Goring**
15 Beeston Palace, Grosvenor Gardens, SW 1
Tel. 7 396 9000, fax 7 834 4393
www.goringhotel.co.uk
Tube: Victoria
75 rooms. Generations of the Goring family have run this Edwardian hotel. Service is low-key but extremely attentive.

▶ ⑨ **Hazlitt's**
6 Frith Street, W 1
Tel. 7 341 1771, fax 7 439 1524
www.hazlittshotel.com
Tube: Tottenham Court Road
23 rooms. In the middle of Soho, and the very antithesis of a sleazy establishment. This was once the house of the Prussian consul and is now furnished in traditional English style but run in an unconventional manner.

▶ ⑥ **The Ritz**
Piccadilly, W 1
Tel. 7 493 8181, fax 7 493 2687
www.theritzhotel.co.uk
Tube: Green Park
129 rooms. A flagship of the London hotel trade, situated right next to Green Park. All rooms are furnished in the Louis XVI style. Tea time in the Palm Court is an institution.

▶ ⑪ **Savoy**
Strand, WC 2
Tel. 7 836 4343, fax 7 240 6040
www.savoy-group.co.uk
Tube: Charing Cross
200 rooms. A legendary Victorian hotel with an art deco foyer where afternoon tea is served. The bathrooms are wonderfully old-fashioned but have modern amenities. Rooms with a view of the Thames are more expensive.

MID-RANGE: £100–200

▶ **Abbey Court Hotel**
20 Pembridge Gardens, W 2
Tel. 7 221 7518, fax 7 792 0858
www.abbeycourthotel.co.uk
Tube: Notting Hill Gate
22 rooms. Small, quiet hotel in country-house style in Notting Hill, ideal accommodation for those who value outstanding service.

▶ **Aster House**
3 Sumner Place, SW 7
Tel. 7 581 5888, fax 7 584 4925
www.asterhouse.com
Tube: South Kensington
12 rooms, restaurant, garden. Kensington elegance at a reasonable price, for non-smokers only.

▶ ① **Durrants Hotel**
26 George Street, W 1
Tel. 7 935 8131, fax 7 487 3510
www.durrantshotel.co.uk
Tube: Bond Street
96 rooms. The oldest London hotel still in operation, privately run since 1790, retains the wood-panelled charm of a coaching inn.

▶ **Five Sumner Place**
5 Sumner Place, SW 7
Tel. 7 584 7586, fax 7 823 9962
www.sumnerplace.com
Tube: South Kensington
13 rooms, garden. Individually decorated rooms close to the South Kensington museums.

▶ **Langorf Hotel**
20 Frognal, NW 3
Tel. 7 794 4483, fax 7 435 9055
www.langorfhotel.com
Tube: Hampstead
32 rooms. Extremely stylish for a mid-range hotel. Not centrally located but in the lovely surroundings of Hampstead and excellent value for money.

▶ **L'Hotel**
28 Basil Street, SW 3
Tel. 7 589 6286
Fax 7 823 7826
www.lhotel.co.uk
Tube: Knightsbridge
12 rooms. An English cottage round the corner from Harrods; intimate atmosphere.

► **Abbey House**
11 Vicarage Gate, W 8
Tel. 7 727 2594
www.abbeyhousekensington.com
Tube: High Street Kensington
Victorian style in Kensington,
friendly service, English breakfast
included.

► **Edward Lear**
28–30 Seymour Street, W 1
Tel. 7 402 5401
Fax 7 706 3766
www.edlear.com
Tube: Marble Arch
31 rooms. Good for families and
close to Oxford Street/Marble
Arch.

► ⑫ **Fielding**
4 Broad Court, Bow Street, WC 2
Tel. 7 836 8305, fax 7 497 0064
www.the-fielding-hotel.co.uk
Tube: Covent Garden
26 rooms. Don't expect luxury
here, as the rooms are small (mini
showers!), but the positives are
English breakfast and the central
location in Covent Garden.

► **Hotel 167**
167 Old Brompton Road, SW 5
Tel. 7 373 0672, fax 7 373 3360
www.hotel167.com
Tube: Gloucester Road
19 rooms. Tastefully and individually furnished rooms make this a
little gem among London's budget
hotels.
In Knightsbridge.

► **Lincoln House Hotel**
33 Gloucester Place, W 1
Tel. 7 486 7630, fax 7 486 0166
www.lincoln-house-hotel.co.uk
Tube: Marble Arch
22 rooms. Friendly Georgian hotel

near Oxford Street and Hyde Park.
English breakfast is included.

► **Norfolk Hotel**
20 Norfolk Square, WC 2
Tel. 7 723 4963
Tube: Paddington
Simple, clean accommodation at a
low price: doubles under £50.
Appeals to a young age-group, not
least because it is close to Paddington Station.

► **The Main House**
6 Colville Road, W 11
Tel. 7 221 9691
www.themainhouse.co.uk
Tube: Notting Hill Gate
Minimalist style with white paint
and wooden floorboards.

► **The Pavilion Hotel**
128–10 Sussex Gardens, W 2
Tel. 7 706 3344, fax 7 262 1863
www.delmerehotel.co.uk
Tube: Paddington
Accommodation of acceptable
standard in a Victorian house only
a few minutes from Paddington
Station.

► ⑧ **Windermere**
142–144 Warwick Way, SW 1
Tel. 7 834 5163, fax 7 630 8831
www.windermere-hotel.co.uk
Tube: Victoria
19 rooms. The hotel, which has a
pleasant breakfast room and clean
guest rooms, is much prettier than
the street.

► **Woodville House**
107 Ebury Street, SW 1
Tel. 7 730 1048, fax 7 730 2574
Tube: Victoria
A small hotel near Victoria Station
with a personal touch and a hearty
breakfast.

Other Types of Accommodation

Hostels The English Youth Hostel Association (YHA) and private operators run hostels, which are not necessarily aimed only at young people. Visit London (►Information) has information about this cheap form of accommodation. It is essential to book in advance!

Bed and breakfast (B & B) Bed and breakfast, i.e. a room in a private home with breakfast, is a cheaper alternative to staying in a hotel. B & B can be booked through agencies or in Visit London offices such as the one in Victoria Station.

 HOSTELS / B&B / CAMPING

YHA YOUTH HOSTELS

► **Central reservations**
www.yhalondon.org.uk

► **City of London**
36–38 Carter Lane, EC 4
Tel. 7 236 4965, fax 7 236 7681

► **Oxford Street**
14 Noel Street, W 1
Tel. 7 734 1618, fax 734 1657

► **Earls Court**
38 Bolton Gardens, SW 5
Tel. 7 373 7083, fax 7 835 2034

► **Hampstead Heath**
4 Wellgarth Road, NW 11
Tel. 8 458 9054, fax 8 209 0546

► **Holland House**
Holland Walk, W 8
Tel. 7 937 0748, fax 7 376 0667

► **Rotherhithe**
Island Yard, Salter Road, SE 16
Tel. 7 232 2114, fax 7 237 2919

OTHER HOSTELS

► **The London Hostels Association**
54 Eccleston Square, SW 1
Tel. 7 834 1545

www.london-hostels.co.uk
Ten hostels with basic facilities and a total of 1,100 beds.

► **The Generator**
Compton Place, WC 1
Tel. 7 388 7666
Fax 7 388 7644
800 beds in 7-bed and 8-bed rooms, large self-service restaurant.

BED AND BREAKFAST

► **Best Bed & Breakfast in London**
PO Box 2070, W 12 8QW
Tel. 8 742 8270
Fax 8 749 8736
www.bestbandb.co.uk

CAMPING

► **Information**
Camping and Caravanning Club
11 Lower Grosvenor Place,
SW 1W 0EY
www.campingandcaravanning
club.co.uk

► **Caravan Harbour**
Crystal Palace Parade, SE 19
Tel. 8 778 7155
In south London via the A 205 near the National Sports Centre.

► **Co-operative Woods Caravan Club**
Federation Road, Abbey Wood,
SE 2, tel. 8 310 2233
In Greenwich; signposted from the
M 25 via the A 2.

► **The Elms**
Lippitts Hill, High Beach,
Loughton, IG10 4AW

Tel. 8 803 6900
North-east of London, via M 25
exit 26 towards Waltham Abbey

► **Lee Valley Campsite**
Sewardstone Road, Chingford,
E 4, tel. 8 529 5689
In north London, via M 25 exit 26,
then A 121 and A 112.

Arrival · Before the Journey

How to get to London

For visitors from overseas, except those who live near a Channel port
or have a good connection to the Eurostar fast rail link, the quickest
and cheapest way to get to London is by air. For those travelling
from the more distant parts of Britain, too, a domestic flight may be
preferable to a long trip on the congested roads or much-criticized
rail network. London´s five airports are served by a huge number of
airlines offering direct flights from major intercontinental destinations, every country in Europe and almost all British airports. Luton
and Stansted airports are the main destinations of low-cost flights.

By air

⏵ INFORMATION ON FLIGHTS

AIRPORTS

► **Heathrow**
Location: 24km/15mi west of the city
Information: Tel. (08 70) 0000 123
www.heathrowairport.com
Terminal 1: domestic flights and British airlines to Europe
Terminal 2: non-British airlines to Europe
Terminal 3: flights to Africa, Asia, America
Terminal 4: British Airways
Tube: Piccadilly Line every 5–10 min (5.04am – 11.33pm daily); journey time approx. 45 min. The cheapest way into London. Note that there are two tube stations (one for terminals 1, 2, 3 and one in terminal 4)!
Rail: Heathrow Express to Pad-dington every 15 min (5.07am – 0.01am daily); journey time 15 min from terminals 1, 2 and 3, 22 min from terminal 4; return ticket £25

Heathrow **express**

Bus: Airbus A 2 via Marble Arch to King's Cross Station every 30 min (5.30am – 10.08pm), journey time approx. 1hr 40 min

Taxi: expensive (approx. £45–50) and not necessarily fast due to congestion – the same applies to the other airports

► **Gatwick**
Location: about 40km/25mi south of London
Information:
Tel. (08 70) 0000 2468
www.gatwickairport.com
Rail: Gatwick Express, 30 min journey time to Victoria Station from 6am to 0.30am. Connex South Central to Victoria Station every 15–30 min (5am–midnight), hourly between midnight and 5am. Thameslink to King's Cross, stops in the City (journey time 35 min).
Bus: National Express 025 to Victoria Station (approx. 65 min).

► **Luton**
Location: 51km/32mi north of London
Information: Tel. (015 82) 40 51 00, www.london-luton.co.uk
Rail: Thameslink every 10 min to King's Cross Station (shuttle bus from terminal to station); journey time about 30 min.
Bus: Green Line 757 to Victoria Station; journey time about 75 min.

► **Stansted**
Location: 55km/35mi north-east of London
Information: Tel. (08 70) 0000 303, www.stanstedairport.com
Rail: Stansted Express every 15/30 min, journey time 45 min to Liverpool Street Station
Bus: A 6 to Victoria Station every 15–20 min (24-hour service, journey time 1hr 40min)

► **City Airport**
Location: 10km/6mi east of city centre in Docklands
Information: Tel. 7 646 0088
www.londoncityairport.com
DLR: DLR station at City Airport, journey time to City about 22 min, to Canning Town tube station 10 min.

AIRLINES

► **British Airways**
Reservations tel. (03 45) 22 21 11
Offices: 156 Regent Street, in Harrods and Selfridges stores
Heathrow, terminal 4 tube station
Tel. (08 70) 850 9850
Gatwick, departures terminal
Tel. (08 70) 850 9850

London phone numbers for some other major airlines in the English-speaking world:

► **Aer Lingus**
Tel. (08 45) 084 44 44

► **Air Canada**
Tel. (08 71) 220 11 11

► **Air New Zealand**
Tel. (08 00) 028 41 49

► **American Airlines**
Tel. (08 45) 778 97 89

► **BMI**
Tel. (08 70) 607 05 55

► **Continental Airlines**
Tel. (08 70) 77 64 64

► **Delta Airlines**
Tel. (08 00) 41 47 67

► **easyjet**
Tel. (09 05) 821 09 05

► **Fly Be**
Tel. (08 710) 700 01 23

► **Qantas Airways**
Tel. (08 45) 774 77 67

► **Ryanair**
Tel. (08 71) 245 00 00

► **South African Airways**
Tel. (08 70) 747 11 11

► **United Airlines**
Tel. (08 45) 844 47 77

► **Virgin Atlantic**
Tel. (08 70) 574 77 47

Trains from the London region and other parts of Britain arrive at one of more than ten railway stations distributed around the perimeter of central London. High-speed Eurostar trains from the European continent via the Channel tunnel between Calais and Folkestone arrive from November 2007 at the newly-built St Pancras International station. Journey times from Paris will then be 2hr 15min, from Brussels around 2hr. Passengers from Europe who prefer a sea crossing take the route Hoek van Holland–Harwich, arriving at Liverpool Street Station, or Calais–Dover, arriving at Victoria Station.

By train

◄ *Eurostar*

◄ *Railway stations*

Journeys from other parts of Britain to London are generally cheaper, and sometimes not much slower, by bus than by rail. National Express runs services from all parts of the country to Victoria Coach Station; the cheapest long-distance connections from major British

By bus

⏵ INFORMATION ON RAIL TRAVEL

INFORMATION

► **In Britain**
Tel. (08 45) 748 4950
www.nationalrail.co.uk

► **From Europe**
Tel. (08 705) 84 88 48
Eurostar Tel. (08 702) 18 81 86
www.eurostar.com

TO THE NORTH

► **Euston**
Euston Road, NW 1

► **King's Cross**
Euston Road, NW 1

► **St Pancras**
Euston Road, NW 1

TO THE EAST

► **Liverpool Street**
Liverpool Street, EC 2

TO THE SOUTH

► **Charing Cross**
Strand, WC 2

► **Victoria**
Victoria Street, SW 1

► **Waterloo**
York Road, SE 1

TO THE WEST

► **Paddington**
Praed Street, WC 2

⏵ ROAD TRAVEL: BUS AND CAR

BUS INFORMATION

▶ **National Express bus**
Tel. (08 705) 80 80 80, www.natio-nalexpress.com

▶ **Victoria Coach Station**
Elizabeth Street/Buckingham Palace Road

▶ **Megabus**
Tel. (09 01) 331 00 31
www.megabus.co.uk

AUTOMOBILE CLUBS

▶ **Automobile Association (AA)**
Norfolk House, Priestley Road,
Basingstoke, Hampshire, RG 24

Tel. (12 56) 2 01 23
Breakdown service:
Tel. (0800) 0289 618

▶ **Royal Automobile Club (RAC)**
RAC House, 89–91 Pall Mall,
London SW 1
Tel. 7 930 2345
Breakdown service:
Tel. (0800) 82 82 82

CHANNEL TUNNEL

Eurotunnel:
Tel. (08 705) 35 35 35, www.euro-tunnel.com

cities are offered by Megabus. National Express/Eurolines also runs services from many European destinations to Victoria Coach Station.

By car
Congestion charge ▶

Traffic in inner London is so heavy that it is not advisable to take a car. If you do so, leave the car in the hotel car park. For private vehicles entering the city centre on working days between 7am and 6.30pm a congestion charge of £8 per day must be paid (e.g. at petrol stations).

Eurotunnel ▶

Drivers from the European continent can choose between the ferry and the Channel tunnel. The shortest ferry routes are Calais–Dover and Dunkirk–Dover. Eurotunnel operates a train service to transport cars through the tunnel every 15 minutes. Passengers stay in the car or can walk about in the carriage. The terminals have motorway connections: in France junction 13 on the A 16, in England junction 11a on the M 20.

Immigration and Customs Regulations

Travel documents

To enter the United Kingdom as tourists, citizens of many English-speaking countries (e.g. Australia, Canada, New Zealand, South Africa, USA) need a valid passport but no visa. Citizens of countries which are members of the EU or European Economic Zone need either a passport or identity card. Information: www.ukvisas.gov.uk.

Driving documents ▶

Drivers must have a valid driving licence and the relevant car registration documents from their country of origin. Cars should be marked with the oval sign showing nationality.

Victoria Station is the terminus for trains from the ferry port of Dover and a major bus station.

Animals

Animals may be brought into the United Kingdom only if a microchip has been implanted for the purposes of identification and a test and vaccination for rabies has been carried out in an authorized laboratory at least six months in advance. Vaccination against ticks and worms is also required one or two days before arrival. Information from Visit Britain (►Information).

Customs-regulations

Travellers from non-EU countries can import the following without paying customs duties: 250g of coffee, 100g of tea, 200 cigarettes or 50 cigars or 250g of tobacco, 2 litres of wine or other drinks with up to 22% alcohol content and 1 litre of spirits with an alcohol content of over 22%, 60cc of perfume, 250cc of eau de toilette and £145-worth of all other goods including gifts and souvenirs.

Travellers within the EU are not subject to restrictions as tourists, though quantities higher than those needed for personal consumption should not be imported (e.g. more than 800 cigarettes, 10 litres of spirits and 90 litres of wine).

Children in London

In London with children

London provides so much entertainment for young visitors that children need never be bored in the city – if they are, it must be the parents' fault. London caters for families: on buses and the tube children under five travel free, and up to the age of 15 they pay only half fare. Museums and other attractions have reduced admission prices for children and family tickets; the big museums, in particular, make great efforts to please children. Many restaurants have a children's menu, and most hotels can help to find babysitters. There is a wide range of information in the magazine *Kids Out*.

Activities with children The Changing of the Guard at Buckingham Palace and Horse Guards is a great treat for children and costs nothing. A sightseeing tour in a double-decker bus is also hard to beat – but only with seats upstairs,

▶ ATTRACTIONS FOR CHILDREN

THEATRE FOR CHILDREN

▶ **Little Angel Marionette Theatre**
14 Dagmar Passage, N 1
Tel. 7 226 1787; tube: Angel
Old-established puppet theatre; booking essential.

▶ **Polka Theatre for Children**
240 The Broadway, SW 19
Tel. 8 543 4888
www.polkatheatre.com
Tube: South Wimbledon
Two theatres for children, clowns, playground and toy shop all in one.

▶ **Puppet Theatre Barge**
Little Venice, W 9
Tel. 7 249 6876,
Tube: Warwick Avenue
Puppet theatre on an old barge in Little Venice.

▶ **Unicorn Arts Theatre**
6 Great Newport Street, WC 2
Tel. 7 836 3334
Tube: Leicester Square

SHOPPING

▶ **Early Learning Centre**
36 Kings Road, SW 3
334–348 Oxford St, W 1
For small children.

▶ **Hamley's**
200 Regent Street, W 1
The world's largest toy shop on six floors.

HOTEL FOR CHILDREN

▶ **Pippa Pop-Ins**
430 Fulham Road, SW 6
Tel. 7 385 2458, fax 7 385 5706
For parents with children between the ages of two and twelve; parents can go out and leave their offspring with childminders.

BABYSITTERS

▶ **Childminders**
6 Nottingham Street, W 1
Tel. 7 935 3000

▶ **Universal Aunts**
Tel. 7 738 8937

FOOD

▶ **Hard Rock Café**
150 Old Park Lane, W 1
Tel. 7 629 0382

▶ **Rock Island Diner**
London Pavilion, first floor
Piccadilly Circus, W 1

▶ **St Martin-in-the-Fields**
Trafalgar Square, WC 2
The café-restaurant in the crypt is cheap and good.

of course, and as near to the front as possible! A boat trip on the Thames is also practically a must; if this seems too expensive, then there are rowing boats on the Serpentine in Hyde Park. There are many other parks, too, such as Regent's Park, Hampstead Heath (kite-flying!), Primrose Hill and Greenwich Park with lots of space for running about and working off energy. Children are the most active visitors at the brass rubbing centres in St Martin-in-the-Fields, Westminster Abbey and elsewhere, where the outlines of brass effigies from medieval graves can be rubbed onto paper.

Toys and childhood are the themes of the Bethnal Green Museum of Childhood, the London Toy and Model Museum and Pollock's Toy Museum. Of the other museums, the best for children are the Natural History Museum, especially the dinosaur and insect departments, and the Science Museum, where they can carry out their own experiments. The London Transport Museum, National Maritime Museum and Docklands Museum also offer activities. Further hits for kids are the *Cutty Sark* in Greenwich, the *Golden Hinde*, the Tower, Madame Tussaud's, the London Planetarium, the London Aquarium and London Zoo. There is a children's zoo in Battersea Park, and farm animals in Crystal Palace Park and Mudchute City Farm in Docklands on the Isle of Dogs.

Museums and other sights

Parents who do not object to military sights find that many children enjoy *HMS Belfast* and the Imperial War Museum, and even the gruesome London Dungeon goes down well with the younger age group, if only because its café is run by a well-known burger chain.

Electricity

The power supply is 240 volts AC at 50 Hz. Visitors from outside Britain should take an adapter for the British three-pin sockets, many of which have to be switched on before use.

Emergency

Tel. 999
Free emergency number for police, fire brigade and ambulance service.

►p.62

Breakdown

►Health

Doctor

Entertainment

Not just Soho In London there is no excuse for being bored in the evening: theatres, cinemas and musicals offer a huge range of entertainment. Everyone should pay a visit to Soho, but Covent Garden and Chelsea buzz just as much. The in-places change so often that only established addresses are given here. The best up-to-the-minute source is *Time Out* magazine. The cinemas, where most Hollywood box-office hits have their European premiere, are in the West End.

⊙ ENTERTAINMENT: ADDRESSES

NIGHTCLUBS AND CABARET

► **Café de Paris**
3 Coventry Street, W 1
Tel. 7 734 7700
Tube: Piccadilly Circus
Dancing in 1920s ambience

► **L'Hirondelle**
Swallow Street, W 1
Tel. 7 734 6666
Tube: Piccadilly Circus

► **Madame Jo Jo's**
8–10 Brewer Street, W 1
Tel. 7 734 2473
Tube: Piccadilly Circus

► **Raymond's Revuebar**
Walker's Court
Brewer Street, W 1
Tel. 7 734 1593
Tube: Piccadilly Circus

Soho by night – nothing to fear, it's the ideal place for an evening out.

Long-established, famous Soho joint

► **Stork Club**
99 Regent Street, W 1
Tel. 7 734 3686
Tube: Piccadilly Circus

CLUBS

► **Bar Rumba**
36 Shaftesbury Avenue, W 1
Tel. 7 287 6933
Tube: Piccadilly Circus
Jazz, Latin, funk, house in one of London's most popular clubs

► **Dingwalls**
Camden Lock
Chalk Farm Road, NW 1
Tel. 7 267 1577
Tube: Camden Town
Easy Listening in Camden Town

► **Fabric**
77 a Charterhouse Street, EC 1
Tel. 7 490 0444
Tube: Farringdon
Enormous club in an old brick-built cold-store with state-of-the-art equipment

► **Heaven**
Under the Arches
Craven Street, WC 2

Tel. 7 930 4480
Tube: Charing Cross
London's most popular spot for gays

► **Marquee**
16 Parkfield Street, N 1
Tel. 7 288 4400
Tube: Angel, Highbury & Islington
Dave Stewart of the Eurythmics is behind the revival of this legendary club, originally founded in 1958, where Jimi Hendrix and many others played.

► **Mass**
St Matthews Peace Garden, SW2
Tel. 7 738 7875
Tube: Brixton
Super-club in an old church

► **Neighbourhood**
12 Acklam Road, W 10
Tel. 7 524 7979
Tube: Ladbroke Grove
This new club in the west of London has become a yardstick by which others are judged.

► **Notting Hill Arts Club**
21 Notting Hill Gate, W 11
Tel. 7 460 4459
Tube: Notting Hill Gate
Not too large and not too expensive, younger age-group

► **Scala**
275 Pentonville Road, N 1
Tel. 7 833 2022
Tube: King's Cross
Disco, cinema, live concerts, bars in a Victorian theatre

► **333**
333 Old Street, EC 1
Tel. 7 739 5949
Tube: Old Street
The definitive East End club. The music ranges from punk and drum 'n' bass to reggae and house.

JAZZ

► **100 Club**
100 Oxford Street, W 1
Tel. 7 636 0933
Tube: Tottenham Court Road
Intimate club with everything from trad jazz to rock, including well-known names.

► **Jazz Café**
5 Parkway, NW 1
Tel. 7 916 6060
Tube: Camden Town

► **Bull's Head**
Barnes Bridge, SW 13
Tel. 8 876 5241
Tube: Hammersmith, bus 209
The journey out to Hammersmith is worth the effort: big names in American and British jazz perform in this Thames-side pub.

► **Ronnie Scott's**
47 Frith Street, W 1
Tel. 7 439 0747
Tube: Leicester Square
Legendary jazz club, still the best in town.

COMEDY

London has a host of small comedy clubs. Consistently one of the best:

► **Comedy Store**
1 a Oxendon Street, WC 2
Tel. 7 344 0234,
bookings 7 344 4444
Tube: Leicester Square

CINEMA – MAINSTREAM

► **Chelsea Cinema**
206 King's Road, SW 3
Tel. 7 351 3742

The cover of »Yellow Submarine« from the Beatles' psychedelic period

SWINGING LONDON

The sound of Britain took the world by storm in the 1960s and had such a lasting influence on rock music that two guitars, a bass, percussion, long hair and outlandish clothing almost became the definition of a rock band. The success of the Beatles kick-started this movement, which centred on London.

When Alexis Korner opened his Rhythm & Blues Club on Ealing Broadway in 1962, traditional jazz was the dominant force on the music scene, and Lonnie Donegan's skiffle and the instrumental music of the Shadows were all the rage. Korner's club was where Mick Jagger, Keith Richards and Brian Jones first performed. It was the place that inspired Eric Clapton, John Mayall and Ray Davies to start up such legendary bands as the Yardbirds, the Blues-breakers and the Kinks. The Decca label, which had turned down the Beatles in 1962 as »not commercial enough«, took care not to miss out on the Rolling Stones, whose record sales soon reached unimaginable levels. It was not long before the entertainment industry was signing up practically every group on the scene, provided they had long hair and electric guitars.

Sacred Sites

The leading R&B clubs in London were the cradle of European rock music. The most important venue for the Beatles, after the Cavern Club in Liverpool and the Star Club in Hamburg, was he Marquee at 90 Wardour Street in the heart of Soho. This was where the Rolling Stones were first paid to perform and The Who destroyed their equipment to the sound of *My Generation*. Until well into the 1970s every band with a reputation had to do a gig at the Marquee at least once a year as a matter of prestige. The queues to get in were long, but alternatives were not far away in Wardour Street: in the Roundhouse on the corner of Brewer Street fans could listen to Manfred Mann or newcomers calling themselves the Hoochie Goochies, whose singer, Rod Stewart by name, shared the mike with Long John Baldry; and the Flamingo Club at number 33 staged groups whose style was more influenced by the likes of Ray Charles or James Brown. The bands who played there regularly included the Graham Bond Organization with Jack Bruce, Ginger Baker and John McLaughlin, and Rod Stewart's Steam Packet with Brian Auger and Julie Driscoll. It was only a short walk from

Thin is in: Twiggy set a trend that not everyone could follow.

Wardour Street to the 100 Club in Oxford Street, the main base for the Pretty Things, to Studio 51 in Great Newport Street or to The Scene in Ham Yard, where Eric Burdon and the Animals made their London debut. Some way out of the city centre, in West End Lane in West Hampstead, was Klooks Kleek, the home of John Mayall's Bluesbreakers. The Crawdaddy Club, which had two establishments, one in Richmond and another in Croydon, was almost as famous as the Marquee. The owner, Giorgio Gomelsky, presented his new finds here – the Yardbirds, for example, who took over from the Stones as resident band playing one night every week.

Pop Aristocracy

By 1965 Swinging London was the mecca of the self-styled pop aristocracy. The award of the MBE (Member of the British Empire) to the Beatles, who had long since moved to London, put the seal on social acceptance of the aristocrats of the pop world, even though the queen was not at all amused to hear, years later, that John, Paul, George and Ringo had passed a joint around in the Buckingham Palace toilets. By now the mods were the trendsetters. They reacted against the established bands, wearing suits and ties on principle and listening to the Small Faces and The Who instead of the Beatles and Rolling Stones. The more eccentric their efforts to be different, the more they were copied. Boutiques previously known only to insiders, such as those of Mary Quant in Carnaby Street and John Stephen in King's Road, had so many imitators that Pete Townshend's jacket made from the Union Jack, which prompted outrage in conservative circles when The Who appeared on the TV show *Ready, Steady, Go!*, was soon available on every street corner. Op Art, Pop Art and crazy fashion became an

A revolutionary fashion designer: Mary Quant (below right) invented the mini-skirt.

integral part of pop culture, and models such as Twiggy, who wore unprecedentedly short mini-dresses from Mary Quant's store Bazaar, elevated the anorexic look to an aesthetic ideal.

Waterloo Sunset

As the record companies had their headquarters in London, up-and-coming talent from the provinces headed for the capital city. They were eager to make a name for themselves, and clubs pulled in the fans with new sensations such as the Hollies from Manchester, The Move and Spencer Davis Group from Birmingham, the Troggs from Andover and Van Morrison's Them from Belfast. London bands reacted to this by putting local colour in their songs. Ray Davies, the frontman of the Kinks, was particularly adept at this. He not only dedicated songs to Berkeley Mews, Denmark Street and Willesden Green, but recorded a lasting memorial to evening on the Thames with *Waterloo Sunset* and commemorated his home area by declaring *I'm a Muswell Hillbilly Boy*. Although the Kinks, especially Ray's brother Dave, were notorious London swingers, they made fun of themselves and fashion-mania with *Dedicated Follower of Fashion*. In *Play with Fire* Mick Jagger relished the social demise of a nou-

veau-riche lady, now forced to find her lovers in Stepney instead of Knightsbridge, while John Lennon, in *A Day in the Life*, speculated about how many holes it takes to fill the Albert Hall. It was the Small Faces, four born-and-bred Cockneys, who did the most appealing demolition-job on Londoners' pride when, describing the small pleasures of East Enders in *Lazy Sunday*, they used so much local slang that people in Kensington had difficulties understanding the song.

Tea and Acid

From 1967 the scene slowly started to change, even though new blues bands such as Fleetwood Mac, Savoy Brown and Ten Years After still notched up great successes in the old clubs. Flower power and frilly shirts pushed out Op Art and Courège. Tea and acid – marijuana and LSD, that is – replaced whisky-and-coke and Guinness as the way to get high. The best-known places to go to achieve a new state of consciousness were UFO in Tottenham Court Road, Speakeasy in Margaret Street, Middle Earth in Covent Garden and the new Round-house in Chalk Farm Road. While the Beatles were still proclaiming that *All You Need is Love*, Pink Floyd were already taking their fans into galactic space with *Interstellar Overdrive*.

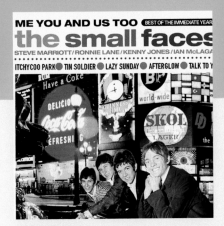

Cream, The Nice, Soft Machine and many other groups were turning with growing success to long, improvised instrumental passages, at which they were all outshone by the new star in the London club heavens: Jimmy Hendrix, who was brought to London in 1967 by Chas Chandler, the former bass player of the Animals, was now the benchmark.

Young and Wild

By 1968 British youth was preoccupied with contemplating its own navel. Tolkien fans made their pilgrimages to Stonehenge and grew magic mushrooms, while the jet-set jumped on the Beatles bandwagon to find fulfilment with swamis, yogis and gurus. It was a little embarrassing when Mick Jagger, who by now only moved in well-to-do circles, sang »In sleepy London town there's just no place for a street-fighting man«, but he was not far from the truth. At the end of the decade, when sound systems became more elaborate and loud-speakers towered higher and higher, the intimate atmosphere of the smaller clubs no longer suited the latest trend: hard rock. New bands like Yes and Genesis were more effective in concert halls or converted theatres. Exorbitant rents and high payments to the bands closed down many inner-city clubs, and new talent like Dr Feelgood, Elvis Costello and Graham Parker played in pubs. In musical terms this pub rock had little in common with punk rock, but it paved the way for bands such as The Clash and the Sex Pistols, who brought about a brief renaissance of the club scene from 1976 and challenged the established bands.

The Legacy

London remains one of the world's top cities for music. Those who are not put off by sky-high prices and big venues are spoilt for choice by a remarkable number of superstar events. However, it is far more exciting to visit the countless pubs and clubs outside the city centre, where undiscovered talent of every description tirelessly performs, dreaming of the big breakthrough. After all, most of the heroes of British rock now commemorated at Madame Tussaud's started out in just the same way more than 40 years ago.

► **Odeon**
Leicester Square
Leicester Square, WC 2
Tel. 7 930 6111
Cinema with 2,000 seats.

► **Ritzy Cinema**
Brixton Oval, Cold Harbour
Lane, SW 2, Tel. 7 733 2229

► **Screen on the Hill**
199 Haverstock Hill, SW 3
Tel. 7 453 3366

CINEMA – ARTHOUSE
AND REPERTORY

► **BFI London**
Imax
1 Charlie Chaplin Walk, SE 1
Tel. 7 902 1234
New venue run by the British Film
Institute with Britain's biggest 3D
screen.

► **Electric Screen**
191 Portobello Road, W 11
Tel. 7 908 9696
Worth a visit not just for the films:

this is the oldest operating cinema
in London with an art deco foyer.

► **Everyman**
1 Hollybush Vale, NW 3
Tel. 7 435 1525

► **ICA Cinema**
Nash House, The Mall, SW 1
Tel. 7 930 0493
The programme is definitely not
mainstream.

► **National Film Theatre**
South Bank, SE 1
Tel. 7 928 3232
Film buffs appreciate the NFT's
high-class programme.

► **Prince Charles**
7 Leicester Place, WC 2
Tel. 7 437 7003
Enormous cinema with double
seats for lovers.

► **Screen on Baker Street**
Baker Street, W 1
Tel. 7 486 0036

Festivals, Holidays and Events

Events and listings
The city magazine *Time Out*, published every Tuesday evening, lists a huge range of events. Visit London and Visit Britain produce a monthly brochure, the *London Planner*.

● INFORMATION ON HOLIDAYS AND EVENTS

PUBLIC HOLIDAYS

1 January: New Year's Day
Good Friday
Easter Monday
First Monday in May
Early May Bank Holiday

Last Monday in May: Spring
Bank Holiday
Last Monday in August:
Summer Bank Holiday
25 December: Christmas Day
26 December: Boxing Day

EVENTS IN JANUARY

► **London Parade**
to see in the New Year (1 January).

► **Charles I Commemoration**
A wreath is laid at the statue of Charles I on Trafalgar Square and a service of remembrance is held for the royal martyr in front of Whitehall Palace (last Sunday in January).

► **Chinese New Year**
in Chinatown (end of January).

IN FEBRUARY

► **Cruft's Dog Show**
at Earl's Court: enormous show of pedigree dogs.

► **Tossing the Pancake**
in Westminster School (Shrove Tuesday).

► **Great Spitalfields Pancake Day Race**
This is no ordinary obstacle race: contestants carry a pan with a pancake (Shrove Tuesday).

► **Stationers' Company Service**
in the crypt of St Paul's Cathedral. Members of a City guild, the Worshipful Company of Stationers, attend a service in historic dress (Ash Wednesday).

► **Trial of the Pyx**
in Goldsmith's Hall: a tradition dating from the 13th century, in which the coins produced by the Royal Mint are tested (end of February or early March).

IM MARCH

► **Oranges and Lemons Service**
Distribution of oranges and lem-
ons in St Clement Danes Church according to ancient tradition.

► **Chelsea Antiques Fair**
in Chelsea Old Town Hall (second half of March).

► **Head of the River Race**
About 400 teams of rowers take part in a race on the Thames from Mortlake to Putney.

► **Oxford and Cambridge Boat Race**
The same course but only two teams: the world's most famous boat race (end of March or early April).

EASTER

► **Royal Maundy Ceremony**
in Westminster Abbey. In accordance with an ancient tradition specially coined Maundy money in white leather purses is handed to deserving persons by the monarch (every two years on Maundy Thursday, the day before Good Friday).

► **London Harness Horse Parade**
in Battersea Park: picturesque parade of old horse-drawn carriages (Easter Monday).

IN APRIL

► **London Marathon**
One of the world's largest marathons (early April, sometimes May).

► **Queen's Birthday**
Gun salute for the queen's birthday (21 April).

► **Pilkington Cup**
Rugby League cup final (end of April).

▶ **Tyburn Walk**
Procession led by the Roman Catholic bishop from Newgate Prison to the old place of execution at Tyburn (last Sunday in the month).

IN MAY

▶ **FA Cup Final**
National football cup final.

▶ **Royal Windsor Horse Show**
Dressage, show jumping, carriage driving and more (second week in May).

▶ **Chelsea Flower Show**
Major event organized by the Royal Horticultural Society (end of May).

IN JUNE

▶ **Coronation Day**
Gun salute to celebrate the coronation of the queen (2 June).

▶ **Beating the Retreat**
Colourful parade of the Household Cavalry on Horse Guards Parade.

»Trooping the Colour«: guards in bearskin hats at the Queen's birthday parade

▶ **Epsom Derby**
Horse races (early June).

▶ **Royal Academy Summer Exhibition**
Art exhibition

▶ **Trooping the Colour**
Official birthday parade for the queen on Horse Guards Parade. The royal family drives down the Mall from Buckingham Palace to the parade ground (mid-June).

▶ **Royal Ascot Race Meeting**
Horse races (mid-June).

▶ **Election of Sheriffs**
Public election of the sheriffs of the City of London in an impressive ceremony in Guildhall (24 June).

▶ **The Garter Ceremony**
The Knights of the Order of the Garter attend a service in St George's Chapel in Windsor. Parade of the Household Cavalry and Yeomen of the Guard.

▶ **City of London Festival**
Music and drama, until July Start of street theatre festival in Covent Garden (until July).

IN JULY

▶ **All England Lawn Tennis Championships**
The world's most famous tennis tournament in Wimbledon (first half of July).

▶ **Cricket Test Matches**
The English cricket team plays a test match at Lord's Cricket Ground.

Revellers at Notting Hill Carnival

▶ Road Sweeping by the Vintners' Company

Procession of the Worshipful Company of Vintners from Vintners' Hall to St James-Garlickhythe Church. They are preceded by the »wine porter« in white jacket and black top hat, who sweeps the route with a birch broom (mid-July).

▶ Doggett's Coat and Badge Race

Boat race upstream from London Bridge to Chelsea Bridge, a tradition established in the 18th century by the Irish comedian Thomas Doggett when he could find no-one to take him home after a night on the town. Eventually he found a young man willing to row him upstream against the tidal current.

▶ Swan Upping

By custom the swans on the Thames belong to the Crown, the Company of Dyers and the Company of Vintners. In this colourful boat procession representatives of the three groups row upstream, count the swans and mark the cygnets.

▶ Royal Tournament

at Earl's Court: military parades (second half of July).

▶ Henry Wood Promenade Concerts

in the Royal Albert Hall (end of July to mid-September).

IN AUGUST

▶ Notting Hill Carnival

Carnival of the London Caribbean community, after the Rio de Janeiro carnival the world's largest event of this kind (bank holiday weekend).

IN SEPTEMBER

▶ Battle of Britain Day

Fly-past of military aircraft to commemorate the air battle over England in the Second World War (15 September, 11am–noon).

▶ London Open House Annual Weekend

500 to 600 historic or architecturally significant buildings are open to the public (mid-September).

▶ Great River Race

Regatta on the Thames from Ham House to the Docklands with a wide variety of vessels.

▶ Chelsea Antiques Fair

in Chelsea Old Town Hall.

▶ Last Night of the Proms

Final concert in the series of Henry Wood Promenade Concerts in the Royal Albert Hall (end of September).

IN OCTOBER

▶ Costermongers' Harvest Festival

Service of »pearly kings and queens« in the church of St Martin-in-the-Fields at 3.30pm (first Sunday in the month).

A »pearly« in his traditional costume

▸ **Trafalgar Day**
Naval parade at Nelson's column in memory of the Battle of Trafalgar (21 October).

▸ **Quit Rent Ceremony**
in the Law Courts, a public ceremony for the payment of rent for two properties, The Moors in Shropshire and a forge near St Clement Danes Church. For The Moors the Corporation of London pays a bill-hook and an axe, for the forge six horseshoes and 61 nails. The rent is received by an officer known as the Queen's Remembrancer (end of October).

IM NOVEMBER

▸ **State Opening of Parliament**
The Queen drives from Buckingham Palace to Parliament in the Irish State Coach to open the session of Parliament in the House of Lords. Gun salutes are fired in Hyde Park and the Tower (early November).

▸ **London to Brighton Veteran Car Run**
Veteran car rally starting at Hyde Park Corner (early November).

▸ **Guy Fawkes Day**
Fireworks to mark the Gunpowder Plot of 5 November 1605, an attempt by Guy Fawkes and his supporters to blow up Parliament.

▸ **Admission of the Lord Mayor Elect**
The outgoing Lord Mayor hands over the insignia to his successor in Guildhall on the Friday before the Lord Mayor's Show.

▸ **Lord Mayor's Show**
The new Lord Mayor drives from Guildhall to the Law Courts in the State Coach to take the oaths of office from the Lord Chief Justice (second Saturday).

▸ **Remembrance Day**
Red paper poppies are worn to commemorate the fallen of the two world wars (second Sunday).

IN DECEMBER

▸ **Carol Services**
Church services during Advent with Christmas carols and lessons from the Bible (from mid-December).

▸ **Tower of London Church Parades**
Inspection parade of the Yeomen Warders (Sunday before Christmas).

▸ **New Year's Eve**
Celebrations in Trafalgar Square.

Food and Drink

For visitors to London from other parts of Britain, the food needs no introduction. For visitors from overseas, some basic guidelines may be helpful. The poor international reputation of English cooking is no cause for concern, for two reasons: firstly, the striking characteristic of the London restaurant scene is its cosmopolitan nature. It would be possible to eat food from a different country every night for a whole month without ever tasting an English dish. The variety available goes far beyond the familiar choice between Chinese, Indian, Italian or French to include the cuisine of the Caribbean, South America, Africa, eastern Europe, Australia and almost everywhere else. In parts of central London it is difficult to find a traditional English fish and chip shop.

Better than expected

Secondly, the quality of English cooking has improved, though it is still uneven. There are at the latest count 37 restaurants in the city with one or more Michelin stars, and London is a good place to find out whether the celebrity chefs so often seen on British TV screens can really produce the fine quality they promote. There are many opportunities to taste the modern style of British cooking, which is influenced by the Mediterranean, France and Asia, or to stay with time-honoured favourites such as roast beef with Yorkshire pudding or steak and kidney pie, which some old-established restaurants have been serving in high quality for decades, regardless of the latest culinary fashions.

◀ *British food – traditional and modern*

Fans of afternoon tea have abundant opportunities to indulge themselves. The stylish and expensive way is to take tea in one of the grand hotels, where prices reach £20–25 per person. Here it is advisable to book a table and arrive well-dressed: men should wear a tie but not jeans, women are expected to maintain a similar standard. For those unfamiliar with British habits, it is useful to know the difference between **afternoon tea**, which mainly involves drinking tea and eating cakes, especially scones with jam and cream, and the more substantial but less usual **high tea**, which also includes a variety of sandwiches and savouries and amounts to a main meal.

Afternoon tea

Anyone looking for a quick snack is spoilt for choice. There are great numbers of sandwich bars where customers can eat inside or carry out their food, and the old-fashioned British sandwich has been joined by baguettes and ciabatta. Little snack bars serve up the more exotic flavours of Indian, Arabic, Chinese and other dishes. Vegetarians, too, are well catered-for in London – if not with pub food, then in the countless Asian restaurants.

? DID YOU KNOW …?

- … that the French philosopher Voltaire is partly to blame for the bad reputation of British food? »In Britain there are 60 different religions, but only one sauce«, was his damning verdict.

Pubs

Pub food varies enormously in quality, from the fashionable dishes of so-called gastropubs to fish and chips and other basics. Visitors from overseas who are not acquainted with pub etiquette should know the following: if food is served, this sometimes takes place in a dining room separate from the bar, where there are properly laid tables and waiter service; but more commonly in the pub lounge itself, where there is no waiter service. Instead orders are placed at the bar and paid for immediately, and the meal is eaten at a normal pub table with other drinkers. Drinks, too, are bought at the bar, and when several people go out together, each person in turn buys a round for the whole group.

Beer
Lager and real ale ▶

In many countries the British have an undeserved reputation for drinking warm beer. In fact pubs serve many different kinds of beer at varying temperatures. The biggest-selling brands, mostly known as lager, are served cold. These are based on European beers, or are English versions brewed under licence of beers from other countries. Traditional English ale, by contrast, often of a kind known as bitter, should be served slightly cool, at cellar temperature. Those kinds described as »**real ale**« or »cask-conditioned« have undergone a second fermentation in the cask and are drawn by hand-pump, rather than under gas pressure. They often have a highly individual flavour, which would suffer if they were served ice cold. Two London breweries, Youngs and Fullers, make traditional ales of this kind.

Fish and chips, the national dish

⏵ SOME OF THE BEST PUBS

▶ ㉒ **etc: see plan on p.84 / 85**
Addresses without numbers are outside the centre.

▶ ㉙ **The Anchor Bankside**
34 Park Street, SE 1
Tube: London Bridge
This pub has been in business since the 17th century, since the 18th century in its present condition. Like Dr Johnson, a regular over 200 years ago, guests today can enjoy the view of the Thames.

▶ ㉗ **Black Friar**
174 Queen Victoria Street, EC 4
Tube: Blackfriars
Wonderful art nouveau pub built in 1905.

▶ **Bunch of Grapes**
207 Brompton Road, SE 13
Tube: Knightsbridge, South Kensington
The »snob screens« which shielded gentlemen from the view of the common people are still in place here; the attractive terrace is more democratic.

▶ ㉕ **Cittie of Yorke**
22 High Holborn, WC 1
Tube: Holborn
A 17th-century pub with one of the longest bars in London.

▶ ㉖ **The Fox and Anchor**
115 Charterhouse Street, EC 1
Tube: Farringdon
This is the local for the butchers from Smithfield Market. It serves filling meals from 6.30am – hearty breakfasts for market traders, not suitable for vegetarians.

▶ **Freemasons Arms**
32 Downshire Hill, NW 3
Tube: Hampstead
A pub with a rustic atmosphere, a lovely beer garden and good food.

▶ ㉚ **The George Inn**
77 Borough High Street, SE 1
Tube: London Bridge
London's last coaching inn with a galleried courtyard; the public bar with smooth-polished wooden tables is extremely cosy.

▶ ㉓ **King's Arms**
25 Roupell Street, SE 1
Tube: Waterloo, Southwark
A typical corner pub.

▶ **Prospect of Whitby**
57 Wapping Wall, E 1
Tube: Wapping
The oldest pub on the Thames, established in 1502, was once a smugglers' nest and popular as it offered grandstand seats for the nearby gallows.

▶ ㉑ **Salisbury**
90 St Martin's Lane, WC 2
Tube: Leicester Square
A superb Victorian interior with mirrors.

▶ ㉘ **Samuel Pepys**
Brook's Wharf, Upper Thames Street, EC 4
Tube: Blackfriars
Attractive pub with a view of the Thames.

▶ ㉒ **Sherlock Holmes**
10 Northumberland Street, WC 2
Tube: Charing Cross.
This is where Conan Doyle wrote

A Study in Scarlet. The pub is full of mementoes to the great detective.

▸ **The Head of Steam**
1 Eversholt Street, NW 1
Tube: Euston Station
Railway nostalgia and a wide selection of ales between Euston Station and the British Library.

▸ **The Spaniards Inn**
Spaniards Road, NW 3
Tube: Hampstead
This pub dates from the 16th century and was once the base from which highwayman Dick Turpin put fear in the hearts of London's citizens. Lovely garden.

▸ **Trafalgar Tavern**
Park Row, SE 10

DLR: Cutty Sark
A magnificent Victorian pub right on the Thames in Greenwich, one of Charles Dickens's favourites.

▸ **Windsor Castle**
114 Campden Hill Road, W 8
Tube: Notting Hill Gate, Kensington High St
This pub in Notting Hill has hardly changed since the 19th century.

▸ ㉔ **Ye Olde Cheshire Cheese**
145 Fleet Street, EC 4
Tube: St Paul's
A Fleet Street institution dating from the 17th century, once famous as a journalists' watering-hole.

▶ ADDRESSES: TEATIME

▸ **The Fifth Floor at Harvey Nichols**
Knightsbridge, SW 1
Tel. 7 235 5000
Tube: Knightsbridge
The café and tea room on the fifth floor of Harvey Nichols department store are a London institution serving everything needed for a proper afternoon tea at a fairly reasonable price.

▸ **The Fountain at Fortnum & Mason**
181 Piccadilly, W 1
Tel. 7 7348 040, tube: Green Park
The Fountain Tea Room of the Fortnum & Mason department store is a similar establishment,

where motherly waitresses serve afternoon tea, high tea and champagne tea.

▸ **Pâtisserie Valerie**
44 Old Compton Street, W 1
Tube: Leicester Square
One of London's best-known pâtisseries, much loved since 1926. There are three more branches in addition to this one in Soho: Maison Sagne, 105 Marylebone High Street, W 1; 8 Russell Street, WC 2; 215 Brompton Road, SW 3.

▸ **Brown's Hotel**
33/34 Albemarle Street, W 1
Tel. 7 518 4108, tube: Green Park
The oldest hotel in London,

London Pride: a pint of bitter, brewed in west London →

established in 1837, is one of the classic places to take afternoon tea.

▶ **The Capital**
22 Basil Street, SW 3
Tel. 7 589 5171
Tube: Knightsbridge
The charming tea room in this small hotel is the right place to take a break after shopping in Harrods.

▶ **Claridge's**
Brook Street, W 1
Tel. 7 629 8860
Tube: Bond Street
Claridge's is a venerable institution where tea is served in the foyer, allowing guests to admire the opulent decoration at leisure from the comfort of a settee.

▶ **The Ritz**
Piccadilly, W 1
Tel. 7 493 8181
Tube: Green Park
London's number one choice, at least for the ambience: the Palm Court is a feast for the eyes. The feast for the palate is slightly disappointing by comparison, considering the price. This does not prevent the Ritz from being booked out weeks in advance.

▶ **Savoy**
Strand, WC 2
Tel. 7 8364343
Tube: Charing Cross
Go to the Savoy if you have a healthy appetite: the price is steep, but you can help yourself as often as you wish.

Restaurants

Food from all the world   It is no problem to find a restaurant in London: there is one on practically every corner. Then again, with such an enormous choice ranging from top-price restaurants to snack bars, it is very difficult to know where to go. If you are not keen on English food, there are treats from all over the world. The Chinese and Indian food, in particular, rate highly for quality and authenticity. The average prices given here are for a main course. Bear in mind that eating out in London is expensive, and that in many restaurants it is essential to book a table in advance!

▶ RECOMMENDED RESTAURANTS

▶ ① **etc: see plan on p.84/85**
Addresses without numbers are outside the centre.

▶ **Price classes**
Expensive (I): over £30
Moderate (II): £10–30
Inexpensive (III): up to £10

ENGLISH

▶ **Maggie Jones's (II)**
6 Old Court Place
Kensington Church Street, W 8
Tel. 7 937 6462
Tube: High Street Kensington
The best of English country cooking. The restaurant is perhaps a little old-fashioned, but has been an institution for decades.

▶ ⑳ **Manze's (III)**
87 Tower Bridge Road, SE 1
Tel. 7 739 3603
Tube: London Bridge
London's authentic contribution to international haute cuisine, but only for strong stomachs: a traditional eel, pies & mash shop.

▶ ⑬ **Rules (II)**
35 Maiden Lane, WC 2
Tel. 7 836 5314
Tube: Charing Cross /
Covent Garden
Rules has been upholding the values of British cooking since 1798 – here this means game shot on the restaurant's own estate and Scottish salmon.

▶ ⑰ **St John (II)**
26 St John Street, EC 1
Tel. 7 251 0848, tube: Farringdon
Classic dishes with a modern touch, e.g. pig's head in aspic, in a former smokehouse.

▶ ⑯ **Simpson's-in-the-Strand (I)**
100 Strand, WC 2
Tel. 7 836 9112
Tube: Charing Cross /
Covent Garden
A distinguished and unassailable bastion of English roast beef since 1828.

▶ **Veronica's (II)**
3 Hereford Road, W 2
Tel. 7 229 5079
Tube: Bayswater
Fascinating rediscovery of historic British cooking.

MIX

▶ ① **Orrery (II)**
55 Marylebone High St, W 1
Tel. 7 616 800
Tube: Baker Street

Interior by the design guru Terence Conran. Excellent Sunday lunch for less than £30. British-Mediterranean food.

▶ ⑱ **Oxo Tower Brasserie (I)**
Barge House Street, SE 1
Tel. 7 803 3888
Tube: Blackfriars/
Waterloo
The fantastic panorama makes this restaurant highly popular, to match the high prices. Asian-Australian cooking.

FISH

▶ ⑦ **Café Fish (II)**
36–40 Rupert Street, W 1
Tel. 7 287 8989
Tube: Leicester Square
Two eateries under one roof: a high-class restaurant and a fish canteen; the latter has ample portions at reasonable prices.

▶ ② **North Sea Fish Restaurant (II)**
7–8 Leigh Street, WC 1
Tel. 7 387 5892
Tube: Russell Square
British fish dishes, good for an eat-in version of fish & chips.

FISH & CHIPS

▶ **Costas Fish Restaurant (III)**
18 Hillgate Street, W 8
Tel. 7 727 4310
Tube: Notting Hill Gate

▶ **Fryer's Delight (III)**
19 Theobald's Road, WC 1
Tel. 7 405 4114
Tube: Holborn

▶ ⑲ **Masters Superfish (III)**
191 Waterloo Road, SE 1
Tel. 7 928 6924
Tube: Waterloo

London Hotels and Restaurants

AFRICAN

▶ ⑭ **Calabash (II)**
Africa Centre
38 King Street, WC 2
Tel. 7 836 1976
Tube: Covent Garden
Excellent food from all over Africa
– north and south, east and west.

▶ **Mandola (II)**
139 Westbourne Grove, W 11
Tel. 7 229 4734
Tube: Notting Hill Gate
Sudanese food, bring your own
alcoholic drinks.

▶ ⑩ **Momo (II)**
25 Heddon Street, W 1
Tel. 7 434 4040
Tube: Piccadilly Circus
Authentic North African cooking
with an atmosphere to match.

CHINESE

▶ ⑥ **Chuen Cheng Ku (II)**
17 Wardour Street, W 1
Tel. 7 434 0533
Tube: Leicester Square/
Piccadilly Circus
A large classic dim sum house in
Chinatown.

▶ ④ **Gallery
Rendezvous (II)**
53–55 Beak Street, W 1
Tel. 7 437 4446
Tube: Oxford Circus /
Piccadilly Circus
Peking-style: duck, of course, but
lamb and noodles too.

▶ **Hunan (II)**
51 Pimlico Road, SW 1
Tel. 7 730 5712
Tube: Sloane Square
An excellent choice for hot and
spicy food from Szechuan and
Hunan in the west of China.

▶ ⑫ **Jenny Lo's (II)**
14 Eccleston Street, SW 1
Tel. 7 259 0399
Tube: Victoria
An extremely popular restaurant
with a menu going beyond the
usual favourites and prices that
don't break the bank.

▶ **Magic Wok (II)**
100 Queensway, W 2
Tel. 7 792 9767
Tube: Queensway
A place for the adventurous to try
out unusual specialities not found
in other restaurants.

▶ ⑨ **Mr Kong (II)**
21 Lisle Street, WC 2
Tel. 7 437 7341
Tube: Leicester Square
An old-established and small res-
taurant on two floors in China-
town with a wide-ranging menu.
Try the Mongolian lamb.

▶ **Royal China (II)**
13 Queensway, W 2
Tel. 7 221 2535, tube: Queensway
One of the best places in London
for dim sum.

FRENCH

▶ ③ **Bar du Marche (II)**
19 Berwick Street, W 1
Tel. 7 734 4606
Tube: Piccadilly Circus
A charming small bistro which
does a good bouillabaisse.

▶ **Bibendum (Kat I)**
81 Fulham Road, SW 3
Tel. 7 581 5817
Tube: South Kensington
French cuisine in the Michelin
House, famous for its art deco
architecture. The fish and seafood
are particularly good.

INDIAN / PAKISTANI / NEPALI

▶ **Aladin (II)**
132 Brick Lane, EC 1
Tel. 7 247 8210
Tube: Aldgate East
Dependable Indian food in the
East End.

▶ **Café Lazeez (II)**
93–95 Old Brompton Road, SW 7
Tube: South Kensington,
Gloucester Road
Traditional Indian and fusion
cooking are equally good at
Lazeez.

▶ **Chutney Mary (II)**
535 Kings Road, SW 10
Tel. 7 351 3113
Tube: Fulham Broadway
The Empire in gastronomic terms:
a combination of English and
Indian food.

▶ **Great Nepalese (II)**
48 Eversholt Road, NW 1
Tel. 7 388 6737, tube: Euston
See how Nepalese food differs
from Indian cooking – both are on
the menu here.

▶ **Lahore
Kebab House (III)**
4 Umberston Street, E 1
Tel. 7 481 9738
Tube: Whitechapel
An excellent balti house: Pakistani
and northern Indian dishes pre-
pared in a cast-iron, wok-like balti.

▶ **Shampan (II)**
79 Brick Lane, E 1
Tel. 7 345 0475
Tube: Aldgate East
A Bangladeshi restaurant, which
means the food can be more than
a little spicy.

i Definitely recommended

- Mr Kong: top-quality Chinese food
- Tawana: excellent Thai food
- Chutney Mary: colonial-style Indian
- Veronica's: a new look at English cooking
- Manze's: as British as it comes
- Calabash: the whole of Africa on a plate

ITALIAN

▶ **Arturo (II)**
23 Connaught Street, W 2
Tel. 7 262 9623
Tube: Marble Arch/Lancaster Gate
Bright, modern restaurant, a slice
of Italy in the middle of London.

▶ ⑮ **Bertorelli's (II)**
44a Floral Street, WC 2
Tel. 7 836 3969
Tube: Covent Garden.
Reliable quality.

▶ **Chelsea Kitchen (II)**
98 King's Road, SW 3
Tel. 7 589 1330
Tube: Sloane Square
Extremely popular Italian restau-
rant with an English influence.

JAPANESE

▶ ⑧ **Kulu Kulu (II)**
76 Brewer Street, W 1
Tel. 7 734 7316
Tube: Piccadilly Circus
Sushi heaven: rolled-up goodies
from the conveyor belt and first-
class noodles.

▶ **Noodle Time (III)**
10 / 11 Nelson Road, SE 10
Tel. 8 293 5263
DLR: Cutty Sark, tube: Greenwich
Something between a snack bar
and a restaurant, delicious and
inexpensive, the perfect place for
an informal Japanese meal.

▶ ㉚ **Nobu (I)**
19 Old Park Lane, W 1
(in the Metropolitan Hotel)
Tel. 7 447 4747
Tube: Hyde Park Corner
One of the most authentic Japanese restaurants, and expensive.

CARIBBEAN

▶ **Brixtonian Havana Club (II)**
11 Beehive Place, SW 9
Tel. 7 924 9262
Tube: Brixton
A large bar and a small restaurant with real Caribbean food.

▶ **Fats (II)**
178 Shirland Road, W 9
Tel. 7 289 3884
Tube: Queens Park
The full range of Caribbean dishes from chicken wings to curries.

MALAYSIAN

▶ ⑤ **Melati (II)**
21 Great Windmill Street, W 1
Tel. 7 437 2745
Tube: Piccadilly Circus
Consistently popular Malaysian food in the heart of Soho.

RUSSIAN

▶ **Nikita's (II)**
65 Ilfield Road, SW 10
Tel. 7 352 6326
Tube: Earl's Court
Lovers of bortsch and blini have been coming here for over 20 years. More than 30 kinds of vodka cater for the hard core.

THAI

▶ **Blue Elephant (I)**
4–6 Fulham Broadway, SW 6
Tel. 7 385 6595
Tube: Fulham Broadway
This is admittedly the most expensive Thai restaurant in London, but the food and the Far Eastern atmosphere are incomparable.

▶ **Tawana (II)**
3 Westbourne Grove, W 2
Tel. 7 229 3785
Tube: Bayswater
Excellent Thai dishes and affordable prices.

STARRED, OR FOR THE STARS

▶ ㉛ **Pied a terre (I)**
34 Charlotte Street, W 1
Tel. 7 636 1178
Tube: Goodge Street
Not flashy – just excellent, Michelin-starred modern French cuisine at a realistic price.

▶ ㉜ **The Ivy (I)**
1 West Street, WC 2
Tel. 7 836 4751
Tube: Covent Garden/
Leicester Square
The place to come celebrity-spotting, but if Elton John doesn't happen to be there, the excellent cooking of classic British dishes is a consolation.

▶ **Gordon Ramsay (I)**
68 Royal Hospital Road , SW 3
Tel. 7 352 4441
Tube: Sloane Square
Gordon Ramsay is not just a ubiquitous TV chef, but one of only three British restaurateurs to hold three Michelin stars. Come here to find out why.

▶ **Locanda Locatelli (I)**
8 Seymour Street, W 1
Tel. 7 836 4751
Tube: Marble Arch
The critics call it London's best Italian restaurant. So many stars

come here that the staff are said to be required to sign confidentiality agreements.

▶ **Fifteen Trattoria (II)**
Westland Place, N 1
Tel. 0871 330 1515

Tube: Old Street
Jamie Oliver's venture to train young people serves hearty Italian food at reasonable prices. The restaurant is more expensive than the trattoria section.

Health

Citizens of Australia, New Zealand and some other countries are entitled to free emergency medical treatment through the National Health Service (helpline for nurse advice and health information: tel. 0845 46 47; www.nhsdirect.nhs.uk). Citizens of the European Union receive free medical treatment by the National Health Service and should carry their European health insurance card. Citizens of other countries are advised to take out health insurance.

Doctors

PHARMACIES

▶ **HD Bliss**
5 Marble Arch, W 1
Tel. 7 723 6116, 9am–midnight

▶ **Zafash**
233–235 Old Brompton Road, SW 5, tel. 7 373 2798; 24 St

EMERGENCY

▶ **Ambulance**
Tel. 999

▶ **Private emergency services**
Doctorcall tel. 7 291 6666
Medcall tel. 0800 136 106
SOS Doctors tel. 7 603 3332

Information

USEFUL ADDRESSES

IN NORTH AMERICA

▶ **British organization for tourism**
Visit Britain
551 Fifth Avenue
Seventh Floor #701
New York
NY 10176

Tel. 1 800 462 27 44
(in Canada tel. 1 888 VISIT UK)
www.visitbritain.com

IN LONDON

▶ **Visit London**
http://uk.visitlondon.com
Victoria Station, SW 1

Tube: Victoria
daily 8am–7pm

Liverpool Street Underground
Station, EC 2
Tube: Liverpool Street
Mon–Fri 8am–6pm, Sat and Sun
8.45am–5.30pm

Waterloo Station
Arrivals, SE 1, tube:
Waterloo, daily 8.30am–10.30pm

Heathrow Terminals 1, 2, 3
Underground station
daily 8am–6pm

Southwark
Vinopolis, 1 Bank End
Tube: London Bridge
Mon–Sat 10am–6pm,
Sun 10.30am–5.30pm

Greenwich, Pepys House
2 Cutty Sark Gardens, SE 10
DLR: Cutty Sark
daily 10am–5pm

▶ **City of London
Information Centre**
St Paul's Churchyard, EC 4
Tube: St Paul's
Mon–Fri 9am–5pm,
Sat 10am–4pm

▶ **Britain and London
Visitor Centre**
1 Regent Street, Piccadilly
Circus, SW 1
Tube: Piccadilly Circus
Mon–Fri 9am–6.30pm, Sat and
Sun 10am–4pm

▶ **London Information Centre**
Leicester Square
Tube: Leicester Square
daily 8am–11pm
Tel. 7 292 2333

▶ **Londonline**
Londonline, tel. 0 90 68 33 44,
provides information on everything of interest to tourists for 60
pence per minute!

INTERNET

▶ **www.timeout.com/
london**
Sightseeing, pubs, bars, restaurants, shopping, kids etc. on the
website of the London listings
magazine.

▶ **www.londontown.com**
Claims to be the number one
internet site for London, and
certainly has a wealth of information.

▶ **www.officiallondontheatre.
co.uk**
A comprehensive programme of
London theatre, including shows
and comedy; search function and
ticket information.

▶ **www.londontransport.
co.uk**
Everything you need to know
about public transport, including
timetables.

▶ **www.londoneats.com**
The most comprehensive online
guide to restaurants in London.

▶ **www.capitalFM.com**
Website of London's most popular
radio station with a lot of information on the music scene.

▶ **www.sorted.org/london**
London's techno pages: party listings, bands, DJs ...

▶ **www.royal.gov.uk**
The royals online.

► **www.thebritishmuseum.ac.uk
www.nationalgallery.org.uk**
London's two top museums have excellent websites. The online presentation of the National Gallery, in particular, is brilliant.

INTERNET CAFES

► **Cyberia Internet Café**
39 Whitfield Street, W 1
Tel. 7 681 4200
www.channel.cyberiacafe.net
Chat, surf and mail in London's first cybercafé.

► **EasyEverything**
358 Oxford Street, W 1
9–13 Wilton Road, SW 1
46 Regent Street , W 1
9 Tottenham Court Road, W 1
The Easy group runs internet cafés in convenient locations. The branch in Wilton Road near Victoria Station has over 400 screens and claims to be the world's biggest.

EMBASSIES IN LONDON

► **Australia**
Australia House, Strand WC 2
Tel. 7 379 4334, fax 7 240 5333

► **Canada**
1 Grosvenor Square, W 1
Tel. 7 258 6600, fax 7 258 6333

► **Ireland**
17 Grosvenor Place, SW 1
Tel. 7 235 2171, fax 7 245 6961

► **New Zealand**
80 The Haymarket, SW 1
Tel. 7 930 8422, fax 7 316 8998

► **South Africa**
South Africa House, Trafalgar Square, WC 2
Tel. 7 451 7299, fax 7 451 7824

► **USA**
24 Grosvenor Square, W 1
Tel. 7 499 9000

Literature

Ben Weinreb/Christopher Hibbert: *The London Encyclopaedia*. MacMillan/St. Martin's Press/Papermac 1983
More about London than any other source.

Work of reference

James Boswell: *London Journal, 1762–1763*. Edinburgh University Press 2004.
Vivid portrait of 18th-century London.

Diaries and travel

Samuel Pepys: *Diaries – A Selection*. Penguin, 2003
The vibrant life of 17th-century London in Pepys's famous diaries – not only valuable historical documents, but an extremely good read.

Monica Ali: *Brick Lane*. Black Swan, 2004.
A story about the Bangladeshi community in the Tower Hamlets area set around one of London's most colourful streets.

Sir Arthur Conan Doyle: *The Complete Sherlock Holmes*, Penguin 1981
Many of Holmes's cases were set in Victorian London. Joseph Conrad: The Secret Agent. Everyman, 1992.
Spy story in anarchist circles.

Daniel Defoe: *Journal of the Plague Year*. Penguin, 2003.
An old man looks back on the Great Plague of 1665, 60 years after it devastated the city.

i **London in the movies**

- Frenzy: a murderer stalks women in Covent Garden market
- The man who knew too much: another Hitchcock. James Stewart stars in a thrilling showdown in the Royal Albert Hall.
- A fish called Wanda: a zany comedy with John Cleese set in a criminal milieu. Not suitable for animal-lovers.
- Notting Hill: Julia Roberts and Hugh Grant get romantic. The travel bookshop really exists: no. 13-15 Blenheim Crescent.
- Vera Drake: a tragic masterpiece of social realism set in working-class London of the post-war years

Charles Dickens: *Oliver Twist*.
A Tale of Two Cities.
Charles Dickens more than anyone else captured Victorian London in literary form.

Nick Hornby: *High Fidelity*. Penguin, 2000.
The life of a thirty-something Londoner who works in a record shop.

Hanif Kureishi: *The Buddha of Suburbia*. Faber and Faber, 2000.
Classic novel about growing up in the Asian community.

Colin MacInnes: *Absolute Beginners*. Allison and Busby, 2001.
Cult novel about Fifties youth culture in Notting Hill.

Timothy Mo: *Sour Sweet*. Paddleless Press, 1999.
Chinese immigrants open a restaurant and struggle to cope with life in England.

Zadie Smith: *White Teeth*. Penguin, 2001.
An impressive literary debut about immigrant families in north London.

Barbara Vine: *King Solomon's Carpet*. Penguin, 1992.
The London underground system is the main character in this dark thriller, written under Ruth Rendell's pseudonym.

Peter Ackroyd: *London, the Biography*. Vintage, 2002.
This mammoth but entertaining work on the life and history of London, organized by themes instead of chronology, has acquired the status of a definitive work.

George Orwell: *Down and Out in Paris and London*. Penguin, 2003.
Orwell's report about living rough in the 1930s.

Donald Rumbelow: *The Complete Jack the Ripper*. Penguin Books.
The best book that has been written about London's most notorious
criminal case.

Iain Sinclair: *London Orbital*. Granta Books, 2002.
The author walked right around the perimeter of the city and captured encounters and observations. An instant classic.

Lost Property

Lost property can be reported to police stations. London Transport
has its own lost property office for items lost on buses and the tube.

 ADDRESSES: LOST PROPERTY

TUBE, BUS, TAXI

► **London Transport Lost
Property Office**
200 Baker Street, NW 1
Mon–Fri 9am–4pm
Inquiries in person or in writing
only; forms are available at tube
stations and bus depots to be sent
to fax no. 7 918 1028.

► **National Express
Buses**
In Victoria Coach Station

► **In railway
stations**
Ask in the station.

Money

The United Kingdom is a member of the European Union but not
the EU currency union. The currency remains the British pound
(pound sterling; £), equal to 100 pence (p, colloquially pronounced
»pee«). There are banknotes for £5, £10, £20 and £50, and coins for
1 penny; 2, 5, 10, 20 and 50 pence; and £1 and £2.

Currency

There are no restrictions on the import or export of British or foreign currency.

No restrictions

The normal opening times of banks are Mon – Fri 9.30am to
4.30pm, on main shopping streets until 5.30pm; some banks also
open on Saturday mornings. Branches at Heathrow and Gatwick airports are open 24 hours per day.

*Opening times of
banks*

Credit cards
Credit cards are accepted in almost all hotels, restaurants and shops, **travellers' cheques** at banks and in many hotels.

Cash machines
Cash machines (ATMs) accept bank cards and credit cards. The loss of bank cards and credit cards should be reported immediately to the issuer so that the card can be cancelled.

Changing money
There are bureaux de change in larger hotels, in the department stores Harrods, Dickins & Jones, Selfridges, John Barker and Marks & Spencer (Marble Arch and Oxford Street) and at many tube and railway stations.

As their rates are normally less favourable than the official rate and they often charge high fees, it is advisable to use them only in emergencies.

i **Exchange rates**

- 1 £ = 1.95 US$
- 1 US$ = 0.51£
- 1 £ = 1.47 euros
- 1 euro = 0.68 £

Museums and Exhibitions

Many museums have no admission fee, but a »voluntary contribution« is often expected (▶ Prices and discounts). Last admission is usually 30–45 minutes before closing time.

⏵ LONDON MUSEUMS

HISTORY / ARTS

▶ **Abbey Museum**
▶Westminster Abbey

▶ **Apsley House**
▶Hyde Park · Kensington Gardens

▶ **Bank of England Museum**
▶Bank of England

▶ **Bramah Museum of Tea and Coffee**
▶Southwark

▶ **Bow Street Police Station**
▶Covent Garden

▶ **British Museum**
▶p.148

The Portland Vase, a Roman treasure in the British Museum

▶ **Burgh House**
▶Hampstead Heath

► **Cabinet War Rooms**
►Whitehall

► **Chelsea Royal Hospital**
►Chelsea

► **Clink Prison Museum**
►Southwark

► **Cutty Sark**
►Greenwich

► **Design Museum**
►Docklands

► **Eton College Museum**
►Windsor Castle

► **Fashion and Textile Museum**
83 Bermondsey Street, SE 1
Tue–Sat 10am–4.45pm,
Sun from noon
Tube: London Bridge
All about London as a centre of
fashion

► **Florence Nightingale Museum**
►Imperial War Museum ·
Lambeth

► **Guildhall Library**
►Guildhall

► **House of Detention**
Clerkenwell Close, EC 1
Daily 10am–6pm
Tube: Farringdon
Victorian prison

► **Jewel Tower**
►Houses of Parliament

► **Jewish Museum**
Raymond Burton House
129–131 Albert Street, NW 1
Sun–Thu 10am–4pm
Tube: Camden Town
Jewish culture in England

► **London Dungeon**
►Southwark

► **Museum in Docklands**
►Docklands

► **Museum of London**
►p.210

► **Museum of the Chelsea
Royal Hospital**
►Chelsea

► **Museum of the Knights
of St John**
►Smithfield Market

► **National Archive**
►Kew Gardens, Kew

► **National Maritime Museum**
►Greenwich

► **National Postal Museum**
►Old Bailey

► **Prince Henry's Room**
►Fleet Street

► **Ragged School Museum**
Copperfield Road, E 3
Wed, Thu 10am–5pm, 1st Sun in
the month 2pm–5pm
Tube: Mile End
The museum presents the condi-
tions in a Victorian school for
needy children in the East End.

► **Royal London Hospital
Museum**
St Augustine and St Philip's
Church, Newark Street, E 1
Mon–Fri 10am–4.30pm
Tube: Whitechapel

► **Sikorski Museum**
20 Princes Gate, SW 7
Mon–Fri 2pm–4pm, first Sat in

the month 10am–4pm
Tube: South Kensington
About the Polish government-in-exile in London 1939–1945

▸ **Tower of London**
  ▸p.261

▸ **Wellington Museum**
  ▸Hyde Park · Kensington Gardens

▸ **Wesley's Chapel
  and House**
  49 City Road, EC 1
  Mon–Sat 10am–4pm, Sun
  2pm–4pm
  Tube: Old Street
  House of the Methodist John
  Wesley (1703–1791) and museum
  of Methodism

▸ **Winston Churchill's Britain
  at War**
  ▸Southwark

ART AND ARCHAEOLOGY

▸ **Barbican Art Gallery**
  Silk Street, EC 2
  Mon–Sat 10am–6pm, Wed to
  9pm, Sun noon–6pm
  Tube: Barbican

▸ **Courtauld Institute Galleries**
  ▸p.160

▸ **Crafts Council Gallery**
  44a Pentonville Road, N 1
  Tue–Sat 11am–5.45pm, Sun
  2pm–5.45pm
  Tube: Angel
  Contemporary and traditional
  crafts

▸ **Dalí Universe**
  ▸South Bank, County Hall

▸ **Dulwich Picture Gallery**
  ▸p.170

▸ **Estorick Collection of Modern
  Italian Art o**
  39 a Canonbury Square, N 1
  Wed–Sat 11am–6pm,
  Sun noon–5pm
  Tube: Highbury & Islington
  Excellent collection of Italian Fu-
  turist works

▸ **Geffrye Museum**
  Kingsland Road, E 2
  Tue–Sat 10am–5pm, Sun
  noon–5pm
  Tube: Liverpool Street, then bus
  22 A, 22 B, 149
  English furniture and interiors
  from the 16th to the 20th century
  in the former almshouse of the
  Ironmongers' Company

▸ **Gilbert Collection**
  ▸Courtauld Institute Galleries

▸ **Hayward Gallery**
  ▸South Bank

▸ **Hogarth's House**
  Hogarth Lane, Great West Road
  W 4; April–Oct Tue–Fri
  1pm–5pm, Sat and Sun
  1pm–6pm, Nov–March to 4pm or
  5pm
  Tube: Turnham Green
  Summer house of the artist William Hogarth

▸ **Institute of
  Contemporary Art**
  ▸The Mall

▸ **Leighton House**
  12 Holland Park Road, W 14 tours
  Sat and Sun 11am, 11.15am, 1pm,
  2.15pm, 3.30pm
  Tube: High Street Kensington
  Home of Frederic Leighton, President of the Royal Academy, decorated in the Moorish style.

▶ **Linley Sambourne House**
18 Stafford Terrace, W 8
March–Oct: Wed 10am–4pm, Sun 2pm–5pm; tube: High Street Kensington
House of the artist and *Punch* caricaturist Edward Linley Sambourne

▶ **National Gallery**
▶p.210

▶ **National Portrait Gallery**
▶p.217

▶ **Petrie Museum of Egyptian Archaeology**
University College London, Malet Place, WC 1
Tue–Fri 1pm–5pm, Sat 10am–1pm
Tube: Euston Square
Collection of the Egyptologist Sir Flinders Petrie (1853–1942)

▶ **Queen's Gallery**
▶Buckingham Palace

▶ **Royal Academy of Arts**
▶Piccadilly Circus

▶ **Saatchi Gallery**
Duke of York Hall, Chelsea

▶ **Serpentine Gallery**
▶Hyde Park · Kensington Gardens

▶ **Sir John Soane's Museum**
▶Lincoln's Inn

▶ **Tate Gallery**
▶p.258

▶ **Wallace Collection**
▶p.276

▶ **Whitechapel Art Gallery**
Whitechapel High Street, E 1
Tue–Sun 11am–6pm, Thu to 9pm,
Tube: Aldgate East
One of London's most important galleries for contemporary art

▶ **William Morris Gallery**
Water House, Lloyd Park, Forest Road, Walthamstow, E 17
Tue–Sat and every 1st Sun in the month 10am–1pm and 2pm–5pm
Tube: Walthamstow Central
House of the artist and social reformer William Morris (1834–1896)

▶ **Victoria & Albert Museum**
▶p.272

LITERATURE, THEATRE AND MUSIC

▶ **British Library**
▶p.148

▶ **Carlyle's House**
▶Chelsea

▶ **Dr Johnson's House**
▶Fleet Street

▶ **Dickens House Museum**
48 Doughty Street, WC 1
Mon–Sat 10am–5pm, Sun from 11am
Tube: Russell Square
Charles Dickens lived here from 1837 to 1839 while working on *The Pickwick Papers* and *Oliver Twist*. Letters, furniture and first editions are on display.

▶ **Handel House Museum**
23–25 Brook Street, W 1
Tue–Sun 10am–6pm, Thu to 8pm
Tube: Bond Street, Oxford Circ.
George Frederick Handel lived here from 1723 to 1759 (and later Jimi Hendrix lived next door).

► **Keats House**
►Hampstead Heath

► **Musical Museum**
►Kew Gardens

► **Royal Academy of Music Museum**
Marylebone Road, NW 1
Tue–Fri 12.30pm–6pm, Sat and
Sun 2pm–5.30pm
Tube: Baker Street, Regent's Park
History and instruments of the
Royal Academy of Music

► **Shakespeare's Globe Theatre**
►Southwark

► **Sherlock Holmes Museum**
►Regent's Park

Sherlock Holmes in combat with Professor Moriarty at the Reichenbach Falls

MILITARY

► **Fusiliers' Museum**
►Tower

► **Guards Museum**
►Buckingham Palace

► **HMS Belfast**
►Southwark

► **Imperial War Museum**
►p.198

► **National Army Museum**
►Chelsea

► **Royal Air Force Museum**
►p.230

► **Royal Armouries**
►Tower

► **Royal Artillery Museum**
►Docklands

NATURE AND
TECHNOLOGY

► **BBC Television Centre**
Wood Lane, W 12
Tours Mon–Sat
Tel. 8 225 8832
Tube: White City
Discover BBC Television Centre

► **Guildhall Clock Museum**
►Guildhall

► **Horniman Museum and Library**
100 London Road, Forest Hill,
SE 23; daily 10.30am–5.30pm
Rail: Forest Hill from Victoria or
London Bridge
Musical instruments, ethnology
and stuffed animals from the
collection of the tea merchant
Frederick John Horniman
(1835–1906)

► **Hunterian Museum**
►Lincoln's Inn

► **Kew Bridge Steam Museum**
►Kew Gardens

► **London Aquarium**
►South Bank, County Hall

London Canal Museum
►Regent's Canal

London Transport Museum
►Covent Garden

Museum of Garden History
►Imperial War Museum ·
Lambeth

Natural History Museum
►p.218

Old Operating Theatre
►Southwark

Old Royal Observatory
►Greenwich

Pumphouse Museum
►Docklands

Science Museum
►p.242

Tower Bridge Experience
►Tower Bridge

Wetland Centre
The Lodge, Queen Elizabeth Walk,
Barnes, SW 13
Tube: Hammersmith
Rail: Barnes
Open-air museum with plants and
animals which live in or on the
Thames.

Woolwich Railway Museum
►Docklands

PALACES AND STATELY HOMES

Chiswick House
Burlington Lane, W 4
April–Sept Wed–Sun 10am–6pm,
Oct to 5pm (Sat closes at 2pm)
Tube: Turnham Green
18th-century mansion.

Eltham Palace
April–Sept Wed–Sun 10am–6pm,
Oct to 5pm, Nov–March to 4pm
Court Yard, Eltham, SE 9
Rail: Eltham from Victoria, Char-
ing Cross or London Bridge
Tudor palace with art deco exten-
sion by the Courtauld family

Fenton House
►Hampstead Heath

Ham House
►Richmond

**Kensington State
Apartments**
►Hyde Park · Kensington Gardens

Kenwood House
►Hampstead Heath

Kew Palace
►Kew Gardens

Marble Hill House
Richmond Road, Twickenham
April–Sept daily 10am–6pm, Oct
to 5pm
Rail: St Margaret's from Waterloo
Georgian stately home with col-
lection of chinoiserie

Osterley Park House
Jersey Road, Osterley, Middlesex
April–Oct Wed–Sun 1pm–4.30pm,
March at weekends; tube: Osterley
House and park of Sir Thomas
Gresham, founder of the Royal
Exchange; remodelled by Robert
Adam in the 18th century.

Queen's Cottage
►Kew Gardens

Queen's House
►Greenwich

► **Royal Mews**
►Buckingham Palace

► **Spencer House**
►St James's Park · Green Park

► **Southside House**
►Wimbledon

► **Syon House**
►Kew Gardens · Syon House

TOYS

► **Bethnal Green Museum of Childhood**
►p.147

► **London Toy & Model Museum**
21–23 Craven Hill, W 2
daily 9am–5.30pm; tube: Lancaster Gate, Paddington

► **Pollock's Toy Museum**
41 Whitfield Street, W 1
Mon–Sat 10am–5pm
Tube: Goodge Street

SPORT

► **Cricket Museum**
►Regent's Park

► **Rugby Football Union Museum**
Rugby Road, Twickenham
Tue–Sat 10am–5pm, Sun 2pm–5pm
Rail: Twickenham from Waterloo
Multimedia museum at the head-quarters of the Rugby Football Union

► **Wimbledon Lawn Tennis Museum**
►Wimbledon

OTHERS

► **Baden Powell House**
65–67 Queen's Gate, SW 1

Daily 7am–10pm
Tube: South Kensington
Museum about the founder of the Boy Scouts

► **Commonwealth Institute**
Kensington High Street, W 8
Daily 10am–5pm
Tube: High Street Kensington
Information centre of the Commonwealth

► **Fan Museum**
►Greenwich

► **Freud Museum**
►Hampstead Heath

► **Fuller's Griffin Brewery**
Chiswick Lane South, W 4
Information from tel. 8 996 2063
Tube: Turnham Green
A tour of London's oldest brewery, including samples, of course

A good likeness? Beatles style at Madame Tussaud's

- **Madame Tussaud's**
  ►p.207

- **National Library of Women**
  Old Castle Street, E 1
  Mon–Fri 9.30am–5.30pm, Sat
  10am–4pm, tube: Aldgate
  Europe's largest library of women's literature; with special exhibitions

- **Ranger's House**
  ►Greenwich

- **Twinings Tea Museum**
  ►The Strand

- **Vinopolis**
  ►Southwark

- **Willow Road No. 2**
  ►Hampstead Heath

Newspapers and Magazines

The first news-sheet appeared in Fleet Street in 1501. The conservative papers are *The Times*, *The Daily Mail*, *The Daily Telegraph*, *The Daily Express*, *The Sun* and *The Star*. The left-wing or liberal papers are *The Guardian*, *The Independent* and *The Daily Mirror*. *The Financial Times* is not just for stockbrokers, but also has an excellent culture section. *The Evening Standard* is London's local paper. Sports enthusiasts read *Sporting Life* or *The Racing Post*.

Newspapers

Time Out, published every Tuesday evening, is an unbeatable source for listings of events, night life, entertainment and restaurants. For the online version go to www.timeout.co.uk.

City magazine

There are Sunday versions of most of the daily papers, as well as scandal and sensation in *The Sunday People* and *The News of the World*.

Sunday papers

International newspapers are available at many newsagents, especially in the City. The best-stocked newsagent for international papers is Moroni & Son, 68 Old Compton Street, W 1 (tube: Leicester Square).

International press

Post and Communications

Post

Post offices in London are open Mon–Fri 9am–5.30pm, Sat to 12.30pm. The post office on Trafalgar Square and the main post office in King Edward Street, EC 1 have longer opening hours.

▶ TELEPHONE NUMBERS

CODES AND SERVICE NUMBERS

▶ **In Britain**
Tel. 020

▶ **From abroad**
Tel. +44 20

▶ **From London**
to Australia: tel. 00 61
to Canada: tel. 00 1
to Ireland: tel. 00 353
to New Zealand: tel. 00 64
to South Africa: tel. 00 27
to USA: tel. 00 1

▶ **Operator**
Tel. 100

▶ **Time of day**
Tel. 123

▶ **Directory inquiries**
for London tel. 142
outside London tel. 192
international tel. 153

Still a sight on London streets: the famous old red phone boxes

Stamps   Postcards and letters weighing up to 20g to European countries cost 44p, to all other destinations worldwide 72p. Stamps are on sale at post offices and newsagents.

Telephone

Public telephones   Most public telephones run by British Telecom (BT) can be operated with either coins (10, 20, 50 pence, £1), credit cards or with phonecards, which are on sale in post offices, newsagents and other shops. 10 units cost £1. The payphones operated by other companies take credit cards or phonecards issued by that company.

International calls   Calls abroad from a BT payphone cost at least £1. Charges are lower on weekdays between 6pm and 8am and at weekends.

Mobile phones   The mobile phone network in the UK uses the GM900 system and is compatible with mobile phones from Europe, Australia and New Zealand, but not with the North American system. If your phone is not compatible, consider buying a SIM card usable in Britain at a high-street store.

Prices · Discounts

London is the most expensive city in Europe. Visitors notice this most of all when shopping and if they want to eat something other than fast food. It is a relief to find that many museums, including most of the major ones, do not charge for entry or only ask for a voluntary contribution. On the other hand some of the most popular sights, such as Tower and Madame Tussaud's are very expensive. For a stay of a few days it may therefore be worth buying the **London Pass**, which includes travel by tube, rail and the DLR, free entry to more than 60 attractions (e.g. the Tower) and other discounts. It is sold at all tourist information offices ► Information) and many other outlets. For information about prices and validity: www.londonpass.com.

The most expensive city in europe

! *Baedeker* TIP

London on the cheap

www.londonfreelist.com has a list of free or cheap events, museums etc.

i Tips

- Cloakroom: 20p
- Restaurants: 10–15%
- Pubs: 10–15% for waiter service, no tips at the bar
- Taxi: 10–15% or round up

Shopping

London is – next to Paris – the most exciting and tempting shopping destination in Europe. Antiques and classic English clothing – tweed, cashmere, shirts, shoes, hats – are the city's trump cards, and there are vast numbers of shops ranging from the classic to the outlandish. The widest choice for shoppers is to be found in the West End between Oxford Street, Regent Street and Bond Street, as well as around Piccadilly and Jermyn Street (even Carnaby Street has made a comeback!), around Covent Garden and (for secondhand goods) in Soho; the other main shopping area is Knightsbridge, South Kensington and Kensington around Brompton Road and High Street Kensington. King's Road and Chelsea are less rewarding by comparison, but it is still worth taking a look here, especially at the designer outlets along Sloane Street. Those in search of something out of the ordinary should not miss Camden Town.

Shopping districts

Visitors from abroad have every opportunity to take back something typically British: tea and marmalade (from Fortnum & Mason or Harrods, for example), tobacco or sweets, and in the higher price bracket perhaps a pipe, scarf, woollens or a Burberry trenchcoat.

Souvenirs

The museum shops in the British Museum, Victoria and Albert Museum, National Gallery and Natural History Museum have a lot of attractive items. There is any amount of kitsch and tourist tat; a plastic policeman's helmet goes down well with kids.

Value added tax Most goods and services (including hotels and restaurants) are subject to 17.5% Value Added Tax (VAT). When leaving the country citizens of non-EU countries can reclaim VAT on goods bought at shops displaying the »Tax Free« sign by taking the relevant form from the store.

Opening hours The minimum opening hours for shops are Mon–Sat 9am–5.30pm, and larger stores on the main shopping streets are open for longer. Many shops open for a few hours on Sundays.

▶ ADDRESSES: SHOPPING

DEPARTMENT STORES

▶ **Dickins & Jones**
Regent Street, W 1
Mainly fashion

▶ **Fortnum & Mason**
181 Piccadilly, W 1
Tea, marmalade and jam ...

▶ **Harrods**
87–135 Brompton Road, SW 1

▶ **Harvey Nichols**
109 Knightsbridge, SW 1
An exclusive address for fashion, cosmetics and furniture

▶ **John Lewis**
278–306 Oxford Street, W 1
Reasonably priced branded jeans and much more

▶ **▶Liberty**
210 Regent Street, W 1

▶ **Marks & Spencer**
458 Oxford Street, W 1
Clothing, woollens, underwear

▶ **Selfridges**
400 Oxford Street, W 1
A gigantic store, with the largest jewellery and cosmetic departments in Europe; serious competition for Harrods

No less imposing than Harrods: Selfridges on Oxford Street

BOOKS

► **Books for Cooks**
4 Blenheim Crescent, W 11
Legendary cookbook shop; recipes
are tested in the café

► **Comic Showcase**
63 Charing Cross Road WC 2;
Comics

► **Daunt Books**
83 Marylebone High Street, W 1
Travel books

► **Forbidden Planet**
179 Shaftesbury Ave, WC 2
Fantasy and science fiction

► **Hatchard's**
187 Piccadilly, W 1
Establishment bookshop since
1797

► **Helter Skelter**
4 Denmark Street, WC 2
Eldorado for fans of rock music

► **R.I.B.A. Bookshop**
66 Portland Place, W 1
Architecture

► **The Travel Bookshop**
13–15 Blenheim Crescent, W 11
A cosy travel bookshop. Most
customers are here to see where
Hugh Grant and Julia Roberts met
in *Notting Hill*.

► **Waterstone's**
203–206 Piccadilly, W 1
The biggest bookshop in Europe

CDs AND VINYL

► **Fopp**
1 Earlham Street, W 3
Small but top-quality selection of
CDs and records

---

i Find something unusual

- Books for Cooks: countless recipes
- Honest Jon's: jazz, reggae ...
- Best of British: the Union Jack on everything
- James Smith: walking-sticks and umbrellas
- Oliver Bonas: gifts
- Hyper Hyper: design fashion at bargain prices
- Reiss: trendy, affordable men's fashion

► **Honest Jon's**
276 Portobello Road, W 10
Incredible range of jazz, reggae,
soul

► **His Master's Voice (HMV)**
363 Oxford Street, W 1

► **Music & Video Exchange**
38 Notting Hill Gate, W 11
The best address for secondhand
music

► **Reckless Records**
30 Berwick Street, W 1
Oldies, second hand

► **Tower Records**
1 Piccadilly Circus, W 1
An enormous store

► **Virgin Megastore**
4–30 Oxford Street, W 1
Another enormous store

FINE FOOD

► **Cadenhead's**
3 Russell Street, WC 2
Over 200 sorts of Scotch whisky
and Irish whiskey

► **Charbonnel et Walker**
1 Royal Arcade,

28 Old Bond Street, W 1
Hand-made chocolates

▶ **Harrods**
Food halls

▶ **Neal's Yard Dairy**
17 Shorts Gardens, WC 2
British and Irish cheese

▶ **Paxton & Whitfield**
93 Jermyn Street, SW 1
Supplier of cheese to the royal
family

DESIGN, GIFTS

▶ **Best of British**
27 Shorts Gardens, WC 2
The name says it all.

▶ **The British Museum Company**
22 Bloomsbury Street, WC 1
Excellent reproduction antiques

▶ **The Button Queen**
29 Marylebone Lane, W 1
Buttons, buttons and more buttons

▶ **The Conran Shop**
12 Conduit Street, W 1
Every imaginable design article for
house and home

▶ **L. Davenports & Co.**
51 Great Russell Street, WC 1
For magicians

▶ **The General Trading Company**
2–4 Symons Street, W 1
Exclusive and out-of-the-ordinary
kitchen equipment, Far Eastern
goods ...

▶ **James Smith**
53 New Oxford Street, W 1
Hand-made umbrellas and walking-sticks

▶ **Knutz**
1 Russell Street, WC 2
Joke shop

▶ **Oliver Bonas**
119 Regent Street, W 1
Nothing that anyone needs, but
nevertheless wonderful gifts

▶ **Preposterous Presents**
262 Upper Street, N 1
Off the wall

▶ **Sherlock Holmes Memorabilia**
230 Baker Street, N 1
Be Holmes or read about him:
pipes, deerstalkers, books...

▶ **Waterford Wedgwood**
158 Regent Street, W 1
Famous ceramics

WOMEN'S FASHION

▶ **Agent Provocateur**
Broadwick Street, W 1
Underwear with a difference by
Vivienne Westwood's son John
Corre

▶ **Donna Karan**
19 Old Bond Street, W 1
The definitive designer shop

► **Fenwick**
New Bond Street, W 1
Always up-to-date but
reasonably priced

► **Hyper Hyper**
26–40 Kensington High Street,
W 8
Fashion and designer shopping, a
good place for bargains

► **Laura Ashley**
9 Harriet Street, SW 1
Classically English

► **Nicole Farhi**
158 New Bond Street, W 1
12 St James's Street, SW 1
Nicole Farhi sells designer fashion
with a touch of understatement at
fairly affordable prices.

► **Vivienne
Westwood**
6 Davies Street, W 1
London's fashion queen

► **World's End**
430 King's Road, SW 3
Vivienne Westwood's first outlet;
not cheap

MEN'S
FASHION

► **Burberry's**
18–22 Haymarket, SW 1
Classic trenchcoats

► **Harvie & Hudson**
77 & 97 Jermyn Street, SW 1
Beautiful ties

► **Lock & Co.**
6 St James's Street, W 1
The inventor of the bowler hats
and court supplier – commoners
can at least look at the window
display.

► **Ozwald Boateng**
9 Vigo Street, W 1
The most innovative gentlemen's
tailor, expensive

► **Reiss**
114–116 Kings Road, SW 3
The latest made-to-measure
trends, reasonably priced

► **The Duffer of St George**
27 D'Arblay Street, W 1
Affordable designer fashion

► **Timothy Everest**
32 Elder Street, E 1
A leading light of new British
fashion

► **Turnbull & Asser**
71/72 Jermyn Street, SW 1
Fine shirts

FASHION FOR
MEN AND WOMEN

► **Aquascutum**
100 Regent Street, W 1
Tweed and raincoats

► **Browns**
23–27 Moulton Street, W 1
Leading address for British haute
couture; Brown's Focus has the
latest

▶ **Designer Sale Studio**
241 King's Road, SW 3
Designer remainders

▶ **Kensington Market**
49–63 Kensington High St., W 8
Seventies style

▶ **N Peal**
Burlington Arcade, W 1
Classic style in cashmere and
knitwear

▶ **The Scotch House**
2 Brompton Road, SW 1
Scottish clothing

SECONDHAND

▶ **Souled Out / Suite 20**
both in
Portobello Green Arcade, W 10

▶ **Steinberg and Tolkien**
193 Kings Road, SW 3
Secondhand, including accessories, from 1890 to 1990

PERFUME

▶ **Crabtree & Evelyn**
239 Regent Street, SW 1

▶ **Floris**
89 Jermyn Street, SW 1

▶ **Penhaligon's**
55 Burlington Arcade, WC 2,
66 Moorgate, EC 2 and
110 a New Bond Street, W 1

PIPES AND
TOBACCO

▶ **Astley's**
109 Jermyn Street, SW 1
Pipes only

▶ **Davidoff of London**
35 St James's Street, SW 1

▶ **Dunhill's**
18 Jermyn Street, SW 1

▶ **Fribourg &Tryer**
214 Piccadilly, SW 1

JEWELLERY

▶ **@work**
156 Brick Lane, E 1
Three designers make fashionable
jewellery here.

▶ **Mikimoto**
179 New Bond Street, W 1
A sea of pearls

▶ **Erickson Beamon**
38 Elizabeth Street, SW 1

SHOES

▶ **Camper**
39 Floral Street, WC 2
The address for cool footwear

▶ **Jones the Bootmaker**
15 Fouberts Place, W 1

▶ **Manolo Blahnik**
49–51 Old Church Street, SW 3
Top-of-the-range shoes

▶ **Office**
60 St Martins Lane, WC 2
For funky feet

▶ **Shellys**
14–18 Neal Street, WC 2
Fashionable but not expensive

TOYS

▶ **Hamley's**
200 Regent Street, W 1
Claims to be the world's largest toy
shop.

▶ **The Kite Store**
48 Wardour Street, W 1
For high flyers

SPORTS

► **Lillywhite's**
24–36 Lower Regent Street, SW 1

► **Skate Attack**
95 Highgate Road, NW 5
A huge range of products for
inliners and skateboarders

KNITWEAR

► **Jane and Dada**
20/21 Christopher's Place, W 1
Knitted design

► **N Peal**
Burlington Arcade, W 1
Classically English

► **The Irish Shop**
11 Duke Street, SW 1

TEA

► **The Tea House**
15a Neal Street, WC 2

► **Twinings**
216 Strand, WC 2

MARKETS

► **Berwick Street Market**
Soho, W 1; tube: Piccadilly Circus
Mon–Sat 9am–6pm
Fruit, food, clothing, household
goods

► **Borough Market**
Borough High Street, SE 1; tube:
London Bridge
Fri 10am–6pm, Sat 10am–4pm
Foodies' heaven: organic and
gourmet produce, designer snack-
ing

► **Brick Lane Market**
E 1 / E 2; tube: Aldgate East
Sun 6am–1pm
All kinds of secondhand
goods

! **Baedeker TIP**

Queens Market

A market off the beaten track: Queens
Market in the East End consists of a shopping
street and a market hall. The goods on sale
here are mainly African and Asian, making
the market a world of its own, where the rest
of London seems far, far away (Tube: Upton
Park).

► **Brixton Market**
SW 9
Tube: Brixton
Mon–Sat 8.30am–5.30pm,
Wed to 1pm
Afro-Caribbean: household goods,
clothes, food, music

► **Camden Markets**
►Camden Town

► **Columbia Road**
E 2; tube: Old Street
Sun 8am–12.30pm
Flowers

► **East Street**
SE 17
Tube: Elephant & Castle
Tue, Wed, Fri, Sat 8am–5pm; Thu
and Sun to 2pm
Fruit, clothing; Sun: plants

► **Farringdon Road**
EC 1; tube: Farringdon
Mon–Fri 6am–noon

► **Jubilee Market**
Covent Garden, WC 2
Tube: Covent Garden
Mon 6am–5pm antiques; Tue–Fri
9am–6pm mixed goods; Sat, Sun
9am–6pm crafts

► **Leadenhall Market**
EC 3; tube: Bank, Monument

Mon–Fri 7am–4pm
Meat, poultry, fish in Victorian
market hall

► **Leather Lane Market**
Leather Lane, EC 1
Tube: Chancery Lane
Mon–Fri 10.30am–2pm
Clothes, electrical goods, records
and CDs

► **Old Spitalfields Market**
65 Brushfield Street, E 1
Tube: Liverpool Street
Daily 11am–4pm
Food, crafts

► **Petticoat Lane Market**
Middlesex Street, E 1
Tube: Aldgate
Sun 9am–2pm
Famous street market, crowded
and noisy. Almost anything can be
found here, but the market is
particularly good for clothes.

► **Portobello Road
Market**
W 11; tube: Ladbroke Grove,
Notting Hill Gate
Mon–Fri 9am–5pm,
Thu to 1pm
A top-ranking event and tourist
attraction. Fruit and vegetables
only on weekdays, antiques and
second-hand goods on Saturdays,
when it is unbelievably crowded.

► **Shepherd's Bush Market**
W 12; tube: Shepherd's Bush
Tue–Sat 8.30am–6pm
Caribbean and Indian products,
books

► **Smithfield Market**
EC 1; tube: Farringdon
Mon–Fri 4.30am–9am
One of the world's biggest meat
markets, but other foods, too

Auction Houses, Galleries, Antiques

Auction houses
The headquarters of the leading international auction houses Sotheby's and Christie's are in London. Phillips and Bonham's are the less
well-known players in this business. The auctions are announced in
the press.

Some antique
dealers
There is a concentration of expensive and fabulously expensive dealers selling exclusive items in Mayfair around Old and New Bond
Street and the side-streets: furniture and crafts in the Bond Street
Antiques Centre (124 New Bond Street, W 1), Victoriana at Christo-
pher Wood's (141 New Bond Street, W 1), silver at SJ Philips (139
New Bond Street, W 1), old masters at Richard Green (33 and 147
New Bond Street, 39 Dover Street, W 1), Victorian sculpture and
painting at Tryon and Morland (23 Cork Street, W 1). St James's is
in a similar class, for example Spink & Son (5 King Street, SW 1).
Less expensive – though by no means cheap – dealers are based in
Pimlico Road: Westenholz (68 Pimlico Road, SW 1), for example,
sells furniture and interiors items. Outlets in Kensington such as
those on Kensington Church Street and Christie's salesroom (85 Old

Brompton Road, SW 7) also have a good reputation. Last but not least there is Chelsea, where rows of dealers line King's Road, New King's Road and Fulham Road, and bargains can sometimes be found, for example in Lot's Road Galleries (73 Lot's Road, SW 10).

Galleries

Most of the old-established London galleries have addresses in Mayfair in the streets around Old and New Bond Street, where Cork Street is the place to find dealers in contemporary art; in South Kensington; and in St James's, where Duke Street is the best location. These galleries sell top-class art with prices to match. Many young gallery owners have set up in the East End and around Portobello Market in Notting Hill.

 AUCTION HOUSES AND ANTIQUE MARKETS

AUCTION HOUSES

▶ **Bonham's**
Montpelier Street, SW 7
Tel. 7 584 9161

▶ **Christie's**
8 King Street, SW 1
Tel. 7 839 9060

▶ **Phillips**
101 New Bond Street, W 1
Tel. 7 629 6602

▶ **Sotheby's**
34–35 New Bond Street, W 1
Tel. 7 493 5000

ANTIQUE AND FLEA MARKETS

▶ **Alfie's Antique Market**
13–25 Church Street, NW 8
Tube: Edgware Road
Tue–Sat 10am–6pm
London's biggest antiques market with 370 dealers under one roof

▶ **Antiquarius**
151 Sydney Street, SW 3
Tube: Sloane Square
Mon–Sat 10am–6pm
A large dealers' market in Chelsea

▶ **Bermondsey Market**
Tower Bridge Road, SE 1
Tube: Borough, London Bridge;
Fri 5am–2pm
Every Friday the former New Caledonian Market attracts crowds of dealers and buyers.

▶ **Chelsea Antique Market**
245–253 King's Road, SW 10
Tube: Sloane Square
Mon–Sat 10am–6pm
Not the latest trends, but the prices are reasonable

▶ **Chenil Galleries**
181–183 King's Road, SW 10
Tube: Sloane Square
Mon–Sat 10am–6pm
A high-class address in Chelsea with many 18th-century items

▶ **Greenwich Antiques Market**
High Road, SE 1
DLR/Rail: Greenwich
Sat, Sun 9am–5pm
A high-quality assortment

▶ **Gray's Antique Market**
58 Davies Street, W 1
Tube: Bond Street
Mon–Fri 10am–6pm

200 stalls with quality articles and a bistro

▶ **Portobello Road Market**
W 11, Tube: Ladbroke Grove, Notting Hill Gate
Sat 7am–5.30pm
Antiques and second-hand market on Saturdays, on weekdays only fruit and vegetables

▶ **Silver Vaults**
53 Chancery Lane, WC 2
Tube: Chancery Lane
Mon–Fri 9am–5.30pm, Sat 9am–12.30pm
Old and new silver

London is heaven for collectors of antiques and knick-knacks.

Sport and Outdoors

Football
The number one spectator sport is, of course, football. Arsenal, Chelsea and Tottenham Hotspur (www.arsenal.co.uk, www.chelseafc.uk, www.spurs.co.uk) are the biggest and best-known Premier League clubs; other clubs such as West Ham United, Charlton and Fulham also have a following. The most usual kick-off time is 3pm on Saturday, but many matches are played at other times. The crowning moment of the season is the cup final in May.

Cricket
Cricket is the English summer sport. Lord's Cricket Ground with its Cricket Museum (▶Regent's Park) is the mecca for cricket fans. The other main stadium is the Oval Cricket Ground.

Rugby
The big London rugby clubs are the Harlequins, Wasps and London Irish. The highlight of the season is the Pilkington Cup, the main stadium Twickenham.

Tennis
What Lord's is to cricket, ▶Wimbledon is to tennis. To get tickets for the tournament in late June/early July either join the queue each morning (the earlier the better) for one of the 600 tickets sold each day, or write a year in advance to the **All England Lawn Tennis Club, Church Road, Wimbledon, SW 19** to take part in the draw. For those who want to play tennis themselves there are public courts in all parts of the city. One good place to play is **Holland Park**.

SPORT

SPORTS CENTRES

► **National Sports Centre**
Crystal Palace, SW 19
Tel. 8 778 0131
Rail: Crystal Palace

► **Chelsea Sports Centre**
Chelsea Manor Street, SW 3
Tel. 7 352 6985
Tube: South Kensington,
Sloane Square

► **West Kensington
Sports Centre**
Walmer Road, W 11
Tel. 7 727 7947
Tube: Latimer Road

► **Richmond Golf Course**
Richmond Park, Roehampton
Gate, Priory Lane, SW 15
Tel. 8 876 3205
Tube: Richmond

HORSE-RIDING

► **Hyde Park Horse-Riding**
63 Bathurst Mews, W 2
Tel. 7 723 2813
Tube: Lancaster Gate

► **Wimbledon Village Stables**
24 High Street, SW 19
Tel. 8 946 8579
Tube: Wimbledon

*Spectators at Lord's Cricket Ground need patience and
the right kind of sun hat.*

Horse races   Ascot and Epsom (▶ Festivals, Holidays and Events) are a synonym for exclusive race meets where the British aristocracy gathers. Horse racing in Windsor is more down-to-earth.

Dog races   Going to the greyhounds is »horse racing for the common man«. Dog races in London are held at the Walthamstow Stadium in Chingford Road.

Snooker   Snooker is related to pool, but more complicated. It is played in pubs but is also a professional sport, broadcast on TV. A place to watch or play is Centrepoint Snooker Club, New Oxford Street, WC 1.

Theatre · Concerts · Musicals

Box office   Tickets should be bought direct from the theatre or concert hall or through an authorized agency – though the latter charge a handling fee of about 25%. The offices of Visit London and the British Travel Centre (▶Information) also sell tickets. Unauthorized ticket agencies, which are often close to the major sights, charge up to three times the normal price! Beware too of touts selling tickets in front of the theatre!

Theatre   London has an exciting theatre scene. In addition to such world-famous companies as the Old Vic, National Theatre and Royal Shakespeare Company there are fringe theatres which put on experimental and political drama and workshops. Others specialize in plays by modern authors or break all known records for duration or the number of spectators by staging old favourites, as in the case of the St Martin's Theatre, where Agatha Christie's *The Mousetrap* has been running for 40 years.

▶ THEATRE INFORMATION

TICKET SALES

▶ **tkts**
Leicester Square, WC 2
Mon–Sat 10am–7pm, Sun noon–3.30pm
Half-price tickets for performances on the same day (arrive early, the queue can be long!)

▶ **Top Ticket**
Tel. 01805 44 44
www.topticketline.de

CLASSICAL AND MODERN

▶ **National Theatre**
South Bank, SE 1
Tel. 7 452 3000
Tube: Waterloo
Unsold tickets at cheap rates on the day of performance

▶ **Old Vic**
Waterloo Road, SE 1
Tel. 7 369 1722
Tube: Waterloo

▶ **Royal Shakespeare Company**
Barbican Centre, EC 2
Tel. 0870 609 1110
Tube: Barbican/Moorgate

▶ **Shakespeare's Globe**
New Globe Walk, Bankside, SE 1
Tel. 7 401 9919
Tube: St Paul's, Mansion House,
walk across the Millennium Bridge
Season is May–Sept.

*Shakespeare's Globe: theatre as it was in
the bard's day*

▶ **Theatre Royal Haymarket**
Haymarket, SW 1
Tel. 0870 901 3356
Tube: Piccadilly Circus

**EXPERIMENTAL
AND FRINGE**

▶ **Almeida**
Almeida Street, N 1
Tel. 7 359 4404
Tube: Angel

▶ **Institute of Contemporary Arts**
The Mall, W 1
Tel. 7 930 3647
Tube: Charing Cross

▶ **Lyric Hammersmith**
King Street, W 6
Tel. 0870 060 0100
Tube: Hammersmith

▶ **Riverside Studios**
Crisp Road, W 6
Tel. 8 237 1111
Tube: Hammersmith

▶ **Royal Court**
Sloane Square, SW 1
Tel. 7 565 5000/2554
Tube: Sloane Square

▶ **Young Vic**
66 The Cut, SE 1
Tel. 7 928 6363
Tube: Waterloo

VARIOUS

▶ **Duke of
York's Theatre**
St Martin's Lane, WC 2
Tel. 0870 060 6623
Tube: Leicester Square

▶ **Lyric Shaftesbury**
Shaftesbury Ave., W 1
Tel. 0870 890 1107
Tube: Piccadilly Circus

▶ **Novello Theatre**
Aldwych, WC 2
Tel. 0870 060 2335
Tube: Covent Garden

▶ **Vaudeville**
Strand, WC 2
Tel. 0870 890 0511
Tube: Charing Cross

**COMEDY, FARCE
THRILLERS**

▶ **Apollo**
Shaftesbury Ave., W 1
Tel. 7 494 5070
Tube: Piccadilly Circus

▶ **Comedy**
Panton Street, SW 1
Tel. 7 369 1731
Tube: Piccadilly Circus

▶ **St Martin's**
West Street, WC 2
Tel. 7 836 1443
Tube: Leicester Square
Non-stop hit since 1962: Agatha
Christie's *The Mousetrap*

THEATRE IN PUBS

▶ **Bush**
Shepherd's Bush Green, W 12
Tel. 7 734 3388
Tube: Shepherd's Bush

▶ **Gate at
Notting Hill**
Prince Albert Pub
Pembridge Road, W 11
Tel. 7 229 5387
Tube: Notting Hill Gate

▶ **King's Head**
115 Upper Street, N 1
Tel. 7 226 1916
Tube: Angel

▶ **Old Red Lion**
St John's Street, EC 1
Tel. 7 837 7816
Tube: Angel

Opera and concerts Apart from the Royal Opera House and the English National Opera there are performances of classical music by five top-class symphony orchestras (Philharmonia Orchestra, London Symphony Orchestra, London Philharmonic Orchestra, Royal Philharmonic Orchestra, BBC Symphony Orchestra) and various chamber orchestras (e.g. Academy of St Martin-in-the-Fields, English Chamber Orchestra, London Bach Orchestra) and choirs (Philharmonica Chorus, Ambrosian Singers, Royal Chorus Society and others). On almost any trip to London there is a chance to see a major star of rock, pop, jazz or ethno perform live.

Dance and ballet The Royal Ballet and the English National Ballet perform classical ballet. Sadler's Wells is a venue for ballet, opera performed in English and frequent appearances by ensembles on tour.

Musicals London is the world's musical capital. If you want to see one, bear in mind that performances are often sold out six months or longer in advance.

Proms The promenade concerts (proms), are a high point in the London musical calendar, held each year from July to September in the Royal Albert Hall. The programme ranges from Baroque to modern works. Ticket prices are low, the audiences a mixed group. There is a huge demand for tickets for the last night, when the conductor takes on the role of presenter amidst a boisterous party atmosphere.

Jazz clubs and pub music ▶Entertainment

⏵ INFORMATION ON OPERA, DANCE, MUSIC

OPERA

► English National Opera
London Coliseum, St Martin's
Lane, WC 2
Tel. 7 632 8300
Tube: Leicester Square

► Royal Opera
Royal Opera House, Covent Garden/Bow Street, WC 2
Tel. 7 304 4000
Tube: Covent Garden
World-famous stage for opera and
ballet. 60 »rear amphitheatre«
seats are sold daily from 10am for
up to £10 for performances on the
same evening (only one ticket per
person).

DANCE AND BALLET

► English National Ballet
Venues: London Coliseum (see
below) and South Bank Centre

► Royal Ballet
Covent Garden Royal Opera
House, see above

► Sadler's Wells Theatre
Rosebury Avenue, EC 1
Tel. 7 863 8000
Tube: Angel
In December and January the
London City Ballet; at other times
high-quality performances by
classical, modern and ethnic
groups.

CONCERTS

► Barbican Hall
Barbican Centre, EC 2
Tel. 7 638 4141
Tube: Barbican, Moorgate
London Symphony Orchestra and
English Chamber Orchestra

► London Coliseum
St Martin's Lane, WC 2
Tel. 7 632 8300
Tube: Charing Cross

► Royal Albert Hall
Kensington Gore, SW 7
Tel. 7 589 8212
Tube: South Kensington
A famous concert hall for famous
orchestras

► St Martin-in-the-Fields
Trafalgar Square, WC 2
Tel. 7 766 1100
Tube: Charing Cross
Home of the renowned Academy
of St Martin-in-the-Fields. Mon,
Tue and Fri free lunchtime con-
certs.

► South Bank Centre
SE 1, Tel. 7 960 4242
Tube: Waterloo
Three concert halls – Purcell
Room, Queen Elizabeth Hall and
Royal Festival Hall – for top-class
music.

► Wigmore Hall
36 Wigmore Street, W 1
Tel. 7 935 2141
Tube: Bond Street
Well-known for concerts of
chamber music, solo concerts and
for its popular Sunday morning
concerts.

THE MOST POPULAR MUSICALS

► The Lion King
Lyceum Theatre
Wellington Street, WC 2
Tel. 0870 243 9000
Tube: Covent Garden

▶ **Dirty Dancing**
Aldwych Theatre
Aldwych, WC 2
Tel. 0870 400 0805
Tube: Covent Garden

▶ **We Will Rock You**
Dominion Theatre
268 Tottenham Court Road, W 1
Tel. 7 413 3546
Tube: Tottenham Court Road

▶ **Mamma Mia**
Prince of Wales Theatre
Coventry Street, W 1
Tel. 0870 850 0393
Tube: Piccadilly Circus

▶ **Spamalot**
Palace Theatre
Shaftesbury Ave., W 1
Tel. 0870 895 5579
Tube: Leicester Square

▶ **Phantom of the Opera**
Her Majesty's Theatre
Haymarket, SW 1
Tel. 7 494 5400
Tube: Piccadilly Circus,
Oxford Circus

▶ **Wicked**
Apollo Victoria
17 Wilton Road, SW 1
Tel. 0870 400 0650
Tube: Victoria

▶ **Mary Poppins**
Prince Edward Theatre
28 Old Compton Street, W 1
Tel. 8 70 040 0046

▶ **Billy Elliot the Musical**
Victoria Palace Theatre
Victoria Street, SW 1
Tel. 0870 895 5577
Tube: Victoria

▶ **Cabaret**
Lyric Theatre
Shaftesbury Ave., W 1
Tel. 0870 040 0046
Tube: Piccadilly Circus

▶ **Astoria**
157 Charing Cross Road, WC 2
Tel. 7 434 9592
Tube: Tottenham Court Rd.

▶ **Brixton Academy**
211 Stockwell Road, SW 9
Tel. 7 771 3000
Tube: Bixton

▶ **Earl's Court**
Warwick Road, SW 5
Tel. 7 385 1200
Tube: Earl's Court

▶ **Hammersmith Apollo**
Queen Caroline Street, W 8
Tel. 7 416 6080
Tube: Hammersmith

▶ **London Arena**
Lime Harbour, E 14
Tel. 7 538 1212
DLR: London Arena, tube: Canary
Wharf

▶ **The Garage**
22 Highbury Corner, N 5
Tel. 7 607 1818
Tube: Highbury & Islington

▶ **Royal Albert Hall**
see above

▶ **Shepherd's Bush Empire**
Shepherd's Bush Green, W 12
Tel. 8 740 7474
Tube: Goldhawk

Time

The British time zone is Greenwich Mean Time:
GMT.
From the end of March to the end of October **British Summer Time**
(BST: GMT plus one hour) applies. From the end of October to the
third Sunday in March the clocks are put back again to winter time
(= GMT).

Greenwich
Mean Time

Tours and Guides

Original London Sightseeing Tours and Big Bus Company are just
two of a number of operators who offer hop-on/hop-off tours from
fixed stopping-places such as Baker Street, Speakers' Corner and Piccadilly Circus. Tickets are sold by the driver, commentaries over
headphones are available in various languages.

Bus tours

Guided walks given by experts on the city are entertaining and interesting. They usually have a theme, such as Roman London, medieval

Guided
walks

Trafalgar Square is a must for bus tours.

▶ SIGHTSEEING INFORMATION

BUS TOURS

► **The Big Bus Company**
Tel. 7 233 9533
www.bigbustours.com

► **London Cab Guides**
Tel. 8 349 2299
www.taxiworld.co.uk
Personal tours in classic London taxis

► **Original London Sightseeing**
Tel. 8 877 2120
www.theoriginaltour.com

GUIDED WALKS

► **The Original London Walks**
Tel. 7 624 3978
www.london.walks.com

► **Discover London Classic Pub Walks**
Tel. 8 668 4019

ON THE THAMES

► **London River Services**
Tel. 7 222 1234
A number of different operators combine under this umbrella to offer river trips, including services on a regular timetable.

ON THE REGENT'S CANAL

► **Jason's Wharf**
60 Blomfield Rd.,
Little Venice, W 9,
Tel. 7 286 3428

► **Jenny Wren Cruises**
250 Camden High St, NW 1
Tel. 7 485 4433

► **London Waterbus Company**
Camden Lock, NW 1
Tel. 7 482 2660

London, Victorian London, »in the footsteps of Jack the Ripper«, Sherlock Holmes's London etc. The latest programmes are available from the organizers. Original London Walks has the widest range of subjects.

Waymarked walks For the 25th anniversary of the coronation of Elizabeth II in 1977 the **Silver Jubilee Walkway** was created. Plaques set into the pavement show the way to all the historic sights on both sides of the Thames. Visit London has a city plan with an exact description of the route. The 3km/2mi-long **London Wall Walk** to 21 sites along the old London city wall starts at Tower Hill Underpass. There are displays with background information at each site.

River trips A trip on the river Thames reveals London from a different angle. A number of different operators under the aegis of London River Services run regular boats from April to September every 20 to 30 minutes from Westminster Pier, Charing Cross Pier and Tower Pier downriver via Greenwich to the Thames Barrier and upriver to Hampton Court. Exact departure times are shown and tickets on sale at the piers.

An excursion on the Regent's Canal is gentler than on the Thames. Old barges glide along from Little Venice past Regent's Park to Camden Lock.

Transport

London Transport runs the underground railway (tube), buses and Docklands Light Railway. Tube and bus plans are available in all tube stations. For information round the clock phone **tel. 7 222 1234** or visit **www.tfl.gov.uk**.

London Transport

London's most efficient transport system, for all its age and the problems of modernizing it, remains the underground railway, generally known as »the tube« (►Baedeker Special p.124). Trains run on 12 lines at very short intervals from about 5am to 1am. It is best to avoid the rush-hours: 7.30am–9.30am and 4.30pm–6.30pm.

Underground

The Docklands Light Railway (DLR) connects the Docklands and Greenwich to the City (Mon–Sat 5.30am–0.30am, Sun 7am to 11.30pm).

Docklands Light Railway

London's famous red double-decker buses – now only the modern types – operate from early morning until midnight. Buses always stop at the stops marked with a red or white sign, but at those marked »request« only when a sign is given to the driver.
Night buses operate once or twice per hour after midnight. Most of the routes pass through Trafalgar Square. They are marked N before the bus number and only stop at bus stops marked N.

Bus

The transport network is divided into six zones. There is a fixed price for all journeys in the central zone, with higher prices for journeys into the zones further out. Most of the sights are in zone 1 or zone 2. Single tickets can be bought from machines, at ticket offices or from the bus driver. Children under five travel free, under-fifteens pay half fare.

Tickets

It is almost always worth buying a **Travelcard**. They are on sale at railway stations and most tube stations.
The **Day Travelcard and 3 Day Travelcard** are available as a »peak« card (valid on weekdays from 1am) or an »off-peak« card (weekdays from 9.30am, Saturday and Sunday at any time). The **7 Day Travel-**

! *Baedeker* TIP

Underground animals
The London tube map is world-famous. To find out about the animals that live there, see www.animalsontheunderground.com

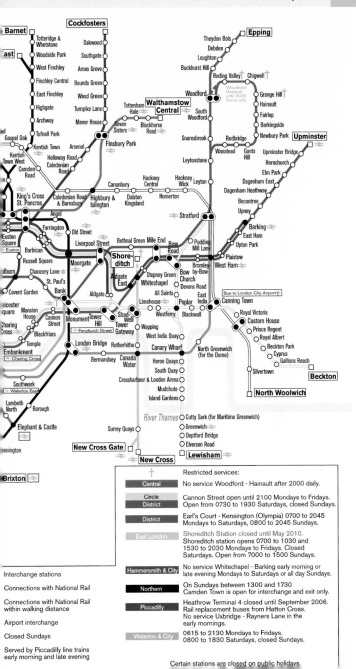

	Restricted services:
†	Restricted services:
Central	No service Woodford - Hainault after 2000 daily.
Circle	Cannon Street open until 2100 Mondays to Fridays.
District	Open from 0730 to 1930 Saturdays, closed Sundays.
District	Earl's Court - Kensington (Olympia) 0700 to 2045 Mondays to Saturdays, 0800 to 2045 Sundays.
East London	Shoreditch Station closed until May 2010. Shoreditch station opens 0700 to 1030 and 1530 to 2030 Mondays to Fridays. Closed Saturdays. Open from 7000 to 1500 Sundays.
Hammersmith & City	No service Whitechapel - Barking early morning or late evening Mondays to Saturdays or all day Sundays.
Northern	On Sundays between 1300 and 1730 Camden Town is open for interchange and exit only.
Piccadilly	Heathrow Terminal 4 closed until September 2006. Rail replacement buses from Hatton Cross. No service Uxbridge - Rayners Lane in the early mornings.
Waterloo & City	0615 to 2130 Mondays to Fridays. 0800 to 1830 Saturdays, closed Sundays.

Interchange stations

Connections with National Rail

Connections with National Rail within walking distance

Airport interchange

Closed Sundays

Served by Piccadilly line trains early morning and late evening

Certain stations are closed on public holidays.

MIND THE GAP!

The train thunders into the station, the doors open with a hiss, a tinny voice says »Mind the gap!«, passengers crowd into the carriage, the doors close and the train is off! To rumbling and screeching sounds it rushes through the tunnel at an infernal speed, then slows to a crawl or even stops for minutes at a time, allowing passengers to see plainly that only a few inches separate the carriage from the tunnel wall and giving them time to wonder how they would get out in case of fire or an accident.

The London Underground is no place for people with claustrophobic tendencies and definitely not the right place for anyone who has a horror of mass transport systems: it is the oldest, largest, most complex, most run-down and in spite of everything one of the most efficient underground railway networks in the world. It is not surprising that the idea of building a railway beneath the ground emerged in London, rather than another city, in the mid-19th century. Traffic problems in what was then the biggest city in the world were getting out of hand. Travellers arriving by train often needed longer to cross London from the station to their goal than to reach the city from their starting point. In 1854 Parliament therefore approved the plan of the Metropolitan Railway Company to construct an underground railway from Paddington via King's Cross to Farringdon Street. The line was built by the »cut and cover« method: a trench was dug along the course of Marylebone Road and Euston Road, retaining walls were put in, the tunnel covered over agfain and the road replaced.

On 10 January 1863 the Metropolitan Line was opened as the world's first underground railway. It bore little similarity to today's Underground, but was simply a train that had been put under the earth with first-, second- and third-class carriages pulled by a special steam engine that had been designed to spout relatively little smoke and steam.

In spite of all prophecies of disaster – who, for heaven's sake, would want to make a train journey under the earth? – the people of London gave this new means of transport such an enthusiastic reception that in 1864 no fewer than 259 projects for new underground railways were being discussed. For the time being the only route to

Whose stocks are rising? Smart operators put their time on the tube to good use.

be opened was the Metropolitan District Railway line, which connected South Kensington with Westminster from 1868.

New Technology

New tunnelling technology brought the breakthrough. As early as 1848 the engineer Marc Isambard Brunel had built the first tunnel ever under the Thames between Wapping and Rotherhithe by driving rectangular frames into the earth to protect the workers as they were digging. Peter William Barlow changed the rectangle into a circle in 1870 to build the Tower Subway between Tower Hill and Bermondsey, through which a train was pulled on a cable – the first underground railway in a tube-like tunnel, even though it operated only for a few months. James Henry Greathead further improved Barlow's method, and the City & South London Railway, opened in 1890, was constructed using his »Greathead Shield«. It is now part of the Northern Line and regarded as the first true modern underground railway, the first »tube«, not only because the method of tunnel construction was new, but also because the trains were completely different: tube-shaped windowless carriages known as »padded cells« pulled by a small electric locomotive taking its power from a

rail that ran parallel to the tracks. After this, one new line followed another: in 1898 the Waterloo and City Line was opened, then the Central Line (1900), the Great Northern and City Line (1904), the Bakerloo and Piccadilly Lines (1906) and the Hampstead Tube (1907). At the terminus the electric locomotive had to be taken back to the other end of the train on a loop, until the introduction in 1903 of the system developed in Chicago by Frank Sprague, by which the locomotive unit was integrated into carriages at both ends of the train. By this means the Underground, as it was officially called, had become established as London's number one transport system by 1907. In the following decades the network was swiftly extended to be capable of transporting hundreds of thousands of passengers each day. During the Second World War the »tube« had to pass a quite different kind of test: tens of thousands of Londoners took refuge in its stations during the German air-raids of 1940/41, and the V1 and V2 rocket attacks of 1944/45.

Bar and Circle

It is hard to go far in London without seeing the sign of the red circle and blue bar that marks a tube station. This, too, is part of the success story:

THE NEXT MOVE
AND TAKE A
SEASON TICKET
UNDERGROUND

London Underground implemented the idea of corporate identity at an early stage. This was the work of Frank Pick, who was responsible for the public face of the tube from 1908. He ensured that the stations, trains, timetables and everything else had a uniform look. He commissioned the calligrapher Edward Johnston to design the official Underground typography introduced in 1916. Pick recruited well-known artists to produce advertising posters. The Second World War saw the appearance of »Billy Brown of London town«, a creation of the cartoonist David Langdon who taught Londoners how to conduct themselves in wartime. The greatest artistic achievement, however, was the work of a low-ranking employee, Harry Beck, in the early 1930s: he devised a revolutionary map of the tracks based on an electric circuit which depicted the tube as a network of lines using only right-angles or 45° angles. This idea was copied all over the world, and the plan of the London Underground is a modern icon of the city.

No Longer Bright and Shiny

Today the London Underground has lost its gloss both literally and metaphorically: most trains are made of unpainted aluminium and, more importantly, the organization Transport for London is financially squeezed. Delays due to outdated track and power failures are a common occurrence, the signalling systems are unreliable, the rolling stock is obsolete, water drips through the tunnel roofs and many stations are in a dreadful condition. Nevertheless, the people of London are attached to their tube – they have no choice, as there is no alternative to it. They complain about delays and the high fares, then make do as best they can, reading a newspaper or a book in the crush and feeling relieved every morning to reach the office in one piece. After decades of under-funding, serious efforts are being made to upgrade track and signals systems and to refurbish run-down stations. For tourists, though, the Underground never ceases to provide an experience, a special mood that comes from wandering through the tunnels to the melancholy accompaniment of a saxophonist, who always seems to be playing just around the next corner – or perhaps the one after that. And anyone who feels inconvenienced by overcrowded trains, building work in the stations or delays ought to be reconciled to the system after a visit to London's Transport Museum in Covent Garden, which tells the fascinating story of the London Underground and other transport systems.

card entitles the holder to unlimited travel at any time with all forms of transport including local trains for one week. The **Visitor Travelcard** is extremely useful. It is purchased not in London but before arrival in the city from travel agents or online at www.london.de, which saves delays on arrival. It is valid for one or three days. The prices for all Travelcards depend on the number of zones selected (zones 1 and 2 usually suffice for visitors whose accommodation is within this area).

At tube stations – at least in the central zones – tickets have to be place in a slot at the barrier to be registered. Always keep single tickets, as they are collected by staff or retained by the machine at the end of the journey.

A feature of London almost as famous as the double-decker buses are the taxis, **black cabs**, which can now be seen in a variety of colours. They can be hailed from the kerbside – if the FOR HIRE sign is lit up, the taxi is free. **Important: licensed taxis have a licence number!** Fares and supplementary costs are displayed in the taxi. The price is doubled for journeys longer than six miles (9.7km); journeys after 8pm also cost more.

Taxis

Black cabs: a classic mode of transport, though not all are black

Travellers with Disabilities

Brochures There are two helpful brochures for travellers with disabilities in London: Access to the Underground (available in tube stations) is a guide to the use of public transport. Access to London has tips on accommodation, transport and access to many public buildings, museums etc (available from RADAR). www.golondon.com/plan_a_visit /disabled is a source of comprehensive information.

⏵ ORGANIZATIONS FOR THE DISABLED

▶ **RADAR**
12 City Forum, 250 City Rd., EC 1, tel. 7 250 3222, www.radar.org.uk

▶ **Artsline**
Tel. 7 388 2227
www.artsline.org.uk
Information about arts and performance venues suitable for persons with disabilities.

▶ **Tripscope**
The Vassall Centre, Gill Avenue, Bristol BS16 2QQ
Tel. (08 45) 7 58 56 41
www.tripscope.org.uk
Information about programmes and transport facilities suitable for persons with disabilities.

Weights and Measures

Metric system with exceptions In 1995 the United Kingdom joined the rest of Europe by adopting the metric system, but with two important exceptions: the pint for beer and milk, and the mile for distances on road signs.

linear measures
1 inch (in;) = 2,54 cm	1 mm = 0,03937 in
1 foot (ft;) = 12 in = 30,48 cm	1 cm = 0,033 ft
1 yard (yd;) = 3 ft = 91,44 cm	1 m = 1,09 yd
1 mile (mi;) = 1,61 km	1 km = 0,62 mi

Surface measures
1 square inch (in²) = 6,45 cm²	1 cm² = 0,155 in²
1 square foot (ft²) = 9,288 dm²	1 dm² = 0,108 ft²
1 square yard (yd²) = 0,836 m²	1 m² = 1,196 yd²
1 square mile (mi²) = 2,589 km²	1 km² = 0,386 mi²
1 acre = 0,405 ha	1 ha = 2,471 acres

Cubic measure
1 cubic inch (in³) = 16,386 cm³	1 cm³ = 0,061 in³
1 cubic foot (ft³) = 28,32 dm³	1 dm³ = 0,035 ft³
1 cubic yard (yd³) = 0,765 m³	1 m³ = 1,308 yd³

1 pint GB (pt) = 0,568 l	1 l = 1,76 pt (GB)
1 pint US (pt) = 4 gills = 0,473 l	1 l = 2,114 pt (US)
1 quart (qt) = 2 pt = 0,946 l	1 l = 1,057 qt
1 gallon (gal) = 4 qt = 3,787 l	1 l = 0,264 gal

Liquid measure

1 ounce (oz;) = 28,365 g	100 g = 2,527 oz
1 pound (lb;) = 453,59 g	1 kg = 2,206 lb
1 cental (cwt;.) = 45,359 kg	100 kg = 2,205 cwt

Weights

Fahrenheit: 0   10 20 32 50 68 89 95
Celsius: -18 -12 -6,5 0 10 20 30 35

Temperature

Conversion:

$$\text{Fahrenheit} = 1,8 \times \text{Celsius} + 32 \qquad \text{Celsius} = \frac{5\,(\text{Fahrenheit} - 32)}{9}$$

Men's clothing / Men's shirts
GB / US: no difference

Clothing sizes

Men's shoes:

GB	8	8,5	9,5	10	10,5
US	8,5	9	10	10,5	11

Women's clothing:

GB	10	12	14	16	18	20
US	8	10	12	14	16	18

Women's shoes:

5,5	6	6,5	7	7,5	8	8,5
7	7,5	8	8,5	9	9,5	10

Children's sizes:

GB (yrs)	2-3	4-5	6-7	8-9	10-11	12	14-16
US (yrs)	2-3	4-5	6-6X	7-8	10	12	14

When to Go

London has a temperate climate. However, as it can be rainy or too hot in summer, the best time for a visit is spring (from May) and early autumn. The fogs for which London was once notorious are now unusual.

Tours

A TOUR
IN A SIGHT-
SEEING BUS TAKES IN
THE HIGHLIGHTS OF LONDON, OF COURSE.
BUT THE REAL WAY TO EXPLORE THE CITY IS
ON FOOT – HERE ARE SOME ROUTES FOR AN
ENTERTAINING WALK.

Open Air Theatre

Bedford College

Mme. Tussaud's

Academy of Music

University of Westminster

MARYLEBONE

Wallace Collection

Selfridges (i)

Roosevelt Memorial

MAYFAIR

Royal Academy

Hyde Park

Hyde Park Corner

Wellington Museum

Wellington Arch

Knightsbridge

Palace

Gardens

BELGRAVIA

Emb. of Germany

St Mary

Euston Tower

Holy Trinity

Circle

Outer

Marylebone

New

Canendish Place

Wimpole St.

Devonshire

Weymouth

George Street

Wigmore

Street

BBC

All Souls

Palladium

SOHO

Broad Street

Grosvenor St.

Newbold

Mount Row

Adam Row

Piccadilly

Green Park

St James's Palace

Lancaster House

Constitution Hill

Buckingham Palace

Queen Victoria Memorial

Queen's Gallery

Royal Mews

Wellington Barracks

Passport Office New Scotland Yard

Westminster Cathedral

Victoria Station

St James's

Birdcage Walk

Park

Wellington Road

Telecom Tower

University College

BLOOMSBURY

University of London

Hospital

Coram Fields

Dicken' Hous Museu

British Museum

Soane's Museum

New Oxford Street

Lincol

ST GILES

Freemasons Hall

Royal Opera House

King Colle

Covent Garden Market

Transport Museum

Courtauld Galleries

Sor Hou

St Martin in-the-Fields

Cleopatra's Needle

Charing Cross Station

Quee Elizabe Ha

National Gallery

Visitor Cen.

Trafalgar Square

Admiralty Arch

Whitehall

Horse Guards

Banqueting House

BA London Eye

SOUTH-

Coun Hall

Roy Festival Ha

ICA

Malborough House

Carlton House Terrace

Downing St.

Parliament Square

Big Ben

Westminster Bridge

St Thomas's Hospital

Westminster Abbey

Jewel Tower

Houses of Parliament

Lambe Palace

St John's Concert Hall

Lambeth Bridge

Tate Britain

PIMLICO

Thames

Lincoln's

Shaftesbury

Regent Street

Oxford Street

Piccadilly Circus

The Mall

Whitehall

Victoria

Leicester Square

Soho Square

Charing Cross Rd

Greek St.

Frith St.

Wardour St.

Rathbone

Charlotte St.

Gower

Tottenham Court

Fitzroy Sq.

Titchfield

Portland St.

Regent Street

Cavendish Square

Berkeley Square

St James's Square

Stanhope Street

Euston Road

Tavistock

Russell Street

Southampton Row

Montague St.

Kings Way

Strand

Northumberland Av.

Victoria Embankment

Lambeth

FINSBURY

CLERKENWELL

St John's Gate

250 m
750 ft

HOLBORN

Chiswell St.

Barbican Arts and
Conference Centre

Broad
Street
Station

Spitalfields
Market

Liverpool
Street
Station

Smithfield

St
Bartholomew

BARBICAN

★ Museum of London

★ Staple Inn

National Postal
Museum

London Wall

London Wall

City Thameslink
Station

★ Guildhall

CITY

Criminal
Court

★★
St Paul's
Cathedral

Bank of
England

Stock
Exchange

Swiss Re
Tower

Royal
Excange ★

★ Lloyd's

Royal Courts

Blackfriars
Station

Mansion
House

Leadenhall
Market

Frenchurch
Street St.

The Temple

Cannon
Street
Station

★ Monument

All
Hallows

★★ Tower

HMS President

HMS
Wellington

OXO
Tower

Blackfriars
Bridge

Millennium
Bridge

Thames

Southwark
Bridge

London
Bridge

Custom
House

National
Theatre

★★
Tate Modern

Shakespeare's Globe
Theatre

Southwark
Cathedral

HMS Belfast ★★

Tower
Bridge

IMAX

London Dungeon

London Bridge
Station

City Hall

Waterloo
Station

TOURS OF LONDON

Four walks. The minimum times given are manageable for
everyone who likes walking. But to get the most out of
them, take your time.

— boundary for
congestion charge
paid by drivers

Baedeker

Getting Around in London

Fast trains and cheap flights mean that a day trip to London is possible from most parts of Great Britain and indeed Europe. But to see the main sights, visit a museum or two and do some shopping, three days is a minimum. For people who like to walk it is not difficult to get around in the City and Westminster. However, it soon becomes tiring to do everything on foot, as London covers an area that makes it one of the largest cities in the world. Fortunately almost every corner of this area can be reached by bus or the underground railway (»tube«). The tube is an indispensable means of transport, even though Londoners are critical of the network, which is in need of modernization. It is certainly advisable to avoid travelling during the rush hour. As far as transport is concerned, any district not too far from the centre is a suitable choice for accommodation; to stay in pleasant surroundings with good places to go out in the evening, the best option is a hotel in the West End, Knightsbridge or Kensington.

i **Highlights of London**

- British Museum – treasures from all over the world
- Westminster Abbey – where English monarchs are crowned
- A walk in Hyde Park – where Londoners relax
- Harrods – legendary department store
- Greenwich – the cradle of British maritime power
- London Eye – a bird's eye view of the city

One more point on transport: when travelling to London, it is advisable to leave the car at home. In 2002 London's mayor introduced the **congestion charge**, a toll of £8 per day for each vehicle that enters the city centre between 7am and 6.30pm from Monday to Friday (see city plan p132 for boundaries of the congestion charge zone). The number plates of vehicles entering the zone system are registered electronically. If this is not a sufficient deterrent, then bear in mind the shortage of parking spaces and the hefty fines for illegal parking.

Ride the London Eye to see the city – including Parliament.

Tour 1 Westminster and the City – Essential London

Start and finish: Westminster Bridge – Tower Bridge (north bank of the Thames)   **Duration:** min. 4 hours

This walk takes in many highlights of the city. To see the Changing of the Guard, plan to be at Horse Guards at 11am (Sunday 10am). To get your bearings take a ride in the London Eye, a 131m/430ft-high observation wheel not far from the starting point.

Start at Westminster tube station. London's famous landmark Big Ben, the clock tower of the ❶ ✳ ✳ **Houses of Parliament**, is in view as you emerge from the underground. The best place to enjoy the magnificent architecture of the Houses of Parliament is from Westminster Bridge. From there cross Parliament Square to take a look at ❷ ✳ ✳ **Westminster Abbey.** Set aside another day to make a thorough visit to the abbey and walk up ❸ ✳ ✳ **Whitehall** passing Downing Street and Banqueting Hall, in front of which Charles II was executed, to Horse Guards, which draws crowds of tourists. A little further on is London's finest square, ✳ ✳ **Trafalgar Square**, which commemorates the British naval hero Lord Nelson. The ✳ ✳ **National Gallery** occupies the north side of the square. Don't feed the pigeons here, but turn round to look back down Whitehall to Big Ben. Then continue along the ✳ **Strand** to the City, passing Waterloo Bridge and Somerset House, home to a first-class collection of paintings in the ✳ ✳ **Courtauld Institute Galleries**. The pubs and cafés of ❹ ✳ **Covent Garden** to the north are the best place to take a break – try the café in the Royal Opera House. The buskers and assorted street performers around Covent Garden Piazza provide plenty of entertainment here. Return to the Strand and the Temple Bar Memorial, where a narrow archway on the right leads to ❺ ✳ **The Temple**. The quiet courtyards and passages of this ancient quarter of the legal profession are a welcome contrast to the city traffic. Beyond Temple Bar is ❻ **Fleet Street**, once the centre of the newspaper business. It leads into Ludgate Hill and a view of ❼ ✳ ✳ **St Paul's Cathedral**. The ascent of the dome is another opportunity to enjoy a bird's-eye view of the city. From the cathedral take Cannon Street and Queen Victoria Street to Bank tube station. Here, in the heart of London's financial world, are the Bank of England and the ❽ ✳ **Royal Exchange**. The last part of this route starts at Bank station. Go down Threadneedle Street or ❾ **Lombard Street** to the Victorian market halls of Leadenhall Market, then along Gracechurch Street to the ✳ **Monument** and on via Lower Thames Street to the ❿ ✳ ✳ **Tower** and ⓫ ✳ ✳ **Tower Bridge**. By this stage you have earned a rest, and the Dickens Inn in St Katharine's Dock is not far away.

Tour 2 South Bank of the Thames

Start and finish: From Westminster Bridge to Tower Bridge (south bank of the Thames)

Duration: min. 2 hours

This walk takes you to a part of London that is becoming more and more attractive and offers wonderful views of Westminster and the City.

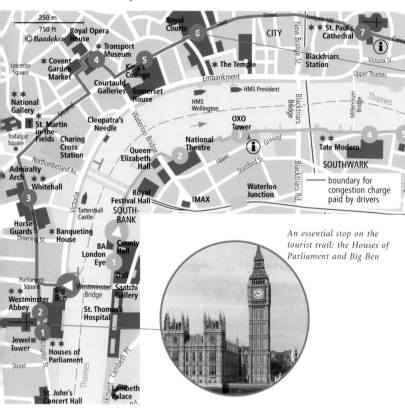

An essential stop on the tourist trail: the Houses of Parliament and Big Ben

Start at Westminster Bridge to get the best view of the ✳ ✳ **Houses of Parliament**. Steps lead down to the path along the south bank near the ❶ ✳ ✳ **London Eye** and on to the South Bank Centre. The Film Café under Waterloo Bridge in the ❷ **National Theatre** complex is a good place for refreshments; further along from the bridge, there is a marvellous view of the City and ✳ ✳ **St Paul's**.

Go on to the ❸ **Oxo Tower**, which contains designer shops, a bar, a restaurant and an observation terrace on the eighth floor. Then walk under Blackfriars Bridge to Southwark. The great bulk of Bankside Power Station, now home to the modern art collection of the ❹ ✱ ✱ **Tate Gallery** is on the right; on the left the intricate structure of the Millennium Bridge leads straight up to St Paul's. Just a little further ❺ ✱ ✱ **Shakespeare's Globe Theatre** provides an opportunity to experience Elizabethan-style theatre. Alternatively stop for a (pricey) glass of wine at Vinopolis or a pint of beer in The An-

The griffin on Temple Bar guards the entrance to the City.

Tours 1 and 2 end at Tower Bridge.

chor pub. Thus fortified, continue to the Gothic splendour of ❻ ✱ **Southwark Cathedral**, then through Borough Market to Borough High Street and the old-world atmosphere of The George Inn. The last stage of the route passes the spectacular new ❼ **City Hall** on the way to ❽ ✱ ✱ **Tower Bridge** and, for the energetic, crosses the river to the ✱ ✱ **Tower**.

Tour 3 The West End

Start and finish: Piccadilly Circus   **Duration:** min. 2 hours

Shopping, parks and royalty is the theme of this walk through some of the most exclusive districts of the city, including places with royal connections.

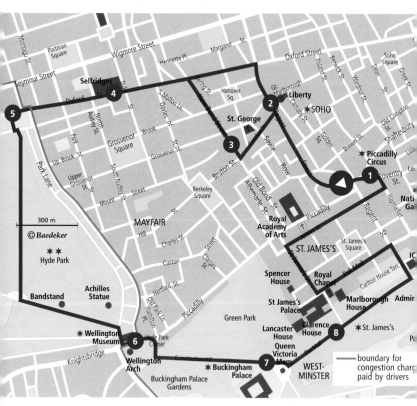

Start at ❶ ★ **Piccadilly Circus** and follow the impressive curve of Regent Street to the main shopping area of the West End. Not to be missed here are the department store ❷ **Liberty** and, if there are children in the group, Hamley's toy shop. Oxford Circus is the junction of Regent Street and the bustle of Oxford Street, which is also lined with shops and department stores. (An alternative route to Oxford Street goes along Conduit Street and New Bond Street, site of the world-famous auction house ❸**Sotheby's**). A »must« for Oxford Street shoppers is ❹**Selfridges**. Continue to the north-east corner of ✳ ✳ **Hyde Park**, well-known for ❺**Marble Arch** and Speakers' Corner. Any route through Hyde Park is a delight. The long way goes west round the Serpentine lake to the Princess Diana Memorial Fountain, with a stop for coffee at the Lido. Whichever route you take, leave the park at ❻**Hyde Park Corner** and cross Green Park to ❼✳ ✳ **Buckingham Palace**. From the palace continue through ✳ **St James's Park** or along the ❽**Mall** to Carlton House Terrace and up the steps to Pall Mall. Turn left along Pall Mall and walk past London's clubs to ✳ **St James's Palace**, one of the city's few Tudor buildings. Finish with a stroll through the St James's district. This can take some time, as high-class gentlemen's outfitters, tobacco and pipe shops and the exclusive department store Fortnum & Mason provide plenty of distractions. Emerge from St James's at ✳ **Piccadilly Circus** and continue to Chinatown for lunch or dinner.

! *Baedeker* TIP

Nostalgic double-decker tour

The red Routemaster double-decker buses were finally taken out of service in December 2005. Now Londoners have to squeeze into the new, enclosed, charisma-free double-deckers or the single-decker »bendy buses«. However, for sightseeing tours two »heritage routes« with the old Routemaster buses will remain: number 9 from Kensington to Aldwych and number 15 from Marble Arch to the Tower. The best seats, of course, are on the top deck as near to the front as possible.

St James's Park, the green heart of London

Tour 4 Holborn · Bloomsbury

Start and finish: Piccadilly Circus – Trafalgar Square

Duration: min. 2 hours

This is a walk through contrasting areas: London's buzzing theatre district between Piccadilly Circus and Soho, and the relative calm of Holborn and Bloomsbury.

Starting at ❶ ✳ **Piccadilly Circus** go west towards ✳ **Soho**, through Chinatown and north to ❷ **Soho Square** – a walk worth repeating in the evening. From Soho Square the route follows a short stretch of New Oxford Street and the signs to the ❸ ✳ ✳ **British Museum**. For a short visit to take in the highlights, see p148ff; to see more than that, spend the rest of the day in the museum. Afterwards enjoy the peace and quiet of the legal quarter ❺ **Lincoln's Inn**. The idiosyncratic ❹ **Sir John Soane's Museum** is here. Return to the West End along Aldwych, stopping to look at the RAF church ❻ **St Clement Danes** and take the ❼ **Strand** to reach ❽ ✳ ✳ **Trafalgar Square** and Nelson's column.

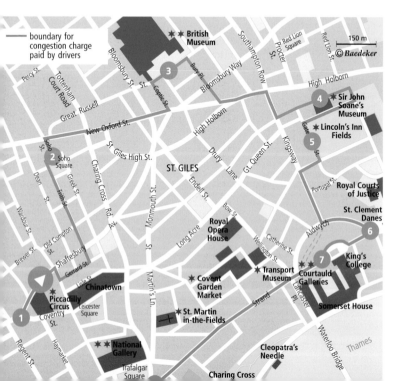

Excursions

The best destinations for a short excursion from the centre of London are ✳ ✳ **Greenwich**, the wonderful park and plant houses in ✳ ✳ **Kew Gardens**, the majestic ✳ ✳ **Hampton Court Palace** or, for a stroll on the banks of the Thames, Richmond. To see a residence of the royal family, take a trip to ✳ ✳ **Windsor Castle**.

Short trips from the city centre

Many places within 100km/60mi of London that are well worth seeing can easily be reached by rail or bus (from Victoria Coach Station).

Longer excursions

Arundel in the South Downs (80km/50mi south of London) is one of the most attractive small towns in the south of England. The castle of the dukes of Norfolk dominates the town (train from Victoria Station).

Ascot, just a few miles to the south-west of Windsor Castle, is the place where high society meets every June to watch the horse races and admire the ladies' hats during Ascot Week. On the Thursday, the day of the Gold Cup race, the royal family comes in coaches from Windsor Castle (trains to Ascot from Waterloo Station).

The attractions of **Brighton**, a popular resort on the south coast (80km/50mi south of London) are the funfair on the Victorian Palace Pier and other seaside pleasures (train from Victoria Station).

In the university town of **Cambridge** (90km/55mi north of London) the medieval colleges are open to visitors (train from Liverpool Street Station).

The city of **Canterbury** (75km/45mi south of London) has one of the most beautiful cathedrals in England (train from Victoria Station or Charing Cross).

Oxford, one of the world's oldest university cities (90km/55mi north-west of London) is in historical and architectural terms arguably England's second most important city after London. Its attractions are the colleges, cathedral, gardens and High Street – not to forget the student life (train from Paddington).

Sights
from A to Z

THE BREATHTAKING GREAT
COURT OF THE BRITISH
MUSEUM AND THE CROWN
JEWELS – JUST TWO
HIGHLIGHTS OF LONDON

All Hallows-by-the-Tower

K 5

Location: Byward Street, EC 3   **Tube:** Tower Hill

London's oldest church

All Hallows is the oldest church in London. It was founded in the 7th century, rebuilt in the 13th to 15th centuries, severely damaged in the Second World War and reconstructed in 1957. It has a 14th-century crypt and a tower dating from 1658 which is typical of the Commonwealth period. Samuel Pepys watched the Great Fire of 1666 from the tower; Admiral Sir William Penn, father of the founder of Pennsylvania, saved All Hallows from the flames by ordering the surrounding houses to be blown up. Inside the church the remains of an arch, partly built from Roman masonry and bearing the date AD 675, are evidence of Anglo-Saxon origins. Two crosses have survived from this period. In the crypt a model of Roman Londinium, items from the Roman and Saxon periods and a font attributed to Grinling Gibbons are on display. The parish register records that William Penn was baptized in All Hallows in 1644 and that John Quincy Adams, sixth president of the USA, married here. The crusader altar in the memorial chapel is from Richard the Lionheart's castle in Palestine.

Crypt ▶

St Olave

Seething Lane, the street in which Samuel Pepys lived, branches off from Byward Street opposite All Hallows and leads to the church of St Olave. It is dedicated to the Norwegian King Olaf, dates from about 1450 and is one of the few churches in the City left untouched by Great Fire. It was Samuel Pepys's parish church (memorial on the south wall). In 1672 Pepys commissioned John Bushnell to produce a bust in memory of his wife Elizabeth, who is buried here. The pulpit is by Grinling Gibbons.

Bank of England · Royal Exchange · Mansion House

J / K 5

Three institutions close to Bank tube station, the Bank of England, the Royal Exchange and the official residence of the Lord Mayor, represent financial power and political authority in the heart of the City.

Bank of England

Location: Threadneedle Street, EC 2   **Tube:** Bank

The Old Lady of Threadneedle Street

The Bank of England, known since James Gillray's caricature at the time of the Napoleonic wars as »The Old Lady of Threadneedle

Three faces of high finance: the Bank of England (left), the Royal Exchange (right), the National Westminster Bank (centre)

Street«, extends along Threadneedle Street and Bartholomew Lane. It was founded in 1694 as a private company on the proposal of the Scotsman William Paterson in order to finance the war against France. This makes it the world's second-oldest central bank, only the Bank of Sweden being older. The bank issues banknotes and sets the base interest rate. The fact that the nation's gold reserves are stored in its vaults has inspired crime novelists to fictional break-ins, but everything kept here is, needless to say, »as safe as the Bank of England«.

Sir John Soane (1753–1837) was the architect of the original, single-storey bank building, which was completed in 1833 and given far-reaching alterations by Sir Herbert Baker from 1924 to 1939. Baker left Soane's façade and Corinthian columns on the south and west fronts untouched but built a new, seven-storey office building behind them.

Admission to the Bank of England Museum (entrance in Bartholomew Lane) is free. Banknotes, coins and a reconstruction of the Stock Office, the banking hall designed by Soane, can be seen inside. (Opening times: Mon–Fri 10am–5pm).

Bank of England Museum
⏱

✱ Royal Exchange

Location: Bank, EC 2   **Tube:** Bank

🕐
Opening times:
visits by arrange-
ment: tel.
7 283 7101

With its imposing Corinthian columns the Royal Exchange domi-nates its surroundings. It was founded by Sir Thomas Gresham in 1565 and awarded the title »royal« by Elizabeth I in 1571. A statue at the back of the building and the weather vane in the shape of Gre-sham's crest, a grasshopper, commemorate the founder. The classical style of the present Royal Exchange, completed in 1844, is the work of Sir William Tite. The first building was destroyed in 1666 during the Great Fire, and in 1838 its successor also burned down. The re-lief by Sir Richard Westmacott in the tympanum represents »Com-merce and the charter of the exchange«. Today only currency and bonds are traded here. The broad steps of the exchange are tradition-ally the place from which a new monarch is proclaimed. In the small but exclusive shops around the ground floor exchange brokers buy their ties and have their umbrellas repaired. Every day at 9am, noon, 3pm and 6pm the **glockenspiel** plays English, Welsh, Scottish, Cana-dian and Australian tunes. The equestrian statue of the Duke of Wellington, without stirrups, that stands in front of the Royal Ex-

Stock Exchange ►

change was cast from captured French cannons. On Old Broad Street the tower of the Stock Exchange, where shares are traded, rises to a height of 110m/360 ft.

Lombard Street

Since the Middle Ages the banking centre of London has been Lom-bard Street to the right of the Royal Exchange. The street takes its name from money-lenders from Lombardy. The bank signs are a re-minder of times past: illiterates could recognize their bank by its coat of arms, such as the horse of Lloyd's (1677), the three crowns of Coutts, the crown and anchor of the National Westminster Bank, the anchor of Williams and Glyn's, Alexander's artichoke and Barclay's eagle. In 1563 Martins took over the grasshopper emblem from Gre-

St Mary
Woolnoth ►

sham, who lived here. Although it is not very attractive from the out-side, St Mary Woolnoth (1716–1727) at the start of Lombard Street is in fact a Baroque gem. With its blue plasterwork ceiling it is de-servedly considered the masterpiece of Nicholas Hawksmoor, a pupil of Wren.

Mansion House

Location: Mansion House Place, EC 4   **Tube:** Bank

Official residence
of the Lord
Mayor

Mansion House, the official residence of the Lord Mayor of London, was built by George Dance the Elder between 1739 and 1753. It lies a short distance to the south of Bank station. During official ceremo-nies the Lord Mayor stands below the Corinthian portico, the pedi-ment of which is decorated with scenes of the rise of London. The sights open to visitors (by arrangement with The Principal's Assistance Office, Mansion House, EC 4, tel. 7 626 25009) include the banqueting hall. Although this is known as the Egyptian Hall, it is modelled not on Egyptian architecture but on the description of an »Egyptian room« in the *Ten Books of Architecture* of the Roman architect and military engineer Vitruvius. Eleven prison cells from the period when Mansion House had the additional function of a court of law can also be viewed.

St Stephen Walbrook

★

St Stephen Walbrook directly adjoins the south side of Mansion House. It is the Lord Mayor's parish church. During the construction of the church between 1672 and 1679, Sir Christopher Wren is thought to have studied the problems of dome-building before he undertook the incomparably larger dome of ► St Paul's Cathedral. The dome of St Stephen Walbrook, borne by Corinthian columns, rises above an altar made from travertine stone by Henry Moore (1987) and derisively known as »the camembert«. Wren's original pulpit and altar are still in place.

Temple of Mithras

Construction work for the Bucklersbury office block on Queen Victoria Street, which leads south-west from the Mansion House, uncovered remains of the Roman Temple of Mithras, which was in use for a period of over 250 years from AD 90. Items found on the site are on view in the ► Museum of London.

London Stone

The purpose and origin of the London Stone on the wall of the Chinese Banking Corporation at 111 Cannon Street are not entirely clear. Does it represent the »navel of London«? One thing is known for certain: the rebel Jack Cade proclaimed himself »Lord of the City« here in 1450.

★ Bethnal Green Museum of Childhood

M 3

Location: Cambridge Heath Road, E 2   **Tube:** Bethnal Green

In 1872 Bethnal Green Museum, a branch of the ► Victoria and Albert Museum, opened in an unusual Victorian building that originally housed items from the Great Exhibition of 1851. After completion of the ► Victoria and Albert Museum, the glass and wrought-iron structure moved to Bethnal Green, and today contains the largest collection of toys in Britain – heaven both for children and collectors of old dolls. The charming exhibits range from games, oriental toy soldiers and European teddy bears to a great variety of dolls and dolls' houses and clothes, including doll's wedding dresses from the 19th and 20th centuries. Temporary exhibitions are held on the upper floor, and of course there is also an interactive area.

🕐
Opening times:
daily except Fri
10am–5.50pm

British Library

Location: Euston Road, NW 1   **Tube:** King's Cross

⏱ Opening times: Mon, Wed, Thu 9.30am–6pm, Tue until 8pm, Sat until 5pm, Sun 11am–5pm; tours: Mon, Wed, Fri, Sun 3pm, Sat 10.30 and 3pm

The British Library was established in 1972 as a merger of several institutions, first and foremost the library of the British Museum. Bequests by Sir Robert Cotton, Robert Harley, Sir Hans Sloane and Charles Townley, in addition to the Royal Library donated by George II in 1757, formed the basis of the collection; in 1823 George III's library was acquired. Owing to the lack of space in the old premises in the ▶ British Museum, a new building designed by Colin St John Wilson was opened in 1997. The glass book-tower at the centre accommodates George III's King's Library .

✴ John Riblat Gallery

Some of the library's greatest treasures are on show in the John Riblat Gallery: an original of the Magna Carta from 1215, the Lindisfarne Gospels from the early 8th century, a Gutenberg bible, a Mercator atlas dated 1569, the original manuscripts of Handel's Messiah and the Beatles song Yesterday in Paul McCartney's hand, Lord Nelson's last letter to Lady Hamilton, notes by Alexander Fleming about the discovery of penicillin, Isaac Newton's first commentaries on gravity and mirror-image notes by Leonardo da Vinci. At the computer terminals visitors can actually leaf through some of the documents – a treat not to be missed!

✴ ✴ British Museum

Location: Great Russell Street
Entrances: Great Russell Street, Montague Place

Tube: Russell Square, Tottenham Court Road
Internet: www.thebritishmuseum.ac.uk

⏱ Opening times: daily 10am–5.30pm, Thu, Fri until 8.30pm; 90-minute tour: daily 10.30am, 1pm and 3pm; »eye opener« (introduction to a room, about 50 min): daily from 11am, programme available at the information desk.

Seven million visitors every year make the British Museum one of London's biggest attractions. It ranks among the world's major collections, comprising art, applied art and everyday items from Egypt, Assyria, Babylon, Greece, the Roman Empire, the rest of Europe and Asia. The origins of the museum are the medieval manuscripts collected by Sir Robert Cotton (1570–1631), a similar collection owned by Robert Harley, Earl of Oxford (1661–1724) and his son, and above all a bequest by the scientist Sir Hans Sloane (1660–1753) that was instrumental in the foundation of the museum by act of parliament in the year of Sloane's death. The money for premises was raised by lottery, and Montague House chosen as the site in 1759. Following the addition of enormous quantities of further items to the collections, it was decided to erect a new building in the classical style. Robert Smirke designed the new museum, which was begun in

A temple dedicated to art and archaeology: the British Museum

1823 and completed in 1843 by Smirke's brother Sydney. When the ▶ British Library moved out, space became available, particularly in the Great Court. This permitted the return of the ethnographical collections from the Museum of Mankind, which no longer exists.

The entrance now leads directly to the Great Court, which Sir Norman Foster has enclosed with a glass dome. The Great Court contains the famous circular Reading Room where, among others, Karl Marx, George Bernard Shaw and Mahatma Gandhi once worked. Here Foster has created the largest covered square in Europe, a breathtaking architectural space. New galleries, a café and museum shops have been placed around and below the Reading Room, which was completed in 1857 to a design by Sydney Smirke. The Reading Room, now of course open to visitors, has been restored to its original appearance and houses the library and COMPASS, the multimedia access system of the British Museum. Room 25 on the floor below presents the African collection from the Museum of Mankind.

★★
Great Court and Reading Room

✔ **DON'T MISS**

- The Rosetta Stone: the deciphering of hieroglyphics (room 4)
- Elgin Marbles: superb sculptures from the Parthenon in Athens (room 18)
- Lion-hunt reliefs: the sport of Assyrian kings (room 10)
- The Mildenhall Treasure: Roman silverware (room 49)
- Egyptian mummies (rooms 61–65)
- Reading room: where Karl Marx and Mahatma Gandhi studied

British Museum

Main Floor

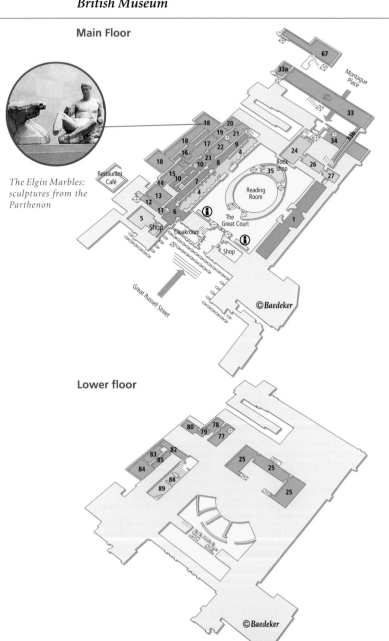

The Elgin Marbles: sculptures from the Parthenon

Lower floor

©Baedeker

Upper Floor

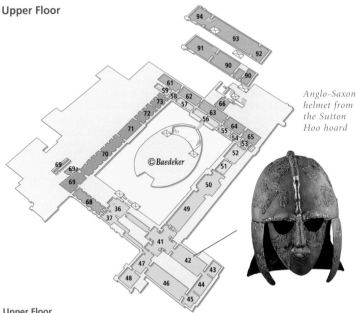

Anglo-Saxon helmet from the Sutton Hoo hoard

Outstanding Exhibits

Only a fraction of the collection, currently estimated to contain 6.5 million items, is on show, and it is quite impossible to visit even this small part in its entirety. The principal rooms are described below.

Room 4
Rosetta Stone ▶

This extensive gallery is devoted to large-scale Egyptian sculpture. The outstanding items are a colossal bust of Ramses II from West Thebes and the Rosetta Stone, found in the Nile delta in 1798 by the French researcher Jean-François Champollion. The inscription in three languages (Egyptian hieroglyphics in the classical and profane styles and a Greek translation) on this tablet of black basalt dating from 195 BC made it possible to decipher hieroglyphics – a milestone of research into ancient history.

Rooms 6–10
Lion-hunt reliefs ▶

Unique treasures of Assyrian civilization are exhibited in these rooms. Room 10 contains reliefs from the reign of Assurbanipal depicting a lion hunt. In the other rooms are reliefs from the palaces of Nimrod and Nineveh, massive winged bulls with human heads from the palace of Sargon in Chorsabad and a black obelisk bearing a description of the deeds of Shalmaneser III.

Powerful: monumental Egyptian sculpture

The Nereid monument is an impressive example of a tomb from Hellenistic Asia Minor.

Room 17

Room 18 contains the famous Elgin Marbles, the sculptures and frieze from the Parthenon in Athens brought to London in the early 19th century by the Earl of Elgin. They include the Horse of Selene from the east pediment of the temple. Selene's triumphal chariot was originally drawn by four horses. Two of them are in Athens and one has been lost. Most of the surviving parts of the Parthenon frieze are also here.

Room 18
◀ Elgin Marbles

This room focuses on Hellenistic art from Asia Minor, with items from the mausoleum of Halikarnassos and the Temple of Artemis in Ephesos.

Room 21

In Room 41 the Sutton Hoo hoard is on display. The ship burial of a 7th-century Anglo-Saxon king (Raedwald or Sigebert) was discovered in Sutton Hoo in Suffolk. It contained weapons, jewellery and coins. Room 42 holds a wonderful treasure: chess pieces of walrus ivory from the Hebridean island of Lewis.

Rooms 41, 42

One of the main attractions in the first of the rooms devoted to Roman Britain is the Mildenhall treasure, found in 1942 by a farmer while ploughing. It comprises 34 pieces of silver plate from the 4th century AD, including the Great Dish, a silver bowl decorated with representations of Bacchus, Hercules and other figures from Roman mythology. The bearded mask at the centre is probably Oceanus, the god of the sea, surrounded by nymphs. The bronze bust of Emperor Hadrian was salvaged from the Thames.

Room 49
◀ Mildenhall Treasure

> ! **Baedeker TIP**
>
> **For bookworms**
> The streets around the British Museum are paradise for bookworms: rows of secondhand bookshops. Two particularly well-stocked stores are Skoob Books (10 Bernard Street) and Any Amount of Books (56 and 62 Charing Cross Road).

The Lindow Man in room 50 is a 2000-year-old mummy of a man thought to have been buried in a bog in Cheshire after being ritually killed by strangling. His stomach contained seeds of mistletoe, the holy plant of the druids.

Room 50

The famous Egyptian collection, with its emphasis on mummies and sarcophaguses, has benefited from a rearrangement.

Rooms 61–63
◀ Mummies

Life in ancient Rome is the theme of these two rooms. The Portland Vase, a masterpiece from the 1st century BC named after the Dukes of Portland, can be seen here. It is one of the finest known examples of Roman glasswork.

Rooms 70/71

Brompton Oratory

D 7

Location: Brompton Road, SW 7 **Tube:** South Kensington

The Roman Catholic Brompton Oratory is the church of the Oratorians, an order founded in Rome in 1575 by St Philip Neri and introduced to England in 1847 by John Henry Newman, later Cardinal Newman, a statue of whom adorns the courtyard of the church. It was built between 1854 and 1884 to a design by Herbert Gribble in the style of the Italian Renaissance. The nave of the church is the third largest in England after ►Westminster Abbey and York Minster. The most notable features of the Oratory are figures of the apostles in Carrara marble, which came from Siena cathedral; the Renaissance altar in the Lady Chapel from the Dominican church in Brescia; and the altar in St Wilfrid's Chapel, which formerly stood in the cathedral of Maastricht. The cemetery in West Brompton is London's largest. Chelsea Pensioners are buried here.

Brompton Cemetery ►

★ ★ Buckingham Palace

F 6/7

Location: The Mall, SW 1 **Tube:** St James's Park, Victoria, Green Park

Opening times:
Aug/Sept
daily
9.30am–4.30pm
ticket reservation
tel. 020
7 766 7300

Buckingham Palace is the London home of the royal family. When the royal standard is flying, the family are at home, attended by a staff of 300. However, the palace has been an official residence only since 1837, when Queen Victoria moved here from ►St James's Palace. It was built on the site of a mulberry orchard laid out for James I and presented to the Duke of Buckingham by Queen Anne. In 1703 the Duke of Buckingham commissioned a modest brick-built house, which King George III bought for his bride Charlotte in 1762. In 1825 George IV gave **John Nash**, his court architect, the task of rebuilding the house, but the costs of the project escalated so much that Nash was dismissed and the work entrusted to Edward Blore, who completed it in 1837. In 1846 the east wing facing ►The Mall was added. The balcony from which the royal family wave to the public is here. In 1913 Sir Aston Webb gave the east wing its classical façade.

Summer opening ►

In late summer visitors are admitted to 19 of the more than 600 rooms, including the Throne Room, the State Dining Room and the remarkably fine private collection in the art gallery. The twelve private apartments of the royal family in the north wing remain closed, of course – though visitors would not meet any blue-blooded residents, as the royal family take their holiday at Balmoral Castle in Scotland at this time of year.

Visitors to London love it: guards parade in front of Buckingham Palace.

The Queen's Gallery occupies the site of the Queen Victoria Chapel, which was destroyed by a bomb in 1940. Items from the extensive royal art collections are exhibited here (opening times: daily except March 10am–5.30pm, last admission 4.30pm).

Queen's Gallery

In front of the palace is the Queen Victoria Memorial planned by Sir Aston Webb and executed by Sir Thomas Brock. The queen is shown surrounded by allegorical figures of Victory, Endurance, Courage, Truth, Justice, Science, Art and Agriculture.

Victoria Monument

The best time of day to visit Buckingham Palace is when the Changing of the Guard takes place. In summer this is normally daily at 11.30am, in winter every other day at 11.30am, except when the weather is bad. At about the same time a squadron of the Household Cavalry coming from changing the guard at the Horse Guards (► Whitehall) rides past the palace on the way to their headquarters in Hyde Park Barracks. Five infantry regiments of the Royal Guard do duty at Buckingham Palace: the Scots Guards (founded in 1642), the Coldstream Guards (1650), the Grenadiers (1656), the Irish Guards (1900) and the Welsh Guards (1913). They all wear the famous bearskin hats and uniforms with scarlet jackets. To learn about their history go to the **Guards Museum** in Wellington Barracks (Birdcage Walk; opening times: daily 10am–4pm, closed mid-Dec–Jan).

✱
Changing of the Guard

The Royal Mews, the stables built by John Nash in 1826 at the south corner of Buckingham Palace park, contain an exhibition of the coaches and automobiles of British monarchs, which are still used

✱
Royal Mews

! **Baedeker** TIP

www.royal.gov.uk
The royal family online: a website for the self-presentation of the house of Windsor. All those who are disappointed not to have met them at Buckingham Palace can look under News/ Engagements to see the official diary of »the firm«, as Prince Philip calls his family – an opportunity, maybe, to get a glimpse of the queen.

on special occasions. Pride of place goes to the Golden State Coach built in 1762 for George III, which has been used for coronations since 1820. Its harnesses and trappings are regarded as the finest in the world. Also on display are the Irish State Coach, bought in 1852 by Queen Victoria and now used for the journey to the opening of parliament, and the glass coach acquired by George V in 1910, which is used by the bride and groom at royal weddings. Needless to say, Rolls Royces and Bentleys bearing the royal coat of arms can also be admired (opening times: March–Oct daily 11am–4pm).

Camden Town

E/F 2

Location: east of Regent's Park   **Tube:** Camden Town

Camden Markets ✱ Until it was discovered by the hippie and alternative scene, Camden Town was just another London suburb. Today it is a magnet for both

In the thick of things: Camden Lock in Camden Town

Londoners and tourists, who come to the shops on the High Street, at Camden Lock (on the Regent's Canal), in Canal Market and in Stables Market under the railway arches to buy outlandish, exotic and in-your-face items at reasonably affordable prices: new and second-hand clothes (the dominant colour is black), shoes and boots, CDs and vinyl records, jewellery and crafts, souvenirs and kitsch, Asian, African and esoteric goods, piercing and tattoos, all the essentials for Goths and punks or for the perfect monster party. In the middle of it all there are a considerable number of good-quality Asian and Arabian food stalls to revive flagging shoppers. Camden markets are an unmissable seven-days-a-week experience, though preferably not at weekends, when the crush is almost unbearable.

Chelsea

B – E 8 / 9

Location: south-west of the city centre   **Tube:** Sloane Square

Chelsea emerged from centuries of obscurity when it caught the eye of Henry VIII, who chose the fishing village as the site of a country palace, now long gone. Thomas More, who lived here for many years, brought high politics to Chelsea. In later centuries scientists, artists and writers such as Joseph Banks, Algernon Charles Swinburne, Oscar Wilde and Thomas Carlyle followed his example. They made Chelsea what it is today: an attractive residential district for the well-to-do. The quiet atmosphere came to an end in the Sixties and Seventies, when Chelsea was the centre of Swinging London – it was in King's Road that Mary Quant opened her boutique and invented the mini-skirt. Mick Jagger and Keith Richards moved in and, when they got older, Johnny Rotten and Sid Vicious took their place. One celebrity has never left: James Bond, whose London address is Royal Avenue, Chelsea.

From a fishing village to a top address

King's Road takes its name from the fact that from 1719 to 1830 it was reserved for the king on his way to Hampton Court or for those in possession of a royal permit. It starts at Sloane Square, which is named after Sir Hans Sloane. Here, in the Royal Court Theatre the premiere of John Osborne's *Look Back in Anger* was staged in 1956. From Sloane Square the road passes right through Chelsea, bordered by pubs, cafés and shops of every kind, particularly fashion and antiques.

King's Road – memories of Swinging London

The most beautiful building on King's Road is The Pheasantry (no. 152), dating from 1765. Chelsea Old Town Hall, built in 1887, is well-known to antique collectors: the antique and art fairs held here in spring and autumn are among the leading events of this kind in the world. Somewhat further away but well worth a detour is the loveliest art nouveau architecture in London, Michelin House. This building, dated 1911 (corner of Sloane Avenue/Fulham Road), is the home of a top restaurant, Bibendum, an oyster bar and a design store.

! *Baedeker* TIP

King's Road Shopping

Steinberg & Tolkien (no. 193) is the place to go for unusual glamour articles and fantastic secondhand items, Reiss stocks trendy and affordable fashion for men (no. 114–116), Octopus has bags and accessories from all over the world (no. 130, Kings Walk Mall) and Aware is good for underwear (no. 182). World's End (no. 430) was Vivienne Westwood's first shop.

Cheyne Walk · Royal Hospital Road

Old Church Street leads down to the Thames and Cheyne Walk. A selection of past and present residents shows that this is one of the highest-class addresses in the city: Keith Richards (no. 3), George Eliot (no. 4), Gabriel Dante Rossetti and Algernon Charles Swinburne (no. 10), Ian Fleming, author of the James Bond books (no. 21), Mick Jagger (no. 48), James McNeill Whistler (no. 101) and J.M.W. Turner (no. 119).

Crosby Hall Right next to Roper's Garden is Crosby Hall, the remains of a town residence built on Bishopsgate in the 15th century by the wool merchant Sir John Crosby and burned down in the 17th century. The Great Hall, which survived the fire, was brought to this site in 1910.

Lindsey House One of the houses beyond it is Lindsey House (no. 96–100), which has been the London headquarters of the Moravian Brethren since 1752.

✳ **Chelsea Old Church** In 1528 Sir Thomas More had the More Chapel, the burial place of his first wife, built onto the 12th-century Chelsea Old Church. The two Renaissance capitals are said to be the work of his close friend Hans Holbein. In the inscription to be seen in the chapel, More asked to be laid to rest next to his wife – however, after his execution his body was buried in the Tower and his head impaled on London Bridge. There is a plaque to the author Henry James, whose grave is here. The Lawrence Chapel was the scene of the secret marriage between Henry VIII and Jane Seymour. Other notable features are Bernini's monument to Lady Jane Cheyne (1699) on the north wall, the family memorial of the goldsmith Sir Thomas Lawrence in the Lawrence Chapel and the funeral monument of Sarah Colville (1632). The final resting-place of the scientist Sir Hans Sloane is the southeast corner of the churchyard by the seated figure of Sir Thomas More. From here there is a view of the elegant Albert Bridge (1873).

Albert Bridge

From the Old Church to the Royal Hospital ⊙ No. 25 Cheyne Row (walk towards Chelsea Royal Hospital and turn off Cheyne Walk a short distance beyond the church) was the home of the Scottish writer Thomas Carlyle (1795–1881) (opening times: April–Oct Wed–Sun 11am–5pm). Further along Cheyne Walk is no.

19–26. The Tudor palace of Henry VIII, built in 1537 and demolished in 1753, stood here. Its residents included Anne of Cleves, Princess Elizabeth (the future Queen Elizabeth I), Lady Jane Grey and later Sir Hans Sloane. Continue in this direction to Chelsea Physic Garden on the right. It was laid out in 1673 by the Worshipful Society of Apothecaries as a herb garden and for teaching purposes. The first cotton seeds sown in Georgia came from here, as did the first tea plants to be taken to India, after coming to England from China. There is a monument in honour of Sir Hans Sloane (opening times: April–Oct Wed 2pm–5pm, Sun 2pm–6pm). Further on is the National Army Museum, which recounts the history of the British army from 1415 to the present day (opening times: daily 10am–5.30pm).

◄ Henry VIII's Palace

◄ Chelsea Physic Garden

Chelsea Royal Hospital was founded in 1682 by Charles II as a home for army veterans. It still accommodates more than 400 »Chelsea Pensioners«, soldiers over the age of 65 who have served for at least 22 years. They still wear the traditional uniform from the Duke of Marlborough's time: scarlet in summer, dark blue in winter, always completed by a three-cornered hat or a peaked cap and military decorations. The original Royal Hospital building, by Sir Christopher Wren, was extended by Robert Adam from 1765 to 1782; it was finally completed by John Soane in 1819. The museum in the east wing is devoted to the history of the hospital (opening times: April to Sept Mon–Sat 10am–noon and 2pm–4pm, Sun 2pm–4pm).

★ **Chelsea Royal Hospital**

In the main building the Great Hall, the beautifully panelled dining room, is open to visitors. It is adorned with royal portraits, replicas of standards captured in the wars against America and France and a mural depicting Charles II on horseback. The chapel, which remains as Wren built it, has a resurrection scene done in 1710 by the Italian painter Sebastiano Ricco. A colonnade leads to the Figure Court. The centre of the court is occupied by a bronze statue of Charles II, a masterpiece by Grinling Gibbons which is decorated

Chelsea Pensioners spend their retirement at Chelsea Royal Hospital.

Royal Hospital Gardens ▶ with a wreath of oak leaves every year on 29 May, the foundation day of the hospital. This is a reference to Charles II's escape from Cromwell's army by hiding in a hollow oak tree. The pensioners receive double pay on this day. The gardens extend to the River Thames. Each year in May they are the setting for the famous Chelsea Flower Show. Some of the cannon on show here were captured from the French at Waterloo.

Battersea Park Battersea Bridge leads across the river to Battersea Park with its Japanese Pagoda of Peace and children's zoo. The massive bulk of Battersea Power Station, now decommissioned, lies on the other side of **Adrenalin Village ▶** Queenstown Road. Here, in Adrenalin Village, those with nerves of steel can take Britain's highest bungee jump.

★★ Courtauld Institute Gallery

G / H 5

Location: Somerset House, Strand, WC 2   **Tube:** Temple
Internet: www.courtauld.ac.uk

⏲ Opening times: daily 10am–6pm, last admission 5.15pm (Mon free admission until 2pm)

The Courtauld Institute Gallery, one of the world's most exquisite art collections, exhibits paintings belonging to London University. The home of the gallery is Somerset House, which previously accommodated the ▶Royal Academy, the Royal Society and the Society of Antiquaries. Somerset House was built for this purpose between 1777 and 1786 by Sir William Chambers on the site of the 16th-century palace of the Lord Protector Duke of Somerset. Chambers designed a building in the Palladian style with its main entrance on the Strand and an imposing, almost 200m-long façade facing the Thames. For this reason the best view of the building is from Waterloo Bridge. When Somerset House was built, the arcades on Victoria Embankment, intended to be used for market stalls, were from time to time subject to flooding by the Thames; the central arch served as a lock gate. The east wing is occupied by the world-renowned King's College of London University.

✔ **DON'T MISS**

- Lucas Cranach the Elder: *Adam and Eve*
- Edouard Manet: *A Bar at the Folies-Bergère*
- Vincent van Gogh: *Self-portrait with Bandaged Ear*

Exhibition of paintings The core of the gallery, a bequest by Samuel Courtauld (1865–1947), is one of the most important collections of French Impressionist and post-Impressionist works outside France. Further acquisitions were Lord Lee of Fareham's collection of Italian Renaissance painting and British portraiture, Count Antoine Seilerne's Princes Gate Collection

Edouard Manet's »Bar at the Folies-Bergère«

(Renaissance and Baroque), and lastly the Roger Fry Collection of works by British and French artists of the late 19th and early 20th centuries.

 European art from 1300 to 1500 is on the ground floor. The rooms on the first floor cover the early Italian Renaissance through to Baroque painting and British portraitists of the 18th century – outstanding works here include *Adam and Eve* by Lucas Cranach the Elder (room 4), *The Flight to Egypt* by Jan Brueghel the Elder (room 4), Rubens's designs for the *Deposition* in Antwerp cathedral (room 5), an *Ecce Homo* by Jan van Eyck (room 6) and Goya's *Francisco de Saavedra* (room 7). The focal point of the rooms on the upper floor and at the same time the highlight of the gallery are the Impressionist works: Renoir's *La Loge* (room 8), Manet's *Dejeuner sur l'herbe* (room 8) and his famous *Bar at the Folies-Bergère* (room 9), as well as works by Gauguin, Monet, Seurat and van Gogh's *Self-portrait with Bandaged Ear* (room 9). Rooms 10 and 11 are devoted to British and French painting since 1900 respectively.

These rooms are modelled on the Winter Palace in St Petersburg and are used for temporary exhibitions, including the display of works from the Hermitage. **Hermitage Rooms**

The Gilbert Collection in the south wing contains an outstanding collection of silver and gold objects, snuff-boxes, clocks, miniatures and porcelain. **Gilbert Collection**

★ Covent Garden

G 5

Location: Covent Garden, WC 2 **Tube:** Covent Garden, Charing Cross, Leicester Square

From a vegetable market to a piazza
Covent Garden is one of London's liveliest spots, especially at week-ends, when it is a stage for street acrobats and buskers who parade their skills to passers-by heading for the shops and restaurants around the square. The name refers to a medieval »convent garden« granted to John Russell, first Earl of Bedford, by Edward VI. In 1631 the fourth earl commissioned **Inigo Jones** to design buildings for the site. Jones created an Italian piazza. With the exception of St Paul's Church, however, little of this remains today. From 1670 London's flower and vegetable market was situated here. In the 18th century Covent Garden, with its gambling dens, pubs and brothels, was London's main entertainment district. In 1832 the city authorities cleaned up the area and moved the market into the Central Hall; in 1974 the market moved out again, and cafés and shops took up residence in Central Hall (don't miss a look at the Cabaret Mechanical Theatre on the lower floor!). In the Jubilee Hall an antiques market is held on Mondays, on other weekdays a general market and at weekends a crafts market. The wholesale market is now held south of the Thames at Nine Elms.

> ! **Baedeker TIP**
>
> **Frenzy**
> To find out what went on in Covent Garden before 1974, watch Alfred Hitchcock's Frenzy – a great thriller as well as a source information. Hitchcock knew the area well: his father was a Covent Garden merchant.

St Paul's Church
»The handsomest barn in the whole of England« was Inigo Jones's verdict on the church opposite Central Hall that he built in 1633: the Earl von Bedford had said »I would have it not much better than a barn«. St Paul's Church is popularly thought to be »back to front«: Jones originally planned to place the altar in the west, but the clergy opposed this solution and he was forced to close off the portico facing the piazza – the place where Professor Higgins first saw Eliza Doolittle – which he had originally planned as the entrance. Access to the church is therefore from the west, which is regarded as the back of the church. The location of St Paul's Church in London's theatre district has made it the »actors' church«. No place of worship apart from ► Westminster Abbey and ► St Paul's Cathedral has so many graves of well-known Londoners of the 18th and 19th centuries, including many actors. In addition to the floral wreaths carved by Grinling Gibbons on the west entrance (1721), it is worth looking at funeral monuments such as those of Grinling Gibbons and the painter Sir Peter Lely.

Acrobats draw the crowds at Covent Garden.

The Royal Opera towers above the north-western side of the square. It originated as the Theatre Royal Covent Garden founded by John Rich in 1732. The present building was completed in 1856 to designs by E.M. Barry and is the third on the site, its predecessors of 1732 and 1809 having burned down. Today it is home to the Royal Opera and the Royal Ballet. The restoration of 1999 integrated Barry's Floral Hall, which was conceived as a ballroom and concert hall, but let to market traders in 1887 for financial reasons.

★
Royal Opera House

> **!** *Baedeker* TIP

> **Bar with a view**
> The terrace on the second-highest storey of the Royal Opera House provides an excellent view over the roofs of London. To reach it, take the escalator from the bar in the Floral Hall (entrance on Bow Street or from the ticket office).

The classical main façade of the opera house looks out over Bow Street, almost directly onto the former Bow Street Police Station, where Henry Fielding formed London's first police force, the Bow Street Runners, in the 18th century. The station is to be converted into a museum.

Bow Street Police Station

Russell Street leads to the Theatre Royal Drury Lane. From 1663 it was the site of the King's Servants Theatre, where the actress Nell Gwynne, mistress of King Charles II, trod the boards. The original theatre and two successors burned down. The present one was built in 1812 by Benjamin Wyatt. One of the regular theatre-goers here is

Theatre Royal Drury Lane

🕐 a ghost which emerges from the wall on the left and hovers over the auditorium (tours: Sun, Mon, Tue, Thu, Fri 2.15pm and 4.45pm, Wed and Sat 10.15am and noon).

✱ London's Transport Museum

🕐
Opening times:
Sat–Thu 10am–6pm
Fri. 11am–8pm

London's Transport Museum in the eastern corner of the piazza tells the story of passenger transport in London. The totally refurbished collection is more than just a row of old vehicles: visitors are encouraged to enjoy a hands-on experience, and the exhibits beneath the Victorian arches of the market hall have been equipped with state-of-the-art museum technology.

From double-deckers to tube trains

The exhibition covers the period from the 19th century to the present. Many different types of the famous red double-deckers are on show, ranging from a horse-drawn bus of 1870 to a 1930s trolley-bus, a horse-drawn tram dating from 1882 and an electric tram of 1910. The »tube« occupies a prominent place. There is a reconstruction of 19th-century tunnel-building, and on the simulator visitors can try their hand at driving a train through the narrow tunnels beneath the streets of London. The Frank Pick Gallery displays photos and posters, the Ashfield Gallery caricatures, and the Harry C. Beck Gallery, named after the creator of the tube network map that has remained essentially unchanged to this day, traces the development of the underground system.

Nostalgia: buses in London's Transport Museum

✴ Docklands

L – N 5 / 6

Location: East of Tower Bridge

The **Docklands Light Railway (DLR)** connects Tower Gateway and **Getting there**
Bank stations in the City with the Docklands and goes on to ►
Greenwich. The driverless computer-controlled trains move on
raised tracks that trace the route of 19th-century railway lines. The
tube (Jubilee Line) also has a Docklands link but the DLR is a pleas-
anter way to travel. The Docklands
can also be reached by water: most
boats make the journey from Westminster Pier, Charing Cross Pier or
Tower Pier to Greenwich, from
where Greenwich Foot Tunnel
leads beneath the Thames to Island
Gardens.

To the east of the City lies London's largest redeveloped area of
recent times, the »up-stream
docks« of Wapping, Limehouse &
Poplar, Surrey Docks, the Isle of
Dogs and the Royal Docks, which
fell into disuse between 1967 and
1981. They were once the economic heart of Great Britain, a place
where goods from all over the
world were unloaded. Baedeker's
London and its Environs 1900 re-   *The DLR is a convenient link to the Docklands.*
ported as follows:

London Docks, lying to the E. of St. Katharine Docks, were constructed **From: Baedeker's**
in 1805 at a cost of 4,000,000l., and cover an area of 100 acres. They **London and its**
have three entrances from the Thames, and contain water-room for **Environs 1900**
about 400 vessels, exclusive of lighters. Their warehouses can store from
170,000 to 260,000 tons of goods (according to description), and their
cellars 121,000 pipes of wine. At times upwards of 3,000 men are em-
ployed at these docks in one day. Every morning at 6 o'clock may be seen
waiting at the principal entrance a large and motley crowd of labourers
…Nothing will convey to the stranger a better idea of the vast activity
and stupendous wealth of London than a visit to these warehouses, filled
to overflowing with interminable stores of every kind of foreign and col-
onial products; to these enormous vaults, with their apparently inex-
haustible quantities of wine; and to these extensive quays and landing-
stages, cumbered with huge stacks of hides, heaps of bales and long rows
of casks.

Docklands

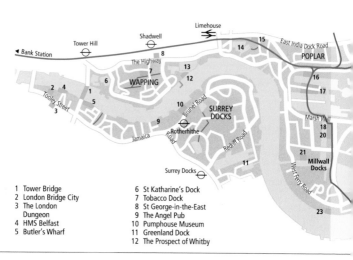

	Docklands Light Railway	
⊖	London Underground	
⤢	Railway	

1 Tower Bridge
2 London Bridge City
3 The London Dungeon
4 HMS Belfast
5 Butler's Wharf

6 St Katharine's Dock
7 Tobacco Dock
8 St George-in-the-East
9 The Angel Pub
10 Pumphouse Museum
11 Greenland Dock
12 The Prospect of Whitby

When the docks moved further downstream, London Docklands lost their purpose, fell into decay and became an area with social problems. From 1981 to 1998 the government authorized the construction of a £25 billion business district with planned employment for 200,000 and housing for 115,000 people. In accordance with the wishes of the then prime minister, Margaret Thatcher, no restrictions were placed on the investors' plans. This gave rise to criticism that the needs of the poor were not considered. Many investors went bankrupt, and millions of square feet of new office space remained empty. However, more and more companies are now moving into the Docklands.

Surrey Docks

Surrey Docks on the south bank of the Thames extend eastwards from ▶Tower Bridge to Greenland Docks in the bend of the river at Rotherhithe. Quays for trade in wood and grain were built on this stretch of the river bank as early as the 14th century. In 1620 the Mayflower left Rotherhithe for Southampton and Plymouth to carry the **pilgrim fathers** to North America.

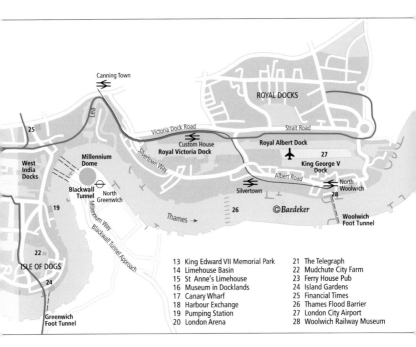

Canning Town

ROYAL DOCKS

25

Victoria Dock Road   Strait Road

Custom House
Royal Victoria Dock   Royal Albert Dock

West
India   Millennium   27
Docks   Dome   King George V
                                                      Dock

Blackwall   North
Tunnel   North   Woolwich
          Greenwich   Silvertown   28
19   Albert Road

                            26   ©Baedeker
Thames →   Woolwich
                                                     Foot Tunnel

22
ISLE OF DOGS

24

Greenwich
Foot Tunnel

13 King Edward VII Memorial Park	21 The Telegraph
14 Limehouse Basin	22 Mudchute City Farm
15 St Anne's Limehouse	23 Ferry House Pub
16 Museum in Docklands	24 Island Gardens
17 Canary Wharf	25 Financial Times
18 Harbour Exchange	26 Thames Flood Barrier
19 Pumping Station	27 London City Airport
20 London Arena	28 Woolwich Railway Museum

The old warehouses of Butler's Wharf and the Anchor Brewery east of Tower Bridge were among the first properties to be converted to a fashionable residential and business complex. The street Shad Thames behind Butler's Wharf conveys a good impression of how the area used to look.

Butler's Wharf

The Design Museum at the end of Butler's Wharf overlooks the Thames. Here everyday articles from vacuum cleaners to coffee cups and cars have been gathered under one roof to show how function determines form, but also how much forms can change. From the café terrace there is a wonderful view of ►Tower Bridge and St Katharine's Dock opposite; the museum shop sells all kinds of design in miniature (opening times: daily 10am–5.45pm).

✷ Design Museum

⊙

Between 1825 and 1843 **Marc Brunel** built the Thames Tunnel, a technical marvel of its time, to connect Wapping with Surrey Docks. The pumphouse is now a museum (opening times: first Sunday in the month, noon–4pm). A good place to stop for a break near the museum is the pub The Angel (101 Bermondsey Wall East), which dates back to the 15th century.

Pumphouse Museum

◄ The Angel

Wapping, Limehouse and Poplar

Wapping, Limehouse and Poplar docks stretch along the north bank of the Thames from Tower Bridge to the Blackwall Tunnel. They were in use from the 16th century and reached their peak in the 18th and 19th centuries, when the main commodities unloaded here were rice, tobacco and wine. Poverty and a high crime rate formed a stark contrast to the hive of commercial activity here: Execution Dock in Wapping was the site of the gallows.

St Katharine's Dock
St Katharine's Dock was opened in late autumn 1827. A number of handsome warehouses such as Ivory House, which was originally used for storing ivory, the harbourmaster's house and the pub Dickens' Inn have been restored. Two historic ships lie at anchor here: the lightship *Nore* and the steam tug *Challenge*, both built in 1931.

Tobacco Dock
The upper floors of Tobacco Dock Warehouse, which dates from 1811, were used to store tobacco and sheepskins, the cellars for wine and rum. Today shops and restaurants occupy the building. Nearby the media magnate **Rupert Murdoch** has built his headquarters, News International, generally known as Fortress Wapping – a brief glance suffices to understand the nickname. The Prospect of Whitby east of Tobacco Dock has been in business since 1502, which makes it the oldest pub on the Thames.

The Prospect of Whitby ▶

Financial Times Printing Press
One of the few new buildings not lambasted by the architectural critics was the printing works of the Financial Times in Poplar, designed by the architect **Nicholas Grimshaw** and built of glass, steel and aluminium.

Isle of Dogs

The Isle of Dogs lay at the centre of the docklands redevelopment. The names of the docks, East India and West India Docks, indicate the trade that was carried on here. However, the Isle of Dogs was not only a place for trade in colonial goods. Its quays and manufacturing works made it London's centre of heavy industry in the mid-19th century. The area has now acquired a completely different character as a place for offices and housing with attractive architecture such as The Cascades, a residential development by **Piers Gough**, the South Quay Plaza office complex and John Outram's Pumphouse on Stewart Street, as well as controversial new buildings such as Canary Wharf.

★ Museum in Docklands
The buildings at the northern end of the West India Docks, which date from 1802 and 1803, are the last remaining multi-storey warehouses from the Georgian period. The Museum in Docklands at no. 1 is devoted to the history of the docks. The atmosphere of the old

Docklands: a laboratory for experiments in postmodern architecture including Britain's tallest building

warehouse and the scenes recreated there give the museum its character. It is superbly equipped, with loving attention to detail. Visitors can stroll through the dark alleys of the harbour quarter to the sounds of singing from a pub and the cries of the street hawkers. Children learn how to load a ship and can take an underwater trip wearing a diving helmet (opening times: daily 10am–6pm).

Canary Wharf

Tomatoes and bananas from the Canary Islands used to be handled at Canary Wharf. Its redevelopment was the most spectacular of the Docklands projects, with a 244m/800ft-high office block designed by **Cesar Pelli**, the tallest building in Britain, towering above it. A shortage of tenants gave the tower the nickname London Space Centre – »space« here meaning not the universe but empty office space.

Millwall Dock

Two buildings stand out at Millwall Dock: the steel-and-glass construction of South Quay Plaza and Harbour Exchange. The London Arena is a multi-purpose hall seating 12,000 people.

Royal Docks

The Royal Docks occupy an area to the east of the River Lea. In 1855 Victoria Dock was opened. Albert Dock followed in 1880. The chemical, cable-manufacturing and food industries set up here, but progress had its price: in January 1917 an explosion in a TNT factory killed 73 people. In 1922 the last of the large docks, King George V Dock, went into service. Since 1987 London City Airport has been

Woolwich
Railway Museum
🕐

in operation. In the old North Woolwich station an attraction for visitors is the Woolwich Railway Museum. Its theme is the Great Eastern Railway, which was founded in 1839 (opening times: in summer Sat–Sun 1pm–5pm).

✳ Thames Barrier

Location: Woolwich, SE 18   **Tube:** Canning Town
Thames boat: Barrier Gardens

🕐
Opening times:
Mon–Fri
10am–5pm,
Sat–Sun
10.30am–5.30pm

On 8 May 1984 the world's largest moving flood barrier, 520m/570yds wide, went into operation in the Thames. Nine piers support a steel barrier consisting of ten enormous gates. It takes about half an hour for the gigantic hydraulic arms to lift the gates into position. This protects large areas of the counties of Essex and Kent from flooding. In the visitor centre there is a fascinating audio-visual show about the construction and the working of the barrier. Boat trips to the barrier gates leave from Barrier Gardens Pier.

Royal Artillery
Museum
🕐

Some distance to the south-east of the barrier is the Royal Arsenal, where the Royal Artillery Museum (opening times: April–Oct Wed–Sat 11am–3.30pm, Nov–March Fri, Sat and Sun 11am–5pm; tube: North Greenwich, then bus to Woolwich) is located.

✳ Dulwich Picture Gallery

Outer suburb

Location: College Road, SE 21   **Tube:** Brixton
Train: West Dulwich from Victoria, North
Dulwich from London Bridge

🕐
Opening times:
Tue–Fri
10am–5pm,
Sat–Sun 11am–5pm

No more than six miles south of the centre of London there is an abrupt change from the city scene to the village atmosphere of Dulwich, the site of lovely Georgian houses, London's only surviving customs barrier and Dulwich College. The college was founded in the early 17th century by Edward Alleyn (1566–1626), a wealthy Shakespearean actor and a bold bear-baiter, as the College of God's Gift for »six poor men and six poor women«.

London's first public art gallery opened here in 1814 in a building designed by Sir John Soane which, through its placement of skylights, was to be a model for the architecture of many later galleries. The bequest of a French art dealer, Noël Desenfans, to his friend Sir Francis Bourgeois in 1807 formed the basis of the collection. Bourgeois and the widow of Desenfans opened the gallery to the public. The works on display include paintings by Rembrandt, Jan van Ruisdael and Aelbert Cuyp, British 17th- and 18th-century portraits by, among others, Sir Peter Lely, Sir Godfrey Kneller, William Hogarth,

Thomas Gainsborough and Sir Joshua Reynolds, paintings by Italian masters (including Raphael, Paolo Veronese, Guercino, Canaletto, Tiepolo), Flemish artists (Rubens, van Dyck, David Teniers) and Spanish masters (Bartolomé Murillo among others) as well as works by French painters (Watteau, Poussin and Le Brun). The pictures are hung close together in the 19th-century fashion. Desenfans, his wife and their friend Bourgeois are buried opposite the main entrance.

Crystal Palace Park (train from Victoria Station) lies further south. This was the site of the Crystal Palace, the focal point of the Great Exhibition of 1851, Sir Joseph Paxton's masterpiece of wrought iron and steel. In 1854 the palace was brought here from Hyde Park and remained a popular attraction until it was destroyed by fire in 1936. A model in the ►Museum of London shows what it looked like. The site of the Crystal Palace is now the National Sports Centre and a park in which life-size plaster casts of prehistoric animals, the last remnants of the Great Exhibition, can be seen.

Crystal Palace Park

Fleet Street

H 5

Location: Between Temple Bar and Ludgate Circus

Tube: Blackfriars, Temple

Fleet Street takes its name from the little Fleet River, down which the bloody effluent from Smithfield Market once flowed into the Thames. It was covered over in the mid-18th century after a drunken butcher fell in and froze to death. Fleet Street used to be the centre of British newspaper publishing. In the late 15th century **Wynkyn de Worde** moved his printing press here from Westminster. In 1702 the Daily Courant was the first daily newspaper to be published in the street. The buildings in which newspaper publishers, their editors and printers once worked are still standing, but they have long been taken over by insurance companies and brokers. Most newspaper publishers have transferred their headquarters out to new business parks, and Fleet Street, the »Street of Ink«, is no longer a synonym for the British press. Reminders of its

»Street of Ink«

? **DID YOU KNOW ...?**

■ ...that the first water-flushed toilet for gentlemen in Britain was opened on 2 February 1852 in Fleet Street? Ladies had to wait more than a week longer: their water closet was inaugurated on 11 February in Bedford Street close to Covent Garden.

golden age as the heart of the newspaper business are the Daily Mail building between Bouverie and Whitefriars Street, the Daily Mirror building on Fetter Lane, the Daily Express building at the corner of Shoe Lane and no. 135 Fleet Street, the Daily Telegraph building. No. 85 was the address of Reuters and AP.

All media institutions have left Fleet Street. Reuters news agency remains – with a monument to its founder.

Temple Bar Temple Bar Memorial, erected in 1880 at the boundary between the City and Westminster and crowned by a griffin, marks the beginning of Fleet Street. Temple Bar, a gate built by Wren in 1680 upon which the heads of decapitated persons were placed on spikes, once stood here. The gate has now been re-erected in Paternoster Square north of ►St Paul's. When the monarch pays a visit to the City, he or she is still obliged to address a formal request for permission to the Lord Mayor at Temple Bar. The entrance to the ►Temple is here.

Child's Bank Child's Bank, the oldest bank in London, was founded in 1671 »at the sign of the marigold« at no.1 Fleet Street, now the Bank of Scotland.

Prince Henry's Room Inside the house at no. 17, opposite Chancery Lane, is Prince Henry's Room with a wooden Tudor ceiling, the centre of which bears the coat of arms of Henry, Prince of Wales and son of James I (opening times: Mon–Sat 11am–2pm); the room is also filled with mementoes to Samuel Pepys. Opposite is St Dunstan-in-the-West with the oldest remaining statue of Elizabeth I (1586) on its south wall.

St Dunstan-in-the-West ►

From 1748 to 1759 Samuel Johnson lived on Gough Square, a little further north. One of the works he wrote here was his famous dictionary (opening times: May–Sept Mon–Sat 11am–5.30pm, Oct–April until 5pm).

Dr Johnson's House

The pub Ye Olde Cheshire Cheese was frequented by many notable writers, while Ye Olde Cock Tavern used to be the haunt of journalists and printers. Both taverns date from the 17th century.

Ye Olde Cheshire Cheese / Ye Olde Cock Tavern

St Bride's is the parish church of the newspaper business. It was first mentioned in the 12th century; the present church was rebuilt in 1957 to Wren's original designs after his building of 1701 burned down in the Second World War. At 70m/230ft the tower of St Bride's is the tallest of any Wren church, prompting London confectioners to use it as the model for their wedding cakes. The church contains memorial plaques to a number of celebrities from the worlds of the press, art and literature. A Roman floor can still be viewed in the museum in the crypt, where there is an exhibition about the history of the church and its connections to the newspaper and printing trades: St Bride's occupies the site of Wynkyn de Worde's printing press.

St Bride's

Gray's Inn

H 4

Location: Gray's Inn Road, WC 2   **Tube:** Chancery Lane

Gray's Inn is one London's four law schools (Inns of Court). The other three are Middle Temple and Inner Temple, situated in the ► Temple, and ► Lincoln's Inn. Gray's Inn is thought to have existed since the 14th century. Its name derives from the former owners of the estate, the Lords de Gray.

The main entrance is on High Holborn beneath a 17th-century arch next to the Cittie of Yorke pub. As the interior of Gray's Inn, including the Great Hall, in which Shakespeare's Comedy of Errors was first performed in 1594, is open to the public only during the London Open House Weekend (► p.75), visits are limited to a walk around the garden, once a popular place for duelling, and a look at South Square with its statue of the philosopher and statesman Francis Bacon, the most famous member of Gray's Inn, who lived here from 1576 to 1626. The garden is open at midday.

Opposite the junction of Gray's Inn Road with High Holborn is Staple Inn. It was once the home and business premises of wool merchants, and later served as student accommodation for future barristers of Gray's Inn. As it stands today, the inn was built in 1586 and is the only surviving Elizabethan timber-framed structure in London.

★
Staple Inn

✶ ✶ Greenwich

Location: east of the city centre
DLR: Cutty Sark, Greenwich

Thames boat: Greenwich Pier from
Westminster or Tower Bridge

Greenwich, situated on the south bank of the Thames about 10km/
6mi from Tower Bridge, is one of the most charming parts of London and well worth a visit. It became world-famous for its observatory, traditionally the lodestar of navigation for sailors from the West, as the world's shipping is governed by Greenwich time and the zero meridian was fixed here. It is thus a place of pilgrimage for everyone who wants to study the history of navigation at first hand, but also an area of wonderful parks.

✶
Cutty Sark

The *Cutty Sark* was the last and most famous of the tea clippers that plied the »tea road« between England and China in the 19th century. It was built in Dumbarton in Scotland in 1869 and was regarded not only as the most beautiful, but also, with its top speed of 17.5 knots, as the fastest ship of its day – in 1871 it took only 107 days from

Shanghai to London, and in 1889 on a voyage to Sydney it overtook the new steamship *Britannia*. It was not taken out of service until 1954. The name, meaning »short shirt«, comes from Robert Burns's poem *Tam O'Shanter*, which describes how the witch Nannie pulls the tail from Tam's grey mare, as shown on the ship's figurehead. Below deck there is an exhibition of old ships' figureheads and mementoes of voyages to China, Ceylon and India. Following severe fire damage during restoration work in May 2007, **the ship is closed to visitors** until further notice.

! *Baedeker* TIP

Rail & River Rover

To make an enjoyable event of the journey to Greenwich, take the DLR to Island Gardens, walk under the Thames through the Greenwich Foot Tunnel of 1902 (but first admire the view which Canaletto painted of the Royal Naval College from the river bank). Return by boat to the Tower or Westminster. London Transport's Rail & River Rover Ticket saves money on this trip.

Close to *Cutty Sark* is the yacht *Gipsy Moth IV*, in which **Francis Chichester** sailed single-handed around the world at the age of 65 in 1966/1967. This took him 274 days, 226 of them spent at sea, and earned him a knighthood.

Gipsy Moth IV

✳ Royal Naval College

The Royal Naval College in the former Greenwich Hospital was the place of training for naval officers. Edward I (1272–1307) had a palace built here. In 1428 the Duke of Gloucester chose the site for his Bella Palace, which Henry VII in turn converted into Placentia Palace. This royal residence and Greenwich had close connections to **Henry VIII**: he was born here, and for 20 years he ruled from here; in Greenwich he married Catherine of Aragon and Anne of Cleves, and signed Anne Boleyn's death warrant. His daughters, Mary I and Elizabeth I, were also born in the palace. Henry ordered the construction of shipyards in Greenwich and in 1512 watched the launch here of the first English four-master, Great Harry. Under Oliver Cromwell the palace was used as a prison and then demolished. From 1696 it was replaced by the King William Building and the Queen Mary Building, which housed a sailors' home founded by Queen Mary II in 1694. These buildings, designed by Sir Christopher Wren but not completed until 1751, were constructed around parts of a new palace for Charles II, begun by John Webb in 1664 but abandoned owing to shortage of money.

Former college for British naval officers

The grounds are open from 8am to 6pm; the public have access to only two rooms (opening times: daily 10am–5pm). The Painted Hall

Visits

← *The figurehead of the Cutty Sark is from Robert Burns's poem »Tam o' Shanter.«*

in the King William Building (south-west side), was completed in 1707 and decorated in the years to 1727 by **Sir James Thornhill** with the paintings to which it owes its name. The ceiling celebrates William of Orange and Mary as peacemakers, triumphing over tyranny in the person of Louis XIV. In the south-west corner there is a portrait of the Royal Astronomer **John Flamsteed**.

The chapel of the Queen Mary Building (on the south-east side) was also built to designs by Wren, but not completed until 1752 by Thomas Ripley. »Athenian« Stuart restored it after a fire in 1779. Benjamin West's altarpiece depicts the shipwreck of St Paul.

★ ★ National Maritime Museum

The National Maritime Museum is probably the largest museum of ships and navigation in the world. Its extremely impressive exhibits tell the story of British sea power. The collections are housed in the west wing of the Queen's House, which was added between 1805 and 1816. Until 1933 the west and east wings were occupied by the Royal Hospital School for sailors' sons. The museum opened in 1937. The Queen's House and Royal Observatory are also part of the National Maritime Museum. Separate and combined admission tickets are available.

Greenwich Citymap

@Baedeker

1 Flamsteed House
2 Flamsteed's Observatory
3 Meridian Building
4 Great Equatorial Building
5 Altazimuth Pavilion
6 South Building
7 Tea House
8 Conduit House

Opening times:
daily 10am–5pm
www.nmm.ac.uk

Exhibition of maritime history
Ground floor ►

The first room beyond the entrance is the Neptune Hall. Displays on the left trace the great voyages of discovery, and the following sections are devoted to passenger transport – here there is a cabin from the *Mauretania* – and freight transport by sea. The central block continues the story of voyages of discovery, and the two other rooms take up the themes of London's role as a port and British naval uniforms. The magnificent **state barge** built in 1732 for Frederick, Prince of Wales is also on display.

Level 2 ►

Level 2 illustrates Britain's rise to world power as a trading nation – with many original items from the great 18th-century voyages of discovery – and presents the Royal Navy, including a life-size reconstruction of a submarine. A section entitled »Art and the Sea« contains **paintings** by van de Veldt, J.M.W. Turner and Muirhead Bone, as well as portraits of famous seamen by such well-known artists as Sir Godfrey Kneller, Sir Peter Lely, William Hogarth, Sir Joshua Reynolds, Thomas Gainsborough and George Romney. From here there is access to the upper level of the Neptune Hall block, where botanical discoveries and the future of marine research are the themes.

✓ **DON'T MISS**

- State barge for Frederick, Prince of Wales
- Maritime paintings
- Mementoes of Lord Nelson
- Model ships for the Admiralty
- Virtual captain's bridge
- Children's section »All Hands«

◄ Level 3

The main subject of level 3 is England's greatest naval hero, Admiral **Horatio Nelson**. The numerous mementoes of Nelson on display include the uniform he wore at the Battle of Trafalgar, at which he died. A particularly fine section is devoted to the construction of warships from 1650 to 1815: every ship in the English fleet started as a model that had to be presented to the Admiralty. The collection contains a large number of these **original models**. The model-makers' attention to detail is astonishing. The two remaining sections allow visitors to make discoveries for themselves: in »**All Hands**« children can find out about the skills needed for a life at sea. This is followed by the **virtual bridge**, where a simulator shows what it is like to pilot a large vessel into harbour.

Inside the National Maritime Museum

✳ ✳ Queen's House

The Queen's House by **Inigo Jones**, a building that inspired the architecture of many other houses but was never surpassed, is a masterpiece of the Palladian style in its symmetry, proportions and the superb quality of its marble floors, wrought-iron balustrades, and carved and painted ceilings. In 1616 Jones was commissioned to build an annexe to Placentia Palace by James I, who wanted a house in Greenwich fit for his queen, Anne of Denmark. James abandoned the project after Anne's death in 1619, but in 1629 Charles I gave Jones the task of completing it for his wife, Henrietta Maria.

The cube-shaped Great Hall represents authentic Palladian style. From here the wonderful Tulip Staircase, designed by Inigo Jones as

🕐 Opening times: daily 10am–5pm

✳

◄ Tulip Staircase

the first winding staircase in England without a central support, leads to the upper floor with the King's Apartment, which was never occupied, and the Queen's Apartment, which was at least used for a few years. Another very beautiful staircase leads down to the Orangery.

Greenwich Park

A place for recreation Next to the grounds of the National Maritime Museum is Greenwich Park, created as a royal garden for Charles II by Le Nôtre, Louis XIV's landscape gardener.

✶ **Old Royal Observatory**
🕐 Opening times: daily 10am–5pm

Flamsteed House, designed by Sir Christopher Wren and named after the first royal astronomer, John Flamsteed, occupies an impressive site on the hill in the middle of the park. There is a wonderful view of the Queen's House and Royal Naval College with the bend of the Thames and the ▶Docklands in the background; further right is the Millennium Dome.

Until 1957 **Flamsteed House** was the home of the Royal Observatory, which Charles II founded in 1675. A mast on the turret bears the time ball, a red sphere that since 1833 has dropped every day at 1pm as a signal for ships on the Thames to set their clocks. Time and navigation are the guiding themes of the exhibition in Flamsteed House. The collection of historic instruments includes three original **Harrison chronometers**, the first chronometers which worked so precisely that they could be used for navigation. Four rooms are furnished as in Flamsteed's time. The problem of determining longitude, for the solution of which the Admiralty established a prize of £20,000 in 1714, is explained for visitors.

The solution was to define a zero (prime) meridian. The British Admiralty naturally fixed its prime meridian on home territory, and so the zero line runs through the **Meridian Building** and divides the world into a western and an eastern hemisphere. To pass from one hemisphere to another, just walk across the steel strip in the ground. The exhibition inside the building contains among other items the Transit Circle, a large instrument designed by the seventh royal astronomer,

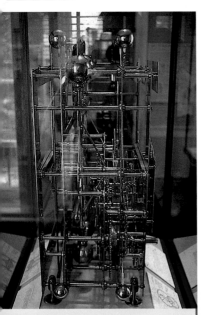

Harrison's revolutionary chronometer

George Bidell Airy, who used it in 1851 to calculate the position of the prime meridian even more exactly than before. The meridian received international recognition at a conference in Washington DC in 1884.

A dome built for a 28-inch telescope installed in 1893, the largest in Great Britain, is the dominant feature of the Equatorial Building.

◄ Equatorial Building

Visitors to the Ranger's House, built in 1688 in the south-east corner of the park, can see paintings, including the outstanding life-size portraits of a 17th-century wedding party by William Larkin, and in the Architectural Study Centre examples of London architecture in the 18th and 19th centuries (opening times: summer daily 10am–1pm and 2pm–6pm, winter Wed–Sun 10am–4pm).

Ranger's House

! *Baedeker* TIP

Trafalgar Tavern

The Trafalgar Tavern (along the bank of the Thames from the *Cutty Sark*) is an excellent place for a rest. The pub has changed little since it opened in 1837. Dickens chose it as the scene for a wedding party in *Our Mutual Friend*. The British cabinet once met in the Nelson Room on the upper floor to dine on whiting.

Millennium Dome

Tube: North Greenwich
Bus von Greenwich: 188, M

Thames boat: Millennium Pier

At the turn of the millennium the wish to express British national pride through architecture was given a new manifestation: the Millennium Dome, planned as a high-tech showcase for a confident nation. A top architect, **Richard Rogers**, sited the world's largest tent on industrial wasteland in northern Greenwich that was previously contaminated by heavy metals. The 50m/164ft-high Teflon roof of the tent, which has a diameter of 365m/1,200ft, is held in place by twelve masts, each 100m/330ft in height. The structure holds 35,000 people, and Wembley Stadium can be fitted into it twice over. A second British star architect, **Norman Foster**, designed North Greenwich tube station, which is also the largest in the world. Most of the costs of the dome, which totalled £758 million (about US$1.5 billion), were raised by a lottery and by private sponsorship, and the rest was intended to come from admission fees. However, the expected stream of visitors failed to materialize. Architecture built for a mil-

A great white elephant: the Millennium Dome

lennium has turned out to be a white elephant. Ambitious plans for its later use came to nothing and potential buyers pulled out. The government, which is responsible for maintaining the dome, has been searching desperately for a purchaser. The Millennium Dome has become the flop of the millennium and is only occasionally open as a venue for events.

Village of Greenwich

Greenwich Market The first port of call in the village is undoubtedly Greenwich Market, a fine old market hall where arts and crafts are the main items on sale.

St Alfege St Alfege was built in 1718 by Nicholas Hawksmoor to replace an older church standing on the site where Danes murdered St Alfege in 1012, in which Henry VIII was baptized. The present church retains some of Grinling Gibbons's wall decoration.

Fan Museum The Fan Museum (no. 12 Croom's Hill) is an unusual institution presenting fans from the 17th century to the present day (opening times: Tue–Sat 11am–5pm, Sun noon–5pm).

★ Guildhall

J 5

Location: Gresham Street, EC 2 **Tube:** St Paul's, Bank

Opening times: inquiries tel. 7 606 3030

The Guildhall, a late Gothic building dating from 1411, is the city hall for the City of London. Only parts of the outer wall, the Great Hall and the crypt remain, as it was devastated in the Great Fire of

1666. Later additions and rebuilding, such as the neo-Gothic south façade of 1789, were destroyed in an air raid in December 1940. After the war the Guildhall was restored. The remains of a Roman amphitheatre from the 1st century AD extending beneath the medieval structure were discovered in the front court in 1988. Remnants of the former Jewish ghetto were also found. Its memory is preserved in the name of the church St Lawrence Jewry, the official church of the Corporation of London to the south of the Guildhall.

The Great Hall is reached from the courtyard, where the coat of arms of London bears the motto Domine dirige nos (Lord guide us). **✳ Great Hall**
The hall, a room for banquets measuring 50m/165ft in length and 29m/95ft in height, is decorated with the banners of the twelve great livery companies, or guilds: seen clockwise these are the grocers, fishmongers, skinners, haberdashers, ironmongers, clothworkers, vintners, salters, tailors, goldsmiths, drapers and mercers. Their coats of arms appear again painted on the moulding, while the names of the Lord Mayors are shown on the windows. At the end of the hall is the minstrels' gallery, adorned with the figures of Gog (right) and Magog (left). On the south side are statues of William Pitt the Younger and Lord Mayor Beckford, an oak dresser with the sword and sceptre of the city, the Royal Fusiliers Memorial and the only remaining 15th-century window. On the north wall there are statues to Sir Winston Churchill, Admiral Nelson, the Duke of Wellington, William Pitt and the Earl of Chatham. Beneath the hall lies the **crypt**, which dates from the 13th to 15th centuries and has one of London's most beautiful groin-vaults (open only for tours).

Guildhall, one of London's few secular Gothic buildings

Part of the art collection of the City of London is in the Guildhall Art Gallery (opening times: Mon–Sat 10am–5pm; Sun until 4pm; free admission Fri and from 3.30pm). **Guildhall Art Gallery**

The greatest treasures of the Guildhall Library are original designs for Shakespeare productions, a map of London from 1591 and a contract for the sale of a house with Shakespeare's signature. The collection of 700 clocks belonging to the Worshipful Company of Clockmakers is also on exhibition in the library (opening times: Mon–Fri 9.30am–4.30pm). **Guildhall Library**

◄ Guildhall Clock Museum

Hampstead · Highgate

Outer suburb

Location: north-west of city centre   **Tube:** Hampstead

Rural London Hampstead possesses great charm. This district in the north of London with its healing springs has always attracted those in need of recuperation, but above all artists and writers such as John Keats, John Constable, Robert Louis Stevenson, D. H. Lawrence, George Orwell, Richard Burton and Peter Sellers have felt at home here. Charles de Gaulle and Sigmund Freud also lived in Hampstead. The countryside around London's highest ground (145 m/475 ft above sea level) is shown in many landscape paintings – works by John Constable, for example.

Hampstead Well There is much to explore on a stroll around the up-and-down lanes of Hampstead Well. On the High Street and Flask Walk there are pretty shops, stylish houses and reminders of the time when Hampstead was a spa; on Church Row a beautiful row of Georgian houses and St John's Church, the burial place of John Constable. Hampstead Cemetery lies a little further away on Finchley Road and there are welcoming pubs like Jack Straw's Castle (12 North End Way). The pub is not very old, but it stands on a historic site: in 1381 Jack Straw, leader of the Peasants' Revolt, marched from here towards the riches of the City of London.

! *Baedeker* TIP

Kenwood Lakeside Concerts

Could there be a more romantic venue for open-air concerts? From June to September classical music is played every Saturday on the lawn of Kenwood House, which slopes like an amphitheatre down to a pond. On 4 July Handel's »Fireworks Music« is performed – with a robust pyrotechnical accompaniment, of course (www.picnicconcerts.com).

Museums ▶ Hampstead Well is notable for its museum houses: **Burgh House** on New End Square, built in 1703, is devoted to the history of Hampstead (opening times: Wed–Sun noon–5pm) and has an excellent cafeteria. **Fenton House** dated 1693, is one of the oldest buildings in Hampstead. It contains a collection of old keyboard instruments, all of which are still in working order (opening times: April–Oct Wed to Fri 2pm–5pm, Sat and Sun 11am–5pm; in March weekends only). The house at **no. 2 Willow Rd.** , which belonged to the architect Ernö **Goldfinger**, is a classic example of 1930s residential architecture (tel. 7 435 6166). If the name seems familiar, that is because Ian Fleming, the creator of 007 and a neighbour, detested Goldfinger and named his arch-villain after the architect. The **Keats House** has many mementoes of the poet John Keatss, who lived here from 1818 to 1829. He found inspiration in the girl next door, Fanny Browne, and wrote such famous verses as Ode to a Nightingale here (opening times: mid April–Oct Tue–Sun noon–5pm; Nov–March until 4pm).

A little to the south of Hampstead Well, there is the house of Sigmund Freud, the founder of psychoanalysis, who fled to London from the Nazis in 1938 (20 Maresfield Gardens). His famous couch is of course the centrepiece (opening times: Wed–Sun noon–5pm). ◄ Freud Museum

Hampstead's open space, the heath, is famous for its wonderful view over London. From Parliament Hill the city seems to lie at one's feet. The Celtic Queen Boudica is said to be buried beneath a fenced-in hill further north-west. Art-lovers should pay a visit to Kenwood House, built in 1616, for the interior decoration done by **Robert Adam** from 1765 to 1769 for the Earl of Mansfield, as well as for the excellent collection of paintings belonging to the Earls of Iveagh, which includes works by Vermeer, Rembrandt, Reynolds, Romney and Gainsborough (opening times: April–Sept daily 10am to 5.30pm, Oct until 5pm, Nov–March until 4pm). For a freshly tapped pint, go to The Spaniards Inn (Spaniards Road), haunt of the highwayman Dick Turpin.

Hampstead Heath

★

◄ Kenwood House

Highgate Cemetery

Location: Swains Lane, N 6

Tube: Archway, then a 15-minute walk via Macdonald Rd. (leaving the tube left, then right), Salisbury Walk, Raydon St and Chester St to Swains Lane.

London's best-known cemetery is located to the east of Hampstead in the well-to-do suburb of Highgate. It was established in 1839. The western part was closed in 1975 and has been cared for by the Friends of Highgate Cemetery since then. This section with its overgrown graves, truly a sequestered spot – **Bram Stoker** found inspiration here for writing Dracula – is like a sample-book of Victorian funerary sculpture. For example, the owner of The Observer newspaper, Julius Beer, had his grave modelled on the mausoleum of Halikarnassos, and the graves on the so-called Egyptian Avenue are based on royal graves from Egypt. The eastern part of the cemetery is the final resting-place of **Karl Marx** and his wife Jenny. To find it take the second left from the entrance. The grave is beyond the second junction of paths.

! *Baedeker* TIP

From Hampstead to Highgate

A visit to Highgate Cemetery alone is not especially rewarding. A better alternative is to combine it with a trip to Hampstead. Starting in Hampstead, take the path through the woods at the end of Well Walk, go straight on across the heath, then between Highgate Ponds and up to Mernon Lane. Then go left up the steep Highgate West Hill, from which Swains Lane branches off to the right, and downhill to the cemetery entrance. The walk from Hampstead takes about 45 minutes and shows that London can be quite hilly. On the way there is a view of the Millennium Dome in the distance in Greenwich. The best place for refreshments is The Flask pub up on Highgate West Hill.

Karl Marx's grave

Only the eastern part of Highgate Cemetery is – for an admission fee – accessible (April–Sept Mon to Fri 10am–4.30pm, Oct–March until 3.30pm; Sat and Sun from 11am); the western section can be visited only as part of a tour (Mon–Fri 2pm, Sat and Sun every hour 11am to 4pm, Oct–March 3pm; Bookings under tel. 8 340 1834). A permit is necessary for photography.

✴ ✴ Hampton Court Palace

Excursion

Location: East Molesey, 25km/16mi south-west of the city centre
Thames boat: Hampton Court Bridge

Train: Hampton Court from Waterloo Station

🕐 Opening times:
March–Oct
Mon 10.15am–6pm,
Tue–Sun
9.30am–6pm
(last admission
5.15pm);
Oct–March
Mon
10.15am–4.30pm,
Tue–Sun
9.30am–4.30pm
(last admission
3.45pm)

Hampton Court is regarded as one of the most beautiful royal palaces in England. It was built between 1514 and 1520 in a bend in the River Thames by the Lord Chancellor, Cardinal Wolsey (1475–1530). Wolsey fell out of favour with Henry VIII by refusing to approve Henry's divorce from Catherine of Aragon, and lost his offices and possessions. The king took Hampton Court Palace for himself and had the Great Hall and extensions around Fountain Court built. Apart from Catherine of Aragon, all of his wives lived here; the ghosts of **Jane Seymour**, his third, and **Catherine Howard**, his fifth wife, are said to haunt the rooms. Elizabeth I, too, liked Hampton Court Palace; it was here that she heard the news of the victory over the Spanish Armada in 1588. Charles I lived here too – as king and as a prisoner of Oliver Cromwell. Major alterations were not made until the period of William and Mary: while the Tudor style of the west façade was preserved, the east wing and Fountain Court with the state apartments were rebuilt by Sir Christopher Wren in the Renaissance style. The palace has been open to visitors since 1838.

State apartments

The way to the state apartments is through Anne Boleyn's Gateway in Clock Court, which takes its name from the large astronomical clock made for ► St James's Palace in 1540 and brought here in the 19th century. After that visitors proceed up the **King's Staircase**, which has magnificent paintings by Antonio Verrio, into the state apartments, all of which were decorated by great artists of the Baroque period: woodcarvings by Grinling Gibbons, frescoes by Antonio Verrio, wrought iron by Jean Tijou, work in marble by John Nost. There are also paintings by Tintoretto and others in the King's Draw-

ing Room and by Sir Godfrey Kneller in the Queen's Guard Chamber. The tour proceeds through the royal chapel, built by Wolsey and redecorated by Wren, and the Haunted Gallery, where the ghost of Catherine Howard walks, to the Tudor rooms. The outstanding room here is the **Great Hall**, built from 1531 to 1536, with its superb hammer-beam roof and wall-hangings, which were produced in the 16th century to designs by the Flemish artist Bernaert van Orley and depict the life of Abraham. The Wolsey Closet still contains the cardinal's furniture.

The beer cellar, wine cellar and the kitchens give an impression of the effort and expense involved in providing for the needs of a palace with 500 residents.

The Tudor period lives on at Hampton Court Palace.

This gallery (entrance in the south-west corner of Clock Court) presents a fine collection of paintings, in-cluding works by Correggio, Parmigianino, Tintoretto and Lucas Cranach (*The Judgement of Paris*).

◄ Renaissance Picture Gallery

A walk around the park and gardens takes in the Privy Garden, a pri-vate garden for the king; the Great Fountain Garden from the time of William of Orange; the Tudor and Elizabethan Knot Garden; and Wren's Broad Walk. The gardens are at their best in mid-May. The

Hampton Court Park

enormous Great Vine, planted over 200 years ago in a greenhouse on the Thames by the famous land-scape gardener Capability Brown, is an especially impressive sight. Everyone visiting with children should venture into the **maze**, which was planted in its present form in 1714. The covered Tudor tennis court on Broad Walk, where tennis is still played to the old rules, is a great rarity.

The Lower Orangery facing the

 DON'T MISS

- King's Staircase
- Great Hall: glorious Tudor architecture
- *The Judgement of Paris*: painting by Lucas Cranach
- The maze: a great place to get lost
- *The Triumphs of Caesar*: cycle of paintings by Andrea Mantegna
- Tudor tennis court: where Henry VIII played

Thames houses a masterpiece of European art: Andrea Mantegna's (1431–1506) *Triumphs of Caesar*, a cycle of nine enormous paintings acquired by Charles I in 1629.

The largest theme park in the south of England, Chessington World of Adventure, is to the south of Hampton Court in Chessington (reached via the A 309/A 243; nearest station: Chessington South).

Chessington World of Adventure

✳ Harrods

D 7

Location: 87–135 Brompton Rd., SW 1   **Tube:** Knightsbridge

Everything for Everybody Everywhere

After the Tower, British Museum, Buckingham Palace, Westminster Abbey and Big Ben, Harrods is the most-visited attraction in London. Nobody should miss a visit to the department store founded in 1849 by Charles Henry Harrod. Mr Harrod's little shop has grown into an institution with a sales areas of 54,000 sq m/580,000 sq ft and a staff of 4,000, who are proud to uphold the company motto: »Everything for Everybody Everywhere«. Harrods is now owned by an Egyptian, **Mohammed Al-Fayed**, the father of Princess Diana's companion Dodi. A shrine to the couple, who died in an accident in Paris in summer 1997, has been placed by the stairway on the ground floor, close to the Egyptian Hall. By claiming that Prince Philip had Diana and Dodi murdered by the secret service, Al-Fayed has achieved the feat of losing Harrods's privileged status as supplier to the royal family.

A theatrical experience

Harrods is a theatrical experience. Fortnum & Mason may have a touch more refinement – the staff at Harrods do not wear frock coats like their counterparts in Piccadilly – but the Brompton Road palace of Mammon excels at capturing the limelight: Harrods is not just a

A palace for gourmets: the Food Halls at Harrods

department store, but has become a brand name. The chief difference between Harrods and its rivals is that Harrods has everything – and it goes without saying that, if something should be unavailable, Harrods will obtain it.

There is no need to worry that shopping at Harrods is only for the well-off – it is also a store for normal purchases. Luxury is the attraction, however, which is why streams of tourists crowd through the portals and are granted admission so long as they are decently dressed, do not wear shorts or have rucksacks on their backs – and take no photographs! Once these conditions have been met, visitors are free to wander through the store and marvel at the nobly furnished Egyptian Hall, the enormous perfumery, the area selling exclusive gifts for gentlemen, the sports department with its top-quality cricket, golf and polo equipment, the departments for toys and school uniforms – the latter typically British in the eyes of foreign visitors – or any other of the almost 300 different departments. The absolute highlight, however, are the Victorian Food Halls on the ground floor. It would be insulting to describe them as a supermarket. The richly decorated halls feel more like a cathedral for gourmets.

◀ Food Halls

> **! Baedeker TIP**
>
> **Picnic in Hyde Park**
> Surrounded by dozens of different kinds of Italian salami, French cheese and English biscuits, who could withstand temptation and walk out without buying anything? What pleasure could be greater than to take a well-filled bag from Harrods Food Halls and walk the short distance to Hyde Park for a picnic?

✶ ✶ Houses of Parliament

G 6/7

Location: Parliament Square, SW 1   **Tube:** Westminster

The seat of the upper and lower houses of Parliament is officially called The Palace of Westminster, because it stands on the site of an old royal palace. The palace was built by Edward the Confessor and enlarged by William the Conqueror and William Rufus, for whom Westminster Hall was constructed between 1097 and 1099. A fire in 1512 spared only Westminster Hall, the 14th-century St Stephen's Chapel and the crypt. Westminster Palace was a royal residence until 1529, when Henry VIII moved to the nearby Whitehall Palace, and became the seat of Parliament in 1547: the House of Commons moved into St Stephen's Chapel, the House of Lords into a chamber at the south end of the courtyard. The architect of the present Houses of Parliament was **Sir Charles Barry** (1795–1860). His neo-Gothic design, built from 1839, pays homage to ▶Westminster Abbey. The first official opening of Parliament in the new buildings

The heart of British democracy

took place in 1852, but construction was not completed until 1888. Following severe damage in the Second World War, Parliament was restored between 1948 and 1950.

Gunpowder Plot There was uproar in 1605, when a group of Catholics led by **Guy Fawkes** tried to blow up Parliament. Fawkes, a staunch Catholic from Yorkshire, left Protestant England in 1593 to hire out his services as a soldier in the Spanish Netherlands. Increasingly repressive measures against English Catholics resulted in a plot against Parliament. For this purpose a man with military experience was needed: Guy Fawkes, who returned to England in 1604. He placed 20 barrels of gunpowder in a cellar below the House of Lords, but on 5 November 1605, before the fuse could be ignited, Fawkes was arrested, tortured, condemned to death and on 31 January 1606 hanged, drawn and quartered in Old Palace Yard. Every year since then a thorough search of the cellars has been made by costumed Yeomen of the Guard before the opening of Parliament (photo p.190/191), and the Fifth of November, Guy Fawkes Day, is celebrated with fireworks and bonfires.

> ! **Baedeker TIP**
>
> **No harm in asking**
>
> Tours of the royal rooms, for which advance booking is necessary, are held on Monday and Tuesday morning and on Thursday and Friday afternoon. The starting point is the Norman Porch entrance of the Victoria Tower. With a little luck and by asking politely it may be possible to join a group spontaneously, paying a contribution.

Big Ben
Victoria Tower Next to Westminster Bridge stands the world-famous clock-tower Big Ben. Along with ▶Tower Bridge it is London's best-known landmark. Big Ben is in fact the bell, named after Sir Benjamin Hall, but quickly became the appellation of the tower as a whole. Since New Year 1923 its chimes have been the signature of the BBC. The architectural counterpoint to Big Ben is the Victoria Tower, which was the world's largest and tallest square tower when it was built. The Union Jack flies from Victoria Tower when Parliament is sitting.

Jewel Tower The Jewel Tower opposite the Victoria Tower is one of the few surviving parts of Westminster Palace. Henry Yevele built it in 1366 as a store-house for the royal treasure. From the early 17th century it served as the House of Lords archive, and from 1869 as 1938 the Weights and Measures Office. It now contains an exhibition about Parliament and the old Westminster Palace (opening times: April to Sept daily 10am–6pm, Nov–March until 4pm, Oct until 5pm).

Westminster Bridge The best view of Parliament is from Westminster Bridge, which was built between 1856 and 1862. The stone structure that it replaced was the second bridge across the Thames after▶ London Bridge. The sculptural ensemble opposite Big Ben represents Queen **Boudica**.

Houses of Parliament

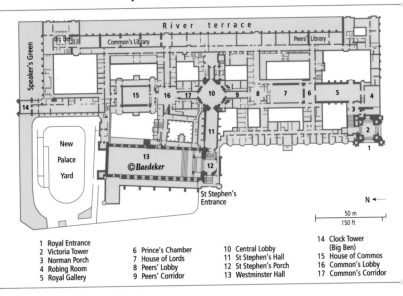

1 Royal Entrance
2 Victoria Tower
3 Norman Porch
4 Robing Room
5 Royal Gallery

6 Prince's Chamber
7 House of Lords
8 Peers' Lobby
9 Peers' Corridor

10 Central Lobby
11 St Stephen's Hall
12 St Stephen's Porch
13 Westminster Hall

14 Clock Tower
    (Big Ben)
15 House of Commos
16 Common's Lobby
17 Common's Corridor

the sergeant-at-arms. The Speaker follows him in gown and wig. A train-bearer, the Speaker's chaplain and a secretary bring up the rear. At the beginning of every session a prayer is held »for God's guidance«.

Westminster Hall Westminster Hall suffered relatively little damage in the fire of 1299 that reduced the old Westminster Palace to rubble. The 79m/ 260ft-long and 30m/98ft-high hall was rebuilt 100 years later in the reign of Richard II by Henry Yevele. Its most impressive feature is the oak hammer-beam roof from the late 14th century. The hall also survived the fire of 1834, after which Parliament was rebuilt in its present form. It has been the scene of some of the most moving events in English history: as the place in which the highest courts in the land met (1224–1882), it saw such famous trials as those of Richard II (1399), Sir Thomas More (1535) and Charles I (1649). In 1653 Oliver Cromwell was appointed Lord Protector in the hall. Westminster Hall is used for ceremonial lying-in-state after the death of leading members of the royal family, most recently for Queen Elizabeth, the Queen Mother, in 2002.

St Stephen's Hall From 1547 until 1834 the House of Commons met in St Stephen's Hall. The mosaics depict the foundation of the chapel by King Stephen. The statues represent Norman and Plantagenet kings and queens and statesmen of the 17th to 19th centuries.

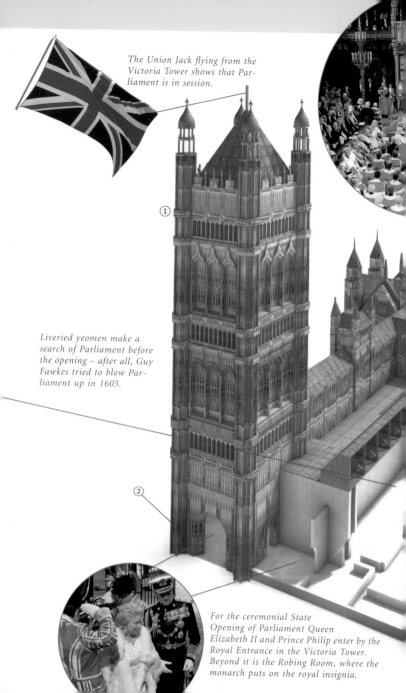

The Union Jack flying from the Victoria Tower shows that Parliament is in session.

①

Liveried yeomen make a search of Parliament before the opening – after all, Guy Fawkes tried to blow Parliament up in 1605.

②

For the ceremonial State Opening of Parliament Queen Elizabeth II and Prince Philip enter by the Royal Entrance in the Victoria Tower. Beyond it is the Robing Room, where the monarch puts on the royal insignia.

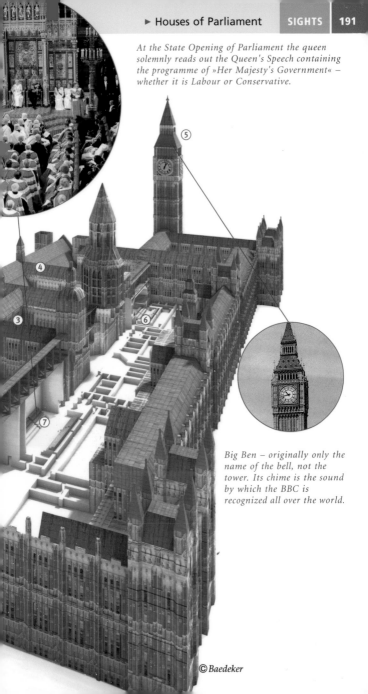

At the State Opening of Parliament the queen solemnly reads out the Queen's Speech containing the programme of »Her Majesty's Government« – whether it is Labour or Conservative.

Big Ben – originally only the name of the bell, not the tower. Its chime is the sound by which the BBC is recognized all over the world.

©Baedeker

HOUSES OF PARLIAMENT

★★ The heart of British democracy beats here – in the House of Commons, where important political decisions are taken, and in the House of Lords, which has lost much of its power in modern times. The annual occasion with the most lavish pageantry is the State Opening of Parliament in November, when the queen opens the session with full ceremony.

⏰ Opening times:

Tours are held in summer: Jul–Aug Mon, Tue, Fri and Sat from 9.15am, Wed and Thu from 1.15pm, Sep–Oct same times, except Tue also from 1.15pm. Ticket office: Abingdon Green opposite Parliament and Victoria Tower Gardens. Visitors are admitted to sessions of both houses: the House of Lords sits Mon–Wed from 2.30pm, Thu and Fri from 11am; the House of Commons Mon from 2.30pm, Tue–Thu from 11.30am, Fri from 9.30am. The visitors' entrance for both houses is St Stephen's Entrance on the west, where a queue forms. It is advisable to arrive well before the session opens, or about two hours after the start.

---

① **Victoria Tower**

With sides 23m/75ft long and a height of 102m/335ft, the Victoria Tower built in 1858 was the world's largest square tower.

② **St Stephen's Entrance**

The entrance for visitors

③ **St Stephen's Hall**

The House of Commons met here from 1547 to 1837.

④ **Westminster Hall**

The only surviving part of Westminster Palace is a historic site. The trials of Richard II and Sir Thomas More, among others, were held here.

⑤ **Big Ben**

London's best-known landmark. The 97.5m/320ft-high tower was built in 1858/1859. The clock-face is almost 8m/26ft in diameter, the hands of the clock are almost 4m/13ft long and the bell weighs 13 tons.

⑥ **House of Commons**

The lower house is known as the House of Commons. Government and Opposition sit opposite each other, neatly divided by a red line on the carpet and exactly two sword-lengths apart.

⑦ **House of Lords**

In the upper house, the House of Lords, the queen reads out the Queen's Speech outlining the government programme at the beginning of every parliamentary year. The murals on the south wall of the chamber depict events from British history, those on the north wall allegories of Justice, Religion and Chivalry. In the window alcoves there are statues of the barons who forced King John to sign Magna Carta in 1215.

Parliament can be seen in all its glory from the opposite side of the Thames.

Inside Parliament

Royal chambers

The queen passes through the 16m/52ft-high **Royal Entrance** in the Victoria Tower for the state opening of Parliament. The Royal Staircase leads up to the Norman Porch, beyond which is the **Robing Room**, where the queen puts on the Imperial State Crown. The **Royal Gallery** is decorated with the coats of arms of the monarchs of England and Scotland. Two enormous frescoes by Daniel Maclise depict *The Death of Nelson* and *Wellington and Blücher after the Battle of Waterloo*. The next room, the **Prince's Chamber**, is the ante-room to the House of Lords. On the panelling are portraits of the Tudors. The reliefs below depict scenes from their reigns. Opposite the entrance is a white marble statue of Queen Victoria, flanked by Justice and Mercy.

House of Lords

The **Peers' Lobby**, immediately to the north of the is paved with glazed tiles. Above the doors are the arms of the royal dynasties of England. From here the Peers' Corridor leads to the **Central Lobby**, an octagonal chamber between the House of Lords and the House of Commons with a 25m/82ft high-vaulted ceiling.

The House of Lords is a magnificent chamber. The peers sit on red leather benches. In November 1999 they acquiesced in the loss of their own power by assenting to a bill introduced by the Blair government that abolished automatic membership for hereditary peers. Until then no less than 646 hereditary peers sat in the House of Lords. The number has now been reduced to 92, who are joined by life peers, the law lords and the Anglican bishops. The Lord Chancellor chairs the sessions from the **Woolsack** in front of the throne – a reminder of the period when England exported wool.

House of Commons

The ante-chamber to the House of Commons, the **Commons' Lobby**, is adorned by statues of 20th-century statesmen, including Winston Churchill and David Lloyd George.

The seat of the Speaker, who chairs meetings of the House of Commons, is placed at the northern end of the chamber. The holder of this office once had the task of negotiating with the sovereign whenever the Crown wished to raise money – a dangerous position. The newly elected **Speaker** still abuses Parliament while making his way to the Speaker's chair, in order to show his reluctance to hold the office. Government and opposition sit opposite each other on parallel rows of benches, which do not provide enough space for all members. The Speaker's mace lies on the table between government and opposition during sessions. Two red lines on the carpet, one on each side, are traditionally two sword-lengths apart. Members of Parliament are not allowed to cross the lines when speaking. The **start of a session** is marked by the call »Mr Speaker! – hats off – strangers!«. All those present stand up to allow a procession to pass. It is led by a man in knickerbockers carrying the golden mace over his shoulder:

Hyde Park · Kensington Gardens

B–E 5/6

Location: west of city centre

Tube: Hyde Park Corner, Marble Arch, Lancaster Gate

✳ ✳ Hyde Park

Hyde Park, once the site of royal hunts, military exercises and duels, is now the place where London relaxes – for a picnic, a walk, sport or just to laze around. A walk through the park is a pleasure at any time of year, but especially in summer. In the morning, before the strollers, joggers and horse-riders arrive, Hyde Park is still quiet; at midday the office-workers of the area eat their sandwiches on the park benches; and after work footballers and sunbathers take over the lawns. In 1536 Henry VIII turned an area originally owned by Westminster Abbey into a park for hunting. In 1635 Charles I opened the park to the people of London, and the better-off residents adopted it as a place to be driven around in their coaches, to see and be seen. In 1851 Hyde Park was the site of the celebrated **Great Exhibition**.

Where London relaxes

Breathing space: Hyde Park is a haven of peace in a busy city.

The main entrance is the triple arch at Hyde Park Corner built in 1828 by Decimus Burton. Its reliefs are scenes from the frieze of the Parthenon (►British Museum). Just behind it is the so-called statue of Achilles, cast from French cannonballs in 1822 by Richard Westmacott in honour of the Duke of Wellington. However, the statue is not the ancient god, but a copy of the horse tamer from the Quirinal in Rome. This did not prevent it from causing a scandal as Britain's first public representation of a naked man. Three main paths cross the park from Hyde Park Corner: the Carriage Road on the left leads to the Albert Memorial, the East Carriage Road on the right to Marble Arch and Speakers' Corner, and the path in the middle to the Serpentine, the lake created for George II's queen, Caroline of Ansbach, in 1730. At the western margin of the Serpentine is the **(Diana) Princess of Wales Memorial Fountain**, to the north of the lake the Bird Sanctuary, in front of which is Epstein's naked spirit of nature, *Rima*. Rotten Row, which runs between the Serpentine and Carriage Road, is reserved for horse- riders. The name is a corruption of the French »Route du Roi«, as it was once the monarch's route to the palace on Whitehall.

Rotten Row ►

Speakers' Corner Since 1872 Speakers' Corner has been the stage for all those who want to air their opinion about any subject on earth without fear of legal consequences. It is at its busiest on Saturdays and Sunday mornings. Jomo Kenyatta, the first president of Kenya, once spoke here and Idi Amin, the notorious former dictator of Uganda, often listened while he was a sergeant in the British army – but neither of them learned their lesson in democracy.

Marble Arch Marble Arch, an island surrounded by traffic, can be seen from Speakers' Corner. The monumental arch was designed in 1828 by **John Nash** in the style of the Roman Arch of Constantine as the main gate to ►Buckingham Palace. When the archway proved to be too narrow for the royal state coach, it was re-erected in 1851 in its present location at Tyburn, a place of execution from the 12th century until 1783. Criminals were brought here from the Tower or Newgate prison to die on the gallows, known as Tyburn Tree. 50,000 people perished here, and every execution drew crowds of onlookers.

Kensington Gardens

Kensington Gardens lie to the west of the bridge across the Serpentine. Again it was Queen Caroline who was responsible for giving the park its – in comparison to Hyde Park – more formal layout from 1728 to 1731. It has been open to the public since 1841.

At the end of the Long Water, the continuation of the Serpentine, is the Italian Garden. Not far away at Victoria Gate is the site of a small (closed) dog cemetery, established in 1880 on the wishes of the Duke of Cambridge. A walk along the west side of the Long Water leads to the most attractive monument in Kensington Gardens, the statue of **Peter Pan** made in 1912 by George Frampton. The little boy who never wanted to grow up is surrounded by all his animal and fairy-tale friends. Further along the path is the **Serpentine Gallery**, which is a showcase for contemporary art (opening times: daily 10am to 6pm).

Albert Memorial

In 1876, on the southern edge of Kensington Gardens, Queen Victoria unveiled Sir George Gilbert Scott's monument to her prince consort,**Albert of Saxe-Coburg-Gotha** (1819–1861). The queen's original wish was to have a colossal monolithic granite obelisk, which was to have been financed by donations. However, the sum collected was insufficient, and a neo-Gothic monument was built instead. The figure of Prince Albert, larger than life size, seated beneath a 58m/190ft-high canopy, holds in his hand the catalogue of the Great Exhibition of 1851, which took place largely on his initiative. On the marble reliefs that decorate the base are 178 figures of famous artists and scientists from all periods of history; the free-standing groups at the corners represent Manufactures, Engineering, Commerce and Agriculture, and the ensembles at the corners of the steps symbolize Europe, Asia, Africa and America.

Prince Albert looks across to the Royal Albert Hall, which he himself initiated. This oval hall with a circumference of over 210m/230yd was completed in 1871 to a design by the military engineers Captain Fowke and General Scott. Although the acoustics were widely known to be poor – they have since been improved – the interior with its enormous glass dome and the high quality of the music performed there made it one of London's most popular concert halls. Among other events, the famous **Proms** are held here each year (▶ Practicalities, Theatre · Concerts · Music).

Royal Albert Hall

✶ **Kensington Palace**   C 6

Kensington Palace, at the east side of Kensington Gardens, was the private residence of English monarchs from 1689 to 1760, but is now known all over the world as the last home of **Princess Diana**. Tens of thousands of mourners laid flowers at the palace gates after her death. The dukes of Kent and Gloucester still live here. It was built as a country house in 1605 and bought by William III, who commissioned Sir Christopher Wren to convert it into his private residence. George I, who made it his official residence, had it altered by Colen Campbell and furnished by William Kent. The last king to reside here was George II. Queen Victoria was born in the palace and learned of her accession to the throne here. Queen Mary, grandmother of Elizabeth II, was also born here. William III, his wife Mary II, Queen Anne and George II all died in Kensington Palace. The statue of William III on the south side was a gift to Edward VII from

🕐 Opening times: March–Oct daily 10am–6pm; Nov–Feb until 5pm (last admission 1hr earlier)

The death of Princess Diana made Kensington Palace world-famous.

Emperor Wilhelm II of Germany. To the east is a monument to Queen Victoria.

Orangery The Orangery on the north side used to be attributed to Sir Christopher Wren, but was probably the work of Nicholas Hawksmoor in 1704. The carvings by Grinling Gibbons that adorn it can today be examined over a cup of tea or coffee.

Royal Ceremonial Dress Collection This exhibition is an opportunity to admire the uniforms and dress of the English court.

State apartments The state apartments on the first floor are mainly furnished in the style of the 17th and 18th centuries. The Queen's Staircase, designed by Wren in 1690, provides access to the oak-panelled Queen's Gallery, which is decorated by portraits of sovereigns. Beyond this are the dining room, living room, study and bedroom of Queen Victoria, Queen Mary and Queen Anne. Through apartments of William III, George I and George II and the King's Grand Staircase, with its trompe-l'oeil paintings by Kent, visitors reach King William's Gallery, which was designed in 1694 by Wren and is decorated with views of London from the 18th and 19th centuries, a painted ceiling by Kent (*The Adventures of Odysseus*) and wood carvings by Grinling Gibbons. The most interesting of the Victorian apartments that follow are the blue-and-gold Cupola Room, in which Queen Victoria was baptized, the King's Drawing Room with its clock of 1730 decorated with allegories of the four ancient empires of Assyria, Persia, Greece and Rome, and the Council Chamber, in which items from the Great Exhibition are displayed.

Hyde Park Corner   E 6

Hyde Park Corner in the south-east corner of the park is dominated by the Wellington Arch, a triumphal gate designed in 1828 by Decimus Burton to celebrate the victory of the Duke of Wellington (1769–1852) at Waterloo. Since 1912 a bronze sculpture of *Peace in a Quadriga* has crowned the massive arch, replacing a monument to Wellington. A new Wellington monument opposite Apsley House portrays the duke on his horse Copenhagen; an English grenadier, a Scottish Highlander, a Welsh fusilier and a northern Irish dragoon occupy the corners. Inside the arch are exhibitions on its history and London monuments; below the quadriga is an observation platform (Wed–Sun from 10am). Three further monuments are placed around Wellington Arch: the Royal Artillery War Memorial (1928), the Machine Gun Corps Memorial (1927) with a figure of the biblical King David, and a new memorial (2003) to the Australians and New Zealanders who fell in the two world wars, inscribed with 24,000 names of the places where they were born and lived.

Wellington Arch Wellington Monument

The victor of Waterloo and later prime minister looks across from his monument to Apsley House, his London residence. It was built by Robert Adam for Baron Apsley between 1771 and 1778 and bought by Wellington after Waterloo. In 1828/1829 he had the house re-faced in Bath stone and added the Corinthian portico and Waterloo Gallery, in which the annual Waterloo banquet was held. The house was known as »No. 1 London«. Since 1952 it has been a museum, but Wellington's descendants still live in part of the house. Many personal items preserve the memory of the **Iron Duke** – supposedly so called not because of his military victories but on account of the iron shutters that he had installed on Apsley House after opponents of his policies smashed the window-panes in 1832. The China and Plate Room on the ground floor is filled with silver and porcelain, including a dinner service from the royal Prussian porcelain manufactory presented to Wellington by the King of Prussia after the battle of Waterloo, and the Egyptian Service that Napoleon intended as a divorce present for Josephine. The sabre that he wore at Waterloo can also be seen. The most impressive item in Wellington's home is in the stairwell: Canova's statue of Napoleon, twice

★
Apsley House Wellington Museum

🕐
Opening times:
Tue–Sun
11am–5pm

◀ Statue of Napoleon

Apsley House: the period furnishings of the home of the Duke of Wellington are the proper setting for the duke's collection of paintings.

life-size,, depicting the French emperor naked except for a fig-leaf. It was brought to London from the Louvre. The first-floor rooms contain paintings of the highest quality, many of which Wellington took from Joseph Bonaparte after the battle of Vitoria (1813). The outstanding works are Velázquez' *Water-seller of Seville*, Correggio's *Agony in the Garden* (Wellington's favourite painting) and an equestrian portrait of the Duke of Goya, which hangs in the Waterloo Gallery, where Wellington entertained his comrades each year at the Waterloo Dinner. The centrepiece of the table, a gift from the King of Portugal, is now in the dining room.

★ Imperial War Museum · Lambeth

H 7

Location: Lambeth Road, SE 1
Internet: www.iwm.org.uk

Tube: Lambeth North, Elephant & Castle

⊙ Opening times: daily 10am–6pm

The Imperial War Museum is dedicated to British wars of the 20th century. It was founded in 1920 and has occupied the former Bethlem Royal Hospital in Lambeth since 1936. The warship *HMS Belfast*

(►South Bank), the Cabinet War Rooms (►Whitehall) and a large collection of planes at Duxford Airfield near Cambridge are also part of the Imperial War Museum.

The centre of the museum is occupied by a large hall in which planes, tanks and artillery-pieces are on display, including Field Marshal Montgomery's command tank, a British Spitfire fighter, a German Focke-Wulf FW 190, an American P-51 Mustang, a German one-man U-boat and the German »flying bombs« V 1 and V 2. An enormous German periscope from the First World War gives a view of ►St Paul's.

The rooms on the lower floor give a chronological account of the world wars, though the historical presentation suffers from the mass of weapons, equipment, medals and uniforms that almost have the character of devotional objects. On the other hand some unique historic items are on display, including Lawrence of Arabia's djellaba (Arab cloak), and a copy of Hitler's

Aircraft of the Second World War in the Imperial War Museum

last testament. »The Blitz Experience« recreates the experience of being in a bunker during a German air-raid. A similar scene conveys the feeling of life in the trenches in the First World War. Other sections are devoted to post-1945 conflicts, secret service activities and the holocaust.

◄ The Blitz Experience

Other Sights in Lambeth

Lambeth Palace is at the eastern end of Lambeth Bridge. It was built in the 12th century and has been the London residence of the archbishops of Canterbury for over 700 years.

Lambeth Palace

The Museum of Garden History is housed in the former church of St Mary-at-Lambeth close to the palace. It is particularly informative about the father and son named **Tradescant**, gardeners to Charles I. Both are buried in the churchyard, which is also the final resting place of **Admiral Bligh**, captain of the famous Bounty (opening times: April–Dec daily 10.30am–5pm).

◄ Museum of Garden History

Further north near Westminster Bridge, this museum tells the story of the life and work of the pioneer of modern nursing (opening times: Mon–Fri 10am–5pm, Sat and Sun 10am–4.30pm).

Florence Nightingale Museum

Kew Gardens · Syon House

Outer suburb

★ ★ Kew Gardens

Location: Kew Road, Kew
Thames boat: Kew

Tube: Kew Gardens

⊙ Opening times:
daily from 9.30am

A day in Kew Gardens, the Royal Botanic Gardens on the south bank of the Thames in the south-west of London, is almost a must. A trip to Kew means escaping from the bustle of the city into a leafy oasis of Victorian leisure. The idyll is spoilt only by the noise of aircraft flying in so low to land at nearby Heathrow airport that visitors to the gardens can almost look in through the windows. Kew Gardens is a place of serious scientific research: every year about 80,000 plants are identified, and over 44,000 are grown here – one sixth of the known species on earth, including 13 that are now extinct in nature and over 1,000 endangered species. In Kew the Brazilian rubber plant was acclimatized to Malaysian conditions and Marquis wheat, which enabled the prairies of north-western Canada to be cultivated, was developed. The idea for the gardens came in 1759 from Princess Augusta, the mother of King George III, in whose reign **Joseph Banks**, who had sailed around the world as a botanist with James Cook, became director in 1773. Banks's time saw the start of the expeditions to all parts of the globe that brought and still bring great numbers of exotic plants to Kew. Sir William Hooker, director from 1841, made Kew Gardens world-famous.

> ！ *Baedeker* TIP
>
> **Kew Explorer**
>
> The Kew Explorer is for everyone who finds the gardens too extensive. It is a gas-powered bus that runs around the gardens on a fixed route, stopping at eight places of interest, where ticket-holders can get on and off as often as they like (tickets at the entrance).

Glasshouses

The two gigantic glasshouses date from the 1840s. Both the Palm House and the Temperate House, which was once the largest in the world, were built by the architect **Decimus Burton** and the engineer **Richard Turner**. Two particularly interesting further features of the garden are the Evolution House and, above all, the Princess of Wales Tropical Conservatory, which presents tropical plants in their natural environment.

Kew Palace

During his period of mental illness King George III lived in the modest-sized Kew Palace , which was built in 1631 for the Fortney family of merchants and is officially known as the Dutch House. The building is undergoing long-term restoration, but its garden in the 17th-century style is open.

The Palm House in Kew Gardens

Queen's Cottage, a wedding present for Queen Charlotte in 1761, was Queen Victoria's favourite cottage. At her wish the wooded character of its garden was preserved.

Queen Charlotte's Cottage

Other charming buildings in the park are the Chinese Pagoda, built by Sir William Chambers in 1761 for his mistress, and the Japanese Gate, a copy of a gate in the Nishi Honganji temple in Kyoto from the Anglo-Japanese Exhibition of 1912.

Pagoda and Japanese Gateway

Three museums in Kew village on the other side of the Thames across Kew Bridge are worth a visit. The Kew Bridge Steam Museum in Green Dragon Lane (look out for its tall tower) contains a collection of 19th- and early 20th-century steam engines, including the »100 inch«, the world's largest piston steam pump (opening times: daily 11am–5pm). The Musical Museum at 368 High Street is a display of automatic musical instruments, from music-boxes to the Wurlitzer (opening times: April–Oct Sat and Sun 2pm–5pm, July and Aug also Wed). The items on show in the museum of the National Archive in Ruskin Avenue include Magna Carta, a letter by Jack the Ripper and the SOS telegram from the Titanic (opening times: daily except Sun 9am–5pm).

Kew village

✳

◀ Kew Bridge Steam Museum

◀ Musical Museum

◀ National Archives

🕐

✳ Syon House · Syon Park

Location: Brentford, Middlesex
Rail: Kew Bridge, Gunnersbury, then bus 237 or 267

Tube: Gunnersbury, then bus 237 or 267

Syon House is in Brentford, immediately south of Kew village. The house was founded as a monastery under Henry V in the 15th century and converted to an aristocratic residence in the 16th century. Over a period of time, its owners turned it into a jewel of interior decoration. This is above all the work of Hugh Smithson, Duke of Northumberland. In the 18th century he hired two of the best men in their fields, **Robert Adam** to design the interior and **Capability Brown** to landscape the park. In six of the rooms Adam created a classical interior unique in London with Roman columns, statues, antique furniture, paintings and elegant wall-coverings.

🕐
Opening times:
Syon House: April–Sept Wed, Thu and Sun 11am–5pm
Syon Park: daily 10am–5.30pm

Syon Park	Syon House is surrounded by a magnificent park in which Charles Fowler, who constructed the Crystal Palace, built a fine glasshouse in 1826/1827. In the Butterfly House tiny Essex Skippers flutter about alongside South American owl moths with wing spans of up to 20cm/8in. The building next to it houses the London Aquatic Experience, where amphibians, snakes and hawks can be seen (opening times: April–Sept daily 10am–5.30pm, Oct–March until 3.30pm).
Butterfly House ►	
London Aquatic Experience ►	

Liberty

F 5

Location: 220 Regent Street, W 1   **Tube:** Oxford Circus

Carpets, furniture, fabrics, porcelain
While ► Harrods boasts that it supplies almost everything, the department store Liberty takes pride in doing exactly the opposite: by no means everything is sold here, but what there is, is all the more refined. Since its foundation in 1875 by **Arthur Lasenby Liberty** the store has been England's best address for fabrics, carpets, furniture and Oriental and Asian porcelain. Liberty made its name with printed silk fabrics of its own design. These products remain classics to this day, and every English country house worth its salt is furnished in the proverbial Liberty Style. The architecture of the store is a sight in its own right, starting with the Tudor façade on Great Marlborough Street and continuing in the wonderful sales areas, which rise as galleries around a spacious inner court. The warm and cosy atmosphere, quintessential Liberty Style, is provided by the wooden panelling. This is not just any old wood: it came from the two last wooden ships of the Royal Navy, *HMS Impregnable* and *HMS Hindustan*.

> **! Baedeker TIP**
>
> **A gift from London**
> A throw, a scarf or a tie from Liberty is a souvenir that ought to please anybody.

Lincoln's Inn

G / H 5

Location: Chancery Lane, WC 2   **Tube:** Holborn, Chancery Lane

Historic college for barristers
Lincoln's Inn, established in the 14th century by the Earl of Lincoln, is one of London's four inns of court (colleges for barristers) along with ► Gray's Inn and the two inns of court in the ►Temple. Its rolls of admission include such famous names as Thomas More, Oliver Cromwell, John Donne, William Pitt, Horace Walpole, Benjamin

Shopping in style at Liberty →

Disraeli, William Gladstone and Margaret Thatcher. The complex of buildings is the best-preserved of its type in London.

For permission to enter, ask the porter in Chancery Lane; entry to the gardens and chapel (both Mon–Fri noon–2.30pm) is unrestricted. The gatehouse of 1518 bears the arms of Henry VIII, the Earl of Lincoln and James Lovell. Beyond it are the Tudor-style Old Buildings, which were altered in 1609. Straight ahead lies the Old Hall, on the right the chapel built by Inigo Jones in 1623 in the Gothic style and thoroughly restored in 1685 by Sir Christopher Wren. The Old Hall was built in 1491 and used until 1883 as the High Court of Chancery. Go past the chapel to reach the Great Hall and the library dating from 1497. Adjoining them are the Stone Buildings with New Square, built in 1680, to the left.

Lincoln's Inn's Fields
Hunterian Museum ▶
🕐

The quiet park behind Lincoln's Inn is a favourite spot for lawyers to take their midday break. Lincoln's Inn Fields was a place of execution in the Tudor and Stuart period. On the south side is the Royal College of Surgeons, home of the Hunterian Museum , the medical collections of Dr John Hunter (1729–1793; opening times: Mon–Fri 10am–5pm).

★
Sir John Soane's Museum

Sir John Soane's Museum is a treat for anyone who likes curiosities. The home of the architect and art collector Sir **John Soane** (1753–1837) is no ordinary museum, but a work of art. Since the

An idiosyncratic art collection: Sir John Soane's Museum

death of Soane nothing has been changed – right down to the positioning of even the smallest piece of bric-a-brac. The rooms seem somewhat untidy and over-full, but this constitutes their charm. The most notable works of art in the house are in the library and dining room: ceiling paintings by Howard, a Reynolds and a portrait of Sir John Soane by Lawrence. Thanks to the ingenious construction of the walls, the Picture Gallery accommodates a large number of paintings, including twelve works by Hogarth (the series **The Rake's Progress** and *The Election*, several works by Canaletto and drawings by Soane. The Monk's Salon holds medieval art and more works by Canaletto in addition to paintings by Alcott and Ruisdael and, in the room next to it, by Watteau. Soane placed the sarcophagus of Seth I, father of Ramses the Great, found in the Valley of Kings in 1817, in the Sepulchral Chamber in the basement (opening times: Tue–Sat 10am–5pm; tours Sat 2.30pm).

! Baedeker TIP

Candlelight museum

The atmosphere of the museum is even more mysterious and enchanting on the first Tuesday of each month from 6pm until 9pm in the evening, when it is illuminated only by candlelight.

Lloyd's of London

K 5

Location: Lime Street, EC 3   **Tube:** Bank, Monument, Aldgate

Lloyd's began from 1688 as Edward Lloyd's coffee house in Tower Street, a meeting-place for captains, shipowners and merchants, who made agreements to insure their ships and cargoes. However, Lloyd's is not an insurance company in the usual sense of the word, but a market in which brokers conclude insurance policies on behalf of the underwriters (known as »names«), who invest capital and are personally liable. The centre of the Underwriting Room, where business is transacted, beneath the rostrum taken from the old Lloyd's Building, is occupied by the bell from the French frigate Lutine, which sank in 1799 and was insured at Lloyd's. The bell is rung still – once for bad news, twice for good news. To this day the name of every Lloyd's-insured ship that sinks is entered into a ledger on a desk next to the bell.

Inside out

Although it was completed in 1986, the Lloyd's Building remains one of London's most spectacular works of architecture. It was designed by a star architect, **Richard Rogers**, the co-designer of the Pompidou Centre in Paris. His ingenious idea was to put the inner parts of the building – lifts, stairs, pipes – on the outside. The only remaining part of the façade of the old building from 1928 is at the Leadenhall Street entrance.

Starship Enterprise? No, just futuristic architecture: Lloyd's Building.

Leadenhall Market At midday office-workers like to escape to the Victorian Leadenhall Market and take a break in a pub there. Here, on the site of the forum of Roman Londinium, there has been a market since the Middle Ages. The present market hall was built in 1881 by Sir Horace Jones.

London Bridge

J / K 5 / 6

Location: King William Street, EC 3 **Tube:** Monument, London Bridge

London's missing sight London Bridge is probably the biggest gap on a tour of the sights of London. The bridge of the famous song, »London Bridge is falling down ...«, no longer stands here. And the bridge never fell down, but was replaced twice.

There was a bridge across the Thames on this site as early as the Roman period. A little further east **Peter de Colechurch** built Old London Bridge between 1176 and 1209. Until the mid-18th century it was the only Thames bridge. Its 20 piers supported not just the roadway, but also houses with shops and even a chapel on either side. Its two halves were joined in the middle by a drawbridge, on the south side of which the heads of the decapitated were placed on spikes. Among those who met this fate was Sir Thomas More. The houses were later pulled down to create passing-places, giving pedestrians refuge from the heavy traffic. An excellent model in the▶ Museum of London shows how London Bridge looked in the Middle Ages. In 1831 John Rennie replaced it with a new bridge further up-river. In its turn this five-arched structure made way for the present, aesthetically boring bridge in 1973. When word got out in 1968 of plans to demolish Rennie's bridge, an American bought it at auction and had it transported to the USA, where it now stands in Lake Havasu, Arizona. The buyer is said to have had ►Tower Bridge in mind and not to have realized his mistake until the bridge was delivered.

✶ Madame Tussaud's

E 4

Location: Marylebone Road, NW 1   **Tube:** Baker Street

In 1802 Marie Tussaud decided to move from Paris to England. She took with her a number of wax figures which she had inherited. This collection, founded by a German doctor named Phillippe Curtius, formed the basis of the exhibition that opened in London in 1835. Today the wax figures are constantly brought up to date. The steep admission price does not prevent Madame Tussaud's from drawing large crowds, who queue at the entrance for an hour or more in summer.

🕐
Opening times:
Mon–Fri
9.30am–5.30pm,
Sat, Sun
9am–6pm

The planetarium attached to Madame Tussaud's screens a three-dimensional journey into space and lets visitors take the controls of an interactive space station for their own voyage of discovery.

London Planetarium

The Mall

F / G 6

Location: Between Admiralty Arch and Buckingham Palace   **Tube:** Charing Cross

The generous width of The Mall makes it London's most impressive avenue, the route taken by the royal family from ►Buckingham Palace for occasions such as Trooping the Colour, the queen's official birthday. The Mall is used for military parades and decorated with flags to greet state guests. At other times four lanes of traffic thunder along it. The street was once much quieter. Until 1911, when **Sir Aston Webb** broadened the avenue to its present width, The Mall was a tranquil place to take a promenade, its original purpose when it was laid out in the reign of Charles II.

London's parade route

Since 1910 the triple gateway of Admiralty Arch has marked the start of The Mall at Trafalgar Square. The Admiralty itself is nearby on Horse Guards Parade (►Whitehall).

Admiralty Arch

A rare sight even for Londoners: the Golden State Coach processes along the Mall in celebration of the Queen's Golden Jubilee

ICA The Institute of Contemporary Art (ICA) is one of London's leading avant-garde galleries. The ICA café is a popular meeting place for the art scene.

✳ Carlton House Terrace This walk along The Mall starts from Admiralty Arch and heads towards Buckingham Palace. The row of brilliant white columns and pediments visible on the right is Carlton House Terrace, a terrace built in two sections by **John Nash** from 1827 to 1832 on the site of the old Carlton House, the residence of George IV before he became king. Carlton House was built in 1709 and demolished in 1829. Its size can be gauged from the portico of the ►National Gallery , which formed part of Carlton House. From the steps between the two halves of Carlton House Terrace the rises to a height of 38m/125ft. It is crowned by the figure of Frederick, Duke of York, who was appointed commander-in-chief of the British army in 1827 and was also notorious for his huge debts. This was said to be the reason for the height of the column – only at the top was the duke safe from his creditors. To meet the costs of erecting it, every soldier in the British army had to forgo one day's pay.

Marlborough House Beyond Carlton House Terrace and set back from the road is Marlborough House, headquarters of the Commonwealth Secretariat. It was built from 1709 to 1711 by Sir Christopher Wren for Sarah, Duchess of Marlborough. In 1850 it became the official residence of the Saxe-Coburg-Gotha family, including the later King Leopold I of

Belgium, then of the future King George V (until 1910) and Queen Mary (from 1936 until her death in 1953).

A little way along, on Stable Yard Road, is Clarence House. It was the home of the Queen Mother until her death and now serves as Prince Charles's apartments. John Nash built the house in 1825 for the Duke of Clarence, the future King William IV.

Clarence House

Lancaster House is almost at the end of The Mall. It is used by the government today but was planned in 1825 by Benjamin Wyatt for the Duke of York, who died before its completion. One of his creditors, the Marquis of Stafford, took over the house after its completion by Robert Smirke and Charles Barry in 1840 and named it Stafford House. The first Lord Leverhulme renamed it Lancaster House and donated it to the nation on the condition that it was used to house the Museum of London, which it did from 1914 to 1951. A comment made by Queen Victoria when she was welcomed to Lancaster House by the Duchess of Sutherland shows the magnificence of the interior: »I have left my house and come to a palace.«

Lancaster House

✳ Monument

Location: Fish Street Hill, EC 3   **Tube:** Monument

As a memorial to the Great Fire of 1666 a column 202 feet (61.50m) in height called simply The Monument was erected between 1671 and 1677, 202 feet from the spot in Pudding Lane where the fire broke out. It has been attributed to Sir Christopher Wren, but was probably designed by Robert Hooke. The Monument once stood in open ground at the northern end of the old ► London Bridge. Although it is the world's tallest free-standing stone column, the surrounding buildings now hem it in and restrict the view from the observation platform. It is surmounted by a 4m/13ft-high urn with a golden ball of fire.

🕐
Opening times:
April–Sept
Mo–Fri 9am–6pm,
Sat, Sun 2pm–6pm;
Oct–March Mon–
Sat 10am–6pm

From the Monument it is a short distance down Fish Street Hill to the Church of St Magnus-the-Martyr, which lies almost unnoticed between modern buildings. A church dedicated to the Norwegian Earl of Orkney, Magnus, who was martyred in about 1100, was recorded on this site at the northern end of London Bridge in the 11th century. The Great Fire destroyed the old church, and Wren replaced it from 1671 to 1676. The features of its fine interior are decorated Ionic columns, a pulpit designed by Wren and a lovely sword-rest made in 1708. The grave of **Henry Yevele,** one of the architects of ► Westminster Abbey and bridge-master of London Bridge, is in St Magnus.

St Magnus-the-Martyr

✳ Museum of London

`J 4`

Location: London Wall, EC 2   **Tube:** St Paul's, Barbican, Moorgate

⏲ Opening times:
Mon–Sat
10am–6pm,
Sun noon–6pm

The Museum of London in the Barbican complex, the largest city museum in the world, is a journey through 2,000 years of history. It presents Roman remains, including wall-paintings from a bath-house in Southwark and an excellent model of the Roman harbour, weapons from the Anglo-Saxon period and furniture, clothing, documents and musical instruments from the Tudor and Stuart periods.

The museum has reconstructions of a Roman kitchen and a cell from the old Newgate prison, as well as a shop and commercial premises from the Victorian and Edwardian periods. There is even an art deco lift from Selfridges department store. The audio-visual presentation »Fire of London«, which includes readings from Samuel Pepys's diaries, recreates the Great Fire of 1666. The sections on the 19th century give a particularly lively and varied impression of the period when London, as the capital city of the empire, was its zenith. The pride and glory of the collection is the golden coach which is taken out of museum once each year to convey the new Lord Mayor through the City.

The Lord Mayor's coach

✳✳ National Gallery

`G 5/6`

Location: Trafalgar Square, WC 2   **Tube:** Charing Cross
Internet: www.nationalgallery.org.uk

⏲ Opening times:
daily 10am–6pm,
Wed until 9pm
Tours daily at
11.30am, 2.30pm,
Wed also 6.30pm

The classical façade of the National Gallery occupies the whole north side of ► Trafalgar Square. The National Gallery was founded in 1824, when the government bought 38 paintings from the merchant John Julius Angerstein and exhibited them in his house at 100 Pall Mall. From 1832 the gallery had its own building on Trafalgar Square to designs by William Wilkins, the work being completed in 1838. Wilkins integrated the colossal portico of Carlton House into the façade. The first extension, with a dome that gave the institution the nickname »national cruet-stand« was made in 1876. The latest addition was the Sainsbury Wing in 1991. It was donated by the Sainsbury brothers, owners of the chain of supermarkets. The museum shop is here.

The National Gallery provides a more or less comprehensive cross-section of European painting from the high Middle Ages until the late 19th century. The most precious parts of the collections are the Dutch masters and the various schools of Italian art of the 15th and 16th centuries.

Before entering the gallery, stop on the terrace to enjoy the wonderful view of Trafalgar Square and ►Whitehall. In front of the building is Grinling Gibbons's statue of James II as a Roman emperor (1686) and a copy in bronze of Houdon's statue of Washington in Richmond, Virginia.

Sainsbury Wing (Painting from 1260 to 1510)

The so-called **Wilton Diptych**, a two-panel altar with a gilded background, which probably originated in France in about 1395, is a masterpiece of late Gothic painting. It shows the kneeling King Richard II (1367–1400), presented to the Virgin by his patron saint, John the Baptist, Saint Edward the Confessor and Saint Edmund. Late Gothic painting from 14th-century Italy is represented by **Duccio di Buoninsegna** from Siena with an *Annunciation* and *Jesus Opens*

Italian painting

One of the world's foremost collections of paintings: the National Gallery on Trafalgar Square

National Gallery (Main Floor)

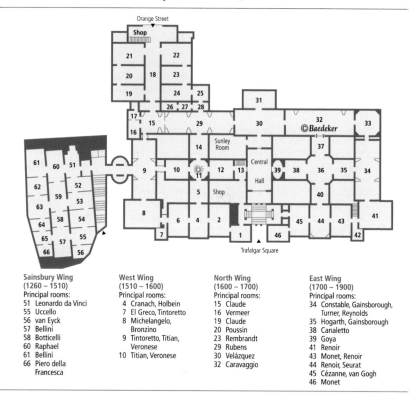

Orange Street

Shop

Sunley Room

Central Hall

©Baedeker

Shop

Trafalgar Square

Sainsbury Wing
(1260 – 1510)
Principal rooms:
51 Leonardo da Vinci
55 Uccello
56 van Eyck
57 Bellini
58 Botticelli
60 Raphael
61 Bellini
66 Piero della
Francesca

West Wing
(1510 – 1600)
Principal rooms:
 4 Cranach, Holbein
 7 El Greco, Tintoretto
 8 Michelangelo,
Bronzino
 9 Tintoretto, Titian,
Veronese
10 Titian, Veronese

North Wing
(1600 – 1700)
Principal rooms:
15 Claude
16 Vermeer
19 Claude
20 Poussin
23 Rembrandt
29 Rubens
30 Velázquez
32 Caravaggio

East Wing
(1700 – 1900)
Principal rooms:
34 Constable, Gainsborough,
Turner, Reynolds
35 Hogarth, Gainsborough
38 Canaletto
39 Goya
41 Renoir
43 Monet, Renoir
44 Renoir, Seurat
45 Cézanne, van Gogh
46 Monet

the *Eyes of a Man Born Blind* with delicate colouring, fine linearity and a balanced, though not perspectival spatial composition. Early Renaissance painting in 15th-century Florence discovered perspective and a new view of man based on the study of anatomy and the ancient ideal of beauty. In this style **Piero della Francesca** painted the 1442 *The Baptism of Christ* against the background of an impressive landscape reflected in the water of the river Jordan. In the 1450s **Paolo Uccello** created the dramatic and in 1432, with extreme foreshortening, *The Battle of San Romano* between Florence and Siena as a tournament-like melée of many combatants. A comparison between **Massaccio**'s life-like, corporeal *Virgin and Child* (1426) and **Sandro Botticelli**'s mannered treatment of the lasciviously reclining figures of *Venus and Mars* (c.1485) illustrates the painting styles of the early and high Renaissance. **Andrea Mantegna** placed *The Agony in the Garden* (c.1460) in a barren, rocky landscape with a many-towered city, including the Colosseum and Trajan's Column in Rome as a backdrop. **Antonello da Messina**'s psychologically sensitive *Portrait of a Young Man* (c.1479) and his equally well-known *Saint Jerome in his Study* form a charming contrast to **Giovanni Bellini**'s official *Portrait of Doge Leonardo Loredan* (c.1500). **Leonardo da Vinci** painted strongly modelled bodies with a subtle treatment of colour and light in intensely atmospheric landscapes, such as the *Virgin of the Rocks* (1483–1508), which depicts St John and the infant Christ in the presence of the Virgin and an angel praying and giving blessings in a rocky landscape. **Raphael** portrays the enthroned Virgin in *The Ansidei Madonna* with St John the Baptist and St Nicholas (1506) in a more contemplative mood as a sacra conversazione. His brilliant *Portrait of Pope Julius II* (1512) is also on view.

✔ DON'T MISS

- Jan van Eyck: *The Arnolfini Portrait*
- Sandro Botticelli: *Venus and Mars*
- Hans Holbein the Younger: *The Ambassadors*
- Leonardo da Vinci: *The Virgin of the Rocks*
- Titian: *Bacchus and Ariadne*
- Rembrandt: *Self Portrait at the Age of 34*
- Diego Velázquez: *The Rokeby Venus*
- John Constable: *The Hay Wain*

Robert Campin's *The Virgin and Child before a Firescreen* (c. 1430) is the starting point of the series of major old masters from the Netherlands. The background to the head of the Virgin, who is offering her breast to the infant Christ, is a wicker firescreen in place of a halo. The scene for **Jan van Eyck**'s life-like *Arnolfini Portrait* of 1434 is an interior which the painter imbues with a remarkable intensity and spatial effect. **Hans Memling**'s *Altarpiece for Sir John Donne* places the enthroned Virgin in the central panel, flanked by St Catherine and St Barbara, who are presenting the donor's family to the Madonna, while John the Baptist and John the Evangelist are shown on the side-panels. There is also a sensitive portrait of a young woman by **Lucas Cranach the Elder** and an expressive interpretation of Christ Mocked (*The Crowning with Thorns*) by **Hieronymus Bosch**.

Early painting from the Netherlands and Germany

West Wing (Painting from 1510 to 1600)

Italian Mannerist painting is represented by **Michelangelo**'s *The Entombment*. The composition of its figures and the muscular bodies are a reference to the sculpture of Laocoön and his sons excavated in 1506. **Agnolo Bronzino** painted his *Allegory* in the 1540s in a coolly erotic manner with naked figures of Venus and Cupid, Jealousy tearing his hair, the mask-like portrayal of Fraud and an old man as the embodiment of Time. **Correggio** depicted his charming *Venus with Mercury and Cupid (The School of Love)* of 1520/1525 in the style of the holy family and a delightful Madonna and child (*The Madonna of the Basket*) with Joseph's carpenter's shop in the background. **Titian**'s meeting between *Bacchus and Ariadne* is full of movement and

Italian and Spanish Painting

drama, while **Andrea del Sarto** lends a pale and introspective face to his *Portrait of a Young Man* (c.1510), a contrast to the self-confident body language of Titian's *Man with a Quilted Sleeve*. **Lorenzo Lotto** presents a well-groomed Venetian lady as *Lucretia* (c.1533). **Paolo Veronese** produced large-format scenes such as *The Adoration of the Kings* and *The Family of Darius before Alexander* in a decorative and ceremonious style. In the 1560s **Tintoretto** painted a *Saint George and the Dragon* incorporating stark contrasts of light and shade and opposing lines of movement. Also by Tintoretto is a spectacular interpretation of *The Origin of the Milky Way* (c.1580): bodies are delineated in pulses of light as Juno casts away the infant Hercules who is drinking from her breast, at which a stream of divine milk is spilt over the heavens. **El Greco** bathes his religious works in flickering coloured light and paints his characteristically Mannerist, elongated figures, as in *The Agony in the Garden of Gethsemane* and *Christ Driving the Traders* from the Temple.

! *Baedeker* TIP

Micro Gallery

The Micro Gallery in the Sainsbury Wing is a fascinating way of gaining orientation among the bewildering number of paintings. Its computer terminals give access to images of all the paintings with explanatory texts, often in the form of animations. There are four paths – works, artists, genres and periods – on which the user can load high-resolution reproductions onto the screen and get information about the works, before printing them on a plan of the gallery for a personalized tour.

Paintings from Germany and the Netherlands

Albrecht Dürer's *Portrait of his Father* is an expressive characterization of old age. **Albrecht Altdorfer** and his *Landscape with a Footbridge* represent the so-called Danube school. In 1533 **Hans Holbein the Younger** from Augsburg painted the *French Ambassadors* at the English court, Jean de Dinteville and Bishop Georges de Selve, in a tour de force of perspective technique with a variety of objects, such as a globe, sundial and musical instruments, that carry a deeper meaning. **Pieter Brueghel the Elder** produced an earthily rustic *Adoration of the Kings*.

North Wing (Painting from 1600 to 1700)

Painting from the Netherlands

Peter Paul Rubens made a contribution to 17th-century Baroque painting with a charming portrait of his sister-in-law Susanne Fourment with a straw hat, *Le Chapeau de Paille*. Moving masses of human figures bathed in light and shade characterize his depiction of Peace and War: Peace naked and voluptuous, followed by Faith and Prosperity; on the right, by contrast, War in armour turns to flee with Discord, Pestilence and the goddess of war. **Anthony van Dyck** was the leading court painter in England at the time of Charles I. His equestrian *Portrait of the King* is one of his greatest works. **Frans Hals** (*Portrait of a Man Holding Gloves*), **Pieter de Hooch** (*A Woman and*

Her Maid in a Courtyard), **Gabriel Metsu** (*A Man and a Woman Seated by a Virginal*), **Jan Vermeer** (*A Young Woman Standing at a Virginal*) and **Jan Steen** (*Skittle Players outside an Inn*), on the other hand, depicted the world of the middle classes. Important landscape painters include **Jan van Goyen** with a river landscape, **Philips Koninck** with a landscape with houses in a wood, and **Jacob van Ruisdael** with a landscape with a ruined castle and a church. **Rembrandt** van Rijn enchants the viewer with his sensitive portraits in soft coloured light – his self portrait, for example, or *Saskia as Flora*. He created a novel combination of a historical painting with a religious theme in his famous early work *Belshazzar's Feast*.

Diego Velázquez, the outstanding Spanish Baroque artist, is represented with a *Portrait of Philip IV of Spain* and with an erotic portrayal of the naked Venus looking at herself in a mirror, known as *The Rokeby Venus* (c.1650). **Francisco de Zurbarán** painted *St Margaret of Antioch* in the contemporary costume of a shepherdess and St Francis in Meditation. **Bartolomé Esteban Murillo** pleases with a cheerful portrait of *A Young Man Drinking* and the harmonious composition of *Christ Healing the Paralytic*. The first high point of Italian Baroque painting were the works of **Caravaggio**, which are characterized by strong contrasts of light and shade and powerful rendering of the body, as in *The Supper at Emmaus* (1602). In France **Claude Lorrain** painted landscapes and architecture with feeling, while **Nicolas Poussin** preferred the severity of classicism. **Louis Le Nain** portrayed the life of lower social classes, for example in *A Woman and Five Children* (1642). **Philippe de Champaigne** confirmed his reputation as a court portrait painter with his official *Portrait of Cardinal Richelieu*.

Spanish, Italian and French painting

East Wing (Painting from 1700 to 1920)

William Hogarth's six-part *Mariage à la mode* (c.1743) ventures a critical look at the hypocrisy of the nobility and bourgeoisie, using marriage customs as an example. **George Stubbs**, on the other hand, painted rustic scenes and thoroughbred horses to please these social classes. **Robert Wilson** is the first major English landscape painter with his atmospheric renderings of the countryside of southern and central England. The portraits of **Joshua Reynolds**, for example *General Sir Banastre Tarleton* or *Lord Heathfield*, combine individuality with a display of status. **Thomas Gainsborough** painted portraits such as *The Morning Walk* for William and Elizabeth Hallet, dissolving forms and colours in a manner that seems almost pre-Impressionist. With his naturalistic treatment of landscapes, **John Constable** stands at the threshold of the 19th century and had a lasting influence on later French outdoor painting. The unfinished *Weymouth Bay*, *The Hay Wain* and *Salisbury Cathedral from the River* are among his great works. The work of **J. M. W. Turner** developed from the romantic

British painting

A masterpiece of English art:
John Constable painted »The Hay Wain« in 1821.

landscapes of the early years to late paintings that are almost non-representational. *The Fighting Temeraire* (1838) with its mood of diffuse light at the closing of the day depicts the last journey of a ship on its way to the breaker's yard; in *Snowstorm* dynamic whirls of colour emphasize the peril of a ship at sea. *Rain, Steam and Speed* is his title for a picture in which a train snakes through a landscape that dissolves and almost disappears in coloured light.

French painting **Jean Baptiste Chardin** painted delightful interior scenes and sensual still-lifes (*The Young Schoolmistress*), while **Antoine Watteau**'s *The Scale of Love* reveals him as an artist of the imaginary fêtes galantes of the Rococo in which dreams mingle with reality. In the early 19th century **Eugène Delacroix** developed a style of painting that combined dynamic forms and colours, while **Jean Auguste Dominique Ingres** maintained a calm, classical manner, as the *Portrait of Madame Moitessier* (1856) illustrates. **Gustave Courbet**'s landscapes place him in the school of French Realism, whereas **Camille Corot** was an early exponent of outdoor painting. The Impressionists include **Edouard Manet** (*Music in the Tuileries Gardens*, 1862), **Claude Monet,** who visited London in 1870 in the company of **Camille Pissarro** (*The Thames below Westminster, Fox Hill, Upper Norwood*), **Pierre Auguste Renoir** (*The Umbrellas*, 1881–1885), **Edgar Degas** (*Ballet Dancers*) and for a time **Paul Cézanne** (*Les Grandes Baigneuses*).

Goya's sceptical view of human nature is particularly clearly expressed in his portraits of the *Duke of Wellington* and the legal scholar *Dr Peral*. Artistic highlights of late 18th-century Venice included the airy Rococo painting of **Giovanni Battista Tiepolo** and veduti by **Canaletto** and **Guardi,** which captured the squares, canals, churches and views of the lagoon in ever-changing variations, often with photographic precision or in melting coloured light.

Spanish and
Italian
painting

✳ ✳ National Portrait Gallery

Location: St Martin's Place, WC 2   **Tube:** Charing Cross
Internet: www.npg.org.uk

What counts in the National Portrait Gallery is not necessarily artistic quality, but the fame of the sitter. The collection founded in 1856 today contains about 10,000 portraits of British subjects who were famous in their time.

🕐
Opening times:
daily 10am–6pm,
Thu, Fri until 9pm

A chronological tour starts in the Tudor period on the upper floor of the new wing (Ondaatje Wing). The outstanding paintings are of Henry VIII, life-size by Hans Holbein the Younger, and a portrait of Elizabeth I by Ditchley, miniatures of Walter Raleigh and Francis Drake by Hilliard and a portrait of Shakespeare by John Taylor, the first acquisition made by the gallery.

In the old part of the building the first section of the upper floor is devoted to 17th-century portraits, including Charles I and Charles II, Nell Gwynne, Oliver Cromwell, the Earl of Arundel (by Rubens) and Samuel Pepys. This is followed by the 18th century, with Sir Christopher Wren, Sir Isaac Newton, the Duke of Marlborough and Sir Robert Walpole (all by Sir Godfrey Kneller). There are self-portraits by William Hogarth and Sir Joshua Reynolds, and a portrait of Captain James Cook by John Webber. The section on the late 18th and early 19th century presents works such as Lord Byron in romantic Albanian dress, portraits of Lord Nelson and Lady Hamilton, Sir

*Portrait of Elizabeth I
in the National Portrait Gallery*

Walter Scott (by Edwin Landseer) and the three Brontë sisters by their brother Branwell.

The Victorian period is well represented on the floor below, with Queen Victoria herself and other notables such as Cecil Rhodes, Benjamin Disraeli, Henry James (by John Singer Sargent) and a caricature of Oscar Wilde. The other rooms and the Atrium Gallery are reserved for figures of the 20th century, ranging from Lawrence of Arabia, James Joyce, Sir Winston Churchill and John Maynard Keynes to John Major, Mick Jagger and Princess Diana.

★★ Natural History Museum

C 7

Location: Cromwell Road, South Kensington, SW 7
Internet: www.nhm.ac.uk

Tube: South Kensington

⊙ Opening times:
Mon–Sat
10am–5.50pm,
Sun 11am–5.50pm
(last admission
5.30pm)

No-one who takes children to London should leave out the Natural History Museum. For entertaining and easily comprehensible explanations of complex matters, this is a marvellous museum.

On his death in 1753 the scientist **Sir Hans Sloane** left his extensive collections (50,000 books, 10,000 stuffed or preserved animals and 334 volumes of pressed plants) to the nation – the basis for the ▶ British Museum. In 1860 it was decided to present the natural sciences separately. Alfred Waterhouse received the commission to design a new museum in Kensington. The result of his work, the Natural History Museum which opened in 1881, resembled a cathedral or a palace in the Romanesque style. The 230m/250yd-long terracotta-clad façade with its two 64m/210ft-high towers dominates this section of Cromwell Road. Expeditions to all parts of the world expanded the holdings. **Sir Joseph Banks**, who sailed around the world with Captain James Cook, was a particularly zealous collector. **Charles Darwin** also returned from his expeditions with new material.

The museum is divided into the Life Galleries in the old building with departments on animal and plant life, the Darwin Centre, the mineralogical collection and the Earth Galleries in an annexe.

✔ **DON'T MISS**

- Dinosaur department
- »Creepy crawlies« – your friends the insects
- Lucy – the oldest ancestor of mankind

Life Galleries

The main entrance leads into the imposing Central Hall. The 26m/85ft-long skeleton of a Diplodocus occupies the middle of the hall.

The 26m/85ft-long skeleton of a diplodocus in the Central Hall gives → a first impression of the wonderful dinosaur department.

In the dinosaur department to the left of the Central Hall, the world of Triceratops and Tyrannosaurus Rex comes to life. Videos, moving models and dioramas explain the evolution, body structure and way of life of these primeval creatures. Among the highlights is a desert scene with life-size velociraptors and oviraptors. The other departments in this part of the building are devoted to human biology – including a larger-than-life model of a human foetus – and the mammals. Fossil species and mammals that mankind has made extinct are on show; the 27m/89ft-long model of a blue whale hangs from the ceiling. The following sections are about fish, reptiles, amphibians and invertebrates.

◄ Dinosaur department

To the right of the Central Hall lies a further highlight: the department for spiders and »creepy crawlies«. The huge model of a scorpion, no.1 Crawley House, containing drawers and cupboards that can be opened to see what kinds of bugs and insects crawl around in the home, and a walk-in termite mound are just two features of this highly entertaining and informative section. The ecology section opposite is less amusing but equally instructive. The exhibits in the next department, devoted to birds, include preserved specimens of extinct species like the dodo.

◄ »Creepy crawlies«

✷

Lucy ►

On the first floor there are rooms on the evolution of species, primates, the varied world of plants and the position of humankind in evolution; the outstanding exhibit here are the remains of »Lucy«, a 1.5- to 5-million-year-old female Australopithecus found in 1974 in Ethiopia. The next part of the museum is given over to minerals and shells. One of the loveliest pieces here is a hand-engraved nautilus shell from Sir Hans Sloane's collection. This area concludes with a section on meteorites, including the three-ton Cranbourne meteor from Australia. The second floor is concerned with the natural history of the British Isles.

Earth Galleries

The Earth Galleries, which take the history of the earth and geology as their theme, are no less spectacular. A lift takes visitors on journeys to the centre of the earth and from the night sky out into the solar system. There are easy-to-understand demonstrations of how earthquakes arise and volcanoes erupt. The section entitled »Restless Surface« shows how the wind and weather shape the surface of the earth. The collection of precious stones is a final treat.

Darwin Centre

The Darwin Centre opened in September 2002. It provides a look behind the scenes at the work of scientists and their passion for collecting: 22 million specimens preserved in alcohol line 25km/16mi of shelves.

Old Bailey

J 5

Location: Newgate Street/
Old Bailey, EC 4

Tube: St Paul's

🕐
Opening times:
public gallery
Mon–Fri
10.30am–1pm,
2pm–4pm

Film classics such as *Witness for the Prosecution* with Marlene Dietrich and Charles Laughton have made the Old Bailey, where all the great criminal trials in England are held, known the world over. The Central Criminal Courts, as they are officially called, were built between 1902 and 1907 and take their popular name from the street on which they are sited. As is only right and proper for a court of law, the dome of the building is crowned by a bronze figure of Justice with a sword and scales – but closer inspection reveals that she is not blindfold, as she usually is. Members of the public can watch proceedings from the gallery. Bags, cameras and mobile phones are not allowed inside the building, but can be left for safe-keeping in the pub opposite.

From the 13th century London's main jail, the infamous Newgate Prison, stood on this site. From 1783 to 1868 criminals were publicly executed in front of the prison, a memorable spectacle that unfailingly brought good business to the landlord of the now-demolished Magpie and Stump opposite. On such days he added a special »Execution Breakfast« to the menu.

◄ Newgate Prison

The former General Post Office is just round the corner in King Edward Street. Since 1966 it has been the home of the National Postal Museum, which has a unique collection of about 350,000 stamps from all parts of the world, including some extremely rare items. They are on display on the second floor; the huge main hall below is used for an exhibition on the history of the British postal service (opening times: Mon–Fri 9.30am–4.30pm).

National Postal Museum

✴ Piccadilly Circus

F 5

Tube: Piccadilly

London's best-known public space, Piccadilly Circus, a synonym for Swinging London in the 1960s, is the »The Hub of the World« for Londoners. The first impression is one of confusion, however, because Piccadilly Circus is a noisy, frenetic place with nose-to-tail traffic: it is the junction of Regent Street, Piccadilly, Haymarket and

The Hub of the World

The hub of the world – a traffic junction and meeting place for Londoners and tourists

Shaftesbury Avenue. It hardly gets quieter in the evening and at night, but after dark Piccadilly Circus takes on its role as the brightly lit heart of the West End. This area is the world of entertainment, starting with the Trocadero Centre and the London Pavilion. The Shaftesbury monument at the centre of the Circus, cast in aluminium by Sir Alfred Gilbert in memory of the Earl of Shaftesbury, is universally known as the Eros fountain, but in fact the figure is intended to represent the angel of Christian charity.

Piccadilly

Gentlemen in high collars

Piccadilly, the street running from Piccadilly Circus towards ▸Hyde Park, owes its name to gentlemen who like to promenade in high collars known as pickadills. Now as then, Piccadilly is the address of some of the longest-established and most exclusive shops in London.

Fortnum and Mason ▸

Fortnum and Mason, a department store founded in 1707, is one of the finest stores on Piccadilly. It is famous for its truly aristocratic food hall with tail-coated staff behind the counters. The specialities here – apart from exorbitantly expensive hampers – are tea, biscuits and preserves.

Royal Academy of Arts

The academy was founded in 1768 and since 1869 has resided opposite Fortnum and Mason in Burlington House, which dates from 1664. In the courtyard is a monument to the first president, Sir **Joshua Reynolds** (1723–1792). The membership consists of 50 Royal Academicians and 25 associates. Such famous artists as Constable, Lawrence, Turner and Millais trained at the Royal Academy. The exhibition of works by contemporary British artists held annually from May until August attracts great attention, and the quality of the special exhibitions is extremely high. The permanent collection is shown in the Private Rooms,

Sculpture by Michelangelo ▸

where the Sackler Galleries hold a treasure of the first order: the only sculpture by Michelangelo in England, a tondo of Mary, Jesus and the infant St John. Michelangelo made it for the Florentine patrician Taddeo Taddei immediately after completing his *David*. In 1823 Sir George Beaumont bought the work and bequeathed it to the academy (opening times: daily 10am–6pm, Fri until 10pm).

Burlington Arcade

Close to the academy is Burlington Arcade, an exclusive shopping arcade built in the Regency style in 1819 for Lord Cavendish. More than 70 small shops supply essential articles for the gentleman and his lady: made-to-measure shirts, cashmere pullovers, hand-made shoes, articles for grooming and tobacco pipes. The house code of behaviour provides the best guide to the style of the arcade: ... *a piazza for the sale of haberdashery, clothing and items, the appearance and smell of which do not cause offence. Whistling, singing, playing of musical instruments, the carrying of large parcels and opening of umbrellas are not allowed.* The arcade has its own guards, known as beadles. In their elegant dress of frock coats and top hats they ensure that visitors respect the rules.

Jermyn Street

The continuation of Burlington Arcade on the other side of Piccadilly (on either side of Fortnum and Mason) are the Piccadilly Arcades and Princes Arcades, which are no less exclusive. They lead to Jermyn Street, where a whole row of high-class outfitters caters for gentlemen of taste.

The Ritz Hotel

Since 1906 the Ritz Hotel at the corner of Piccadilly and Green Park has been one of the foremost addresses among London hotels. It is also a mecca for lovers of afternoon tea, which is taken in the wonderful Palm Court – not a cheap treat, but a stylish occasion for which jacket and tie must be worn!

Regent's Canal

C – N 2–4

A touch of Venice in London

The Regent's Canal was opened in 1820 to connect the Grand Union Canal with London docks. **John Nash** originally planned the canal to

A peaceful scene on the Regent's Canal in Little Venice

cut straight through ►Regent's Park , but it was feared that members of polite society taking a constitutional might be offended by foul-mouthed bargees, and the canal therefore makes a detour around the park. The canal starts in Little Venice, a genuinely romantic and peaceful canal basin where it is hard to believe that the hustle and bustle of London is all around. It is a good place to take a rest in one of the canalside cafés (take the tube to Warwick Ave., or from Paddington Station the exit at the north end of platform 8 and follow the canal for five minutes). From Little Venice the canal passes through London Zoo to Regent's Park and Camden Lock. The following section to the Docklands and the Thames is, with the exception of the

London Canal Museum ►

London Canal Museum (12/13 New Wharf Road; tube: King's Cross), less interesting. The museum is housed in the ice-store of the ice-cream maker Carlo Gatti (opening times: Tue – Sun 10am until 4.30pm).

> ! **Baedeker TIP**
>
> **On the towpath**
>
> An equally enjoyable alternative to a boat trip on the Regent's Canal (see Practicalities p.120) is a walk along the towpath. The stretch from Camden Lock to Regent's Park, for example, takes about 30 minutes.

★ Regent's Park

D/E 2–4

Location: Marylebone, W 1

Tube: Baker Street, Regent's Park, Great Portland Street

Recreation, not royalty

When **John Nash** was commissioned by the royal family to landscape and develop Marylebone Fields, he envisaged a park with two circular avenues and residential terraces, as well as a palace for George, Prince of Wales, and fine villas; Nash also intended the ► Regent's Canal to pass through the park. Work started in 1812, but the plans came to little – no palace was built and only eight villas, of which three remain, were completed. Regent's Park has become a place of recreation with children's playgrounds, tennis courts, grassy areas for cricket and rowing on the boating lake. Plays and concerts are held in summer in the open-air theatre, while Queen Mary's Garden, a lovely rose garden and rockery, and the Victorian Avenue Garden are places to stroll. Since 1978 the principal mosque for London's Muslim community has stood at the western end of the park.

London Zoo

London Zoo occupies the northern end of the park. It was founded in 1826 by Sir Stamford Raffles and Sir Humphrey Davy and is crossed by the ►Regent's Canal. Its main attractions are the birds in the Snowdon Aviary and the children's zoo. The entrances are on the Outer Circle, Prince Albert Road and Broad Walk (opening times:

March–Sept daily 10am–5.30pm, Oct–Feb daily 10am–4pm; last admission 1hr earlier).

Around Regent's Park

Several buildings by Nash close to the park show how Regent's Park might have looked. **Park Crescent**, built on the south-east side in 1821, is a fine example of a curving perspective of colonnaded façades. A tour around the park on the Outer Circle passes a number of Nash's terraces, such as **York Terrace** (1821) to the west of the crescent and, on the east side, **Chester Terrace** (1825), which has the longest uninterrupted colonnaded façade. Adjoining it is **Cumberland Terrace** (1828) with the figure of Britannia on the pediment relief.

Architecture of John Nash

To the north of the zoo, on the far side of the canal, lies **Primrose Hill**, which was formed from the material excavated during the construction of the underground railway. It affords a good view of the city which may be the reason why, in H.G. Well's novel War of the Worlds, the Martians set up camp here.

> **! Baedeker TIP**

Beatlemania

Close to Regent's Park is a sacred place for Beatles fans: the zebra crossing in front of the Abbey Road Studios, shown on the cover of the album of that name. From the entrance to Lord's Cricket Ground go north along Grove End Road, which leads into Abbey Road (to save time take bus no. 39 or 189). The studios are at number three. To find out more, join one of the Beatles tours organized by Original London Walks (tel. 7 624 3978).

A short distance to the west of the park and beyond Regent's Canal is a place of pilgrimage for cricket fans: Lord's Cricket Ground, established in 1814 by the veteran cricketer Thomas Lord and now home of the **Marylebone Cricket Club**, which was founded in 1786. Alongside Wimbledon for tennis and Wembley for football, Lord's completes London's trio of sporting shrines. The Lord's museum tells the story of the ground and the game of cricket. Visitors can take a look at the urn containing the »Ashes«, the trophy for contests between England and Australia (tours: April–Sept daily 10am, noon and 2pm, Oct–March 10am and noon).

Lord's Cricket Ground

221 B Baker Street: everyone who has ever read a Sherlock Holmes story knows this address opposite the south-west entrance to Regent's Park. And indeed there really is a Sherlock Holmes museum there today, though it does not take Holmes's powers of observation to notice that the museum is situated between number 237 and number 239. Visitors – who are greeted not by Mrs Hudson but by a normal doorman – can take a look at Holmes's flat on the first floor, including a violin and his tobacco-pouch in the shape of a Turkish slipper on the mantelpiece.(opening times: daily 9.30am–6pm; see Baedeker Special p.226).

Sherlock Holmes Museum

Essential headwear for Sherlock Holmes: a deer-stalker hat

MR SHERLOCK HOLMES, CONSULTANT DETECTIVE

The life of the greatest sleuth of all time, who described himself as a »consultant detective«, can be reconstructed only on the basis of his own statements and what was recorded by his companion and chronicler, Dr John H. Watson.

Sherlock Holmes was born in Yorkshire on 6 January 1854. In 1881, at St Bartholomew's Hospital in London, he first met **Dr John H. Watson**, who had come to him in search of accommodation. The two men moved into a flat in the house of the widow Mrs Hudson at the now-legendary address 221B Baker Street. Watson describes Holmes as a lean, muscular man with a remarkably acute intellect, who gathered information and possessed deep knowledge about all manner of strange crimes. He was also an outstanding chemist who had published a brilliant monograph on *140 Different Types of Cigarette Ash*, but took little interest in literature and philosophy, subjects on which he was positively ignorant. When he wanted to think, he played the violin – a genuine Stradivarius, though bought at a bargain price – and smoked cheap tobacco. His relationship to women was more or less non-existent, as he preferred his bachelor existence with Watson. However, there was one great exception: **Irene Adler**, »The Woman«, who had proved to be a worthy opponent in the case of *A Scandal in Bohemia*.

Here Sherlock Holmes is not looking at his friend Dr Watson, but at Arthur Conan Doyle, whom he also knew well.

Famous cases

Holmes solved highly complex cases by applying his own method: close examination of the evidence; search for possible explanations; exclusion of what was impossible; consequent deduction. By this means he threw light on such famous criminal cases as *The Hound of the Baskervilles* and – the first jointly investigated case – *A Study in Scarlet*, a bestial murder in Lauriston Gardens near Brixton Road. This and many of his other investigations were carried out in London; one of the most spectacular was the secret of *The Sign of the Four*, a dangerous adventure involving a pact between convicts and a hoard of treasure. Holmes solved the case solved after a thrilling chase down the Thames from Westminster Pier on a steam-boat. In 1891 Holmes succeeded in closing the net around **Professor Moriarty**, the »Napoleon of Crime« and, incidentally, his former private tutor. On 4 May they had a dramatic encounter in Switzerland at the Reichenbach falls near Meiringen. Moriarty gave Holmes time to write and leave behind a letter of farewell. However, after a short fight it was Moriarty who plunged into the abyss; Holmes realized that his own apparent demise represented an opportunity, and allowed even Watson to believe that he, too, had met his death.

Holmes's Secret Life

Only Holmes's **brother Mycroft** knew the truth. By his own account Holmes spent the following three years travelling in the Himalayas and elsewhere and in carrying out research, on which he reported using the pseudonym »Sigerson«. Insiders claim that he went to famous psychoanalyst Sigmund Freud in Vienna to seek a cure for his addiction to morphium; others believe that he took refuge in Cetinje, the capital of Montenegro, where he met Irene Adler again and lived with her for some years. This liaison is said to have produced a son, who went to the USA and had an illustrious career – as a detective. The name Rex Stout is often mentioned in this connection. However, in 1894, to the amazement of Watson, Holmes reappeared in Baker Street and once again successfully tracked down wrong-doers. In October 1903 he left Baker Street for Sussex to keep bees and conduct research into gelée royale. From here he solved his last case, bringing to book the German master-spy von Bork and thus saving the British Empire. Holmes died on 6 January 1957. His last words were reported to have been »Irene«, but devotees of the great man doubt the truth of this, pointing to his confession that »My brain has always governed my heart.«

Regent Street

F 5

Location: between Piccadilly Circus and Langham Place

Tube: Piccadilly Circus, Oxford Circus

London's boulevard

If London has a genuine boulevard, then it is Regent Street. John Nash planned the street to link Carlton House (► p.209) with ► Regent's Park. Little remains from Nash's time, as most of his buildings were demolished in the 1920s, including the Quadrant, an elegant curved colonnade on the section beginning at Piccadilly Circus. A walk from here towards Oxford Circus leads past the opulent Café Royal, where Oscar Wilde was a regular guest, and on to Hamley's, the world's largest toy shop, and a little further the high-class department store ►Liberty.

✱ All Souls

The steeple of All Souls rises beyond Oxford Circus. This church, built between 1822 and 1824, is remarkable for two things: firstly, it is the only church in London by John Nash (1752–1835), and secondly it is conspicuous for its unusual form, a colonnaded rotunda topped with a steeple surrounded by detached columns. All Souls is overshadowed by the BBC building on Portland Place, which leads to ► Regent's Park between beautiful examples of the neoclassical architecture of the Adam brothers.

Richmond

Outer suburb

Location: south-west of the centre
Thames boat: Richmond

Tube, rail: Richmond

Rural peace

Richmond's quiet, rural character make this area on the south bank of the Thames in the south-west of London one of the best residential areas of the city. English monarchs appreciated its charm as long ago as the Middle Ages: in the 12th century Henry I owned a manor house here, which was extended to become Sheen Palace and replaced in 1501 in Henry VII's reign by Richmond Palace. Henry VIII quartered Anne of Cleves there after divorcing her, and Elizabeth I died in the palace. Only a few remains of these buildings survive around Old Palace Yard, including the gatehouse with the arms of Henry VII; Trumpeters' House was built in 1701 on the site of the middle gate of Richmond Palace.

✱ Richmond Green

Richmond Green once served for the recreation of palace residents and is now a pretty place with 17th- and 18th-century houses, narrow lanes, charming shops and pubs such as The Cricketer (1666) and The Prince's Head. The four eye-catching brick-built houses

A sunny day by the river in Richmond

known as Maids of Honour Row were built in 1724 by the future George II for the court attendants of his wife.

To reach Richmond Hill take Hill Rise from Bridge Street, passing the elegant Terrace Gardens. From the hill there is a wonderful view over the green valley of the River Thames, on clear days even as far as ▶Windsor.

Richmond Hill

South of Richmond village lies Richmond Park, an expanse of 660 hectares/1630 acres (bus no. 65 from the tube station). It was enclosed in 1637 in the reign of Charles I; herds of red and fallow deer still roam there. The special attractions are Isabella Plantation, a woodland area created in 1831 in which rhododendrons and azaleas flower, and Prince Charles's Spinney, where some of England's oldest oak trees grow. King Edward VIII was born in the White Lodge, which George II built; it was also the residence of the Duke of York, later King George VI, and today houses the school of the Royal Ballet.

✳
Richmond Park

Ham House, built in 1610 for Sir Thomas Vavasour, lies on the Thames to the west of the park (bus no. 371 from the tube station). Originally a modest country house, it was inherited in the mid-17th century by Elizabeth Dysart – her father was Charles I's »whipping boy«, i.e. he was beaten instead of the prince when Charles had misbehaved – who enlarged it after her marriage to the Duke of Lauderdale. Today it belongs to the ▶Victoria and Albert Museum and re-

Ham House

mains largely as the Lauderdales left it. The house is thus an oppor-tunity to see a typical interior of wealthy aristocrats of the Stuart period. The collection of miniatures in Ham House is itself a treas-ure (opening times: April–Oct Mo–Wed, Sat and Sun 1pm–5pm).

✦ Royal Air Force Museum

Outer suburb

Location: Hendon, NW 9   **Tube:** Colindale

Opening times: daily 10am–6pm

The former factory of an early aviator, Claude Grahame White, in the far north of London is the home of the Royal Air Force Museum. White learned to fly from Louis Blériot, in 1909 the first man to fly across the Channel, and quickly made Hendon one of Europe's lead-ing centres of aviation. In the museum, one of the largest of its kind in the world, more than 100 aircraft from the early days of military aviation to the present day are on show, in addition to documents, medals and displays on technology.

Aircraft hangars

The Historic Hangars are the centrepiece of the museum. The 30 RAF aircraft in the exhibition range from a First World War Avro 504 to a Phantom. A simulator allows visitors to thunder at low-alti-tude above the Welsh mountains or to be shaken about in a bi-plane dogfight. In the Bomber Hall there are 16 British and American bombers, including a Lancaster and a B-17 Flying Fortress; the Battle of Britain Hall houses 15 British, German and Italian planes that took part in the battle for England's skies in summer 1940. In 2003, for the 100th anniversary of motorized flight, a new hall was opened to show milestones in aviation history, including a Blériot XI. Gra-ham White's workshop was also reconstructed to mark the occasion.

Replicas of a Hurricane and a Spitfire in front of the RAF Museum

✳ St Helen's Bishopsgate

K 5

Location: Great St Helen's, EC 3   **Tube:** Bank

The Church of St Helen's, a 12th-century foundation, is one of the loveliest in the City and at the same time one of the most unusual: it has two naves of equal size, because it was used simultaneously by nuns and the laity. The nuns assembled in the northern nave, while the southern one was reserved for the parish congregation. In the northern half the 15th-century steps, which gave access to the church from the nunnery, can still be seen. The most remarkable features are the funerary monuments: Sir Thomas Gresham († 1579), founder of the Royal Exchange, lies next to the nuns' choir. Alongside him is Julius Cesar Adelmare († 1636), an adviser to James I. William Pickering († 1574), ambassador to France and Spain, was laid to rest beneath a canopy tomb. Opposite this is the grave of Sir John Crosby († 1475); the tomb of Lord Mayor John Spencer († 1608) is by the south wall.

A church for nuns and the laity

✳ St James's Palace

F 6

Location: Pall Mall, SW 1   **Tube:** Green Park

St James's Palace, a little to the north of ► The Mall is an excellent example of Tudor-style brick architecture. Its name preserves the memory of a leper hospital founded in the 12th century and dedicated to James the Lesser, Bishop of Jerusalem. Henry VIII ordered its demolition in 1532 and the construction to plans by **Hans Holbein the Younger** of the royal palace in which Charles II, James II, Mary II, Queen Anne and George IV were born. St James's Palace became the monarch's residence in 1698 after the fire in Whitehall Palace. This is the reason why ambassadors are still accredited to the Court of St James's, even though Buckingham Palace took its place as the home of the sovereign in the reign of Queen Victoria. Today Princess Anne lives there.

The home of Princess Anne

From St James's Street there is a view of the Gate House, the sole surviving original part of the Tudor building. Sentries in bearskin hats guard the gate, behind which lies the Colour Court with a 17th-century arcade.

Gate House

To the west of the Gate House, visible from Stable Yard Road, lies Ambassadors' Court with the Chapel Royal of 1532. It is open to the public for Sunday services at 8.30am and for matins at 11.15am. The painting of the coffered ceiling is said to be by Holbein. The wed-

Chapel Royal

dings of William III and Mary II (1677), Queen Anne (1683), George IV (1795), Queen Victoria (1840) and George V (1893) took place in the chapel. **York House** on the north side of the court was the home of Lord Kitchener from 1915 to 1916 and the Duke of Windsor from 1919 to 1930.

St James's Palace was a royal residence until 1837.

Opposite the palace on Marlborough Road is the **Queen's Chapel**. It was built for Henrietta Maria, wife of Charles I; the commission was given to Inigo Jones, who made it the first Palladian church in England. Charles II married Catherine of Braganza here in 1661. 100 years later the chapel was again the scene of a royal wedding, when George III married Charlotte Sophie of Mecklenburg-Strelitz.

Pall Mall – London's clubland St James's Street and Pall Mall, the main thoroughfares of London's clubland, meet in front of the gatehouse of St James's Palace. This district was and remains the home of the most famous London clubs (►Baedeker Special p.233). Pall Mall, in particular – the name derives from a game similar to croquet that was popular in the 17th century, paille maille – is the address of several exclusive institutions: no. 104 is the Reform Club and no. 106 the Traveller's Club, both built by **Sir Charles Barry**, the architect of the► Houses of Parliament, while no. 116, the United Services Club is the work of **John Nash**.

St James's Square ► About halfway along Pall Mall towards ►Trafalgar Square and separated from it by a row of buildings, is one of the finest squares in the West End, St James's Square,. Henry Jermyn, Earl of St Albans, had it laid out in the 1660s. A wooden rotunda designed by John Nash and an equestrian statue of King William III occupy the centre of the square. Two of the surrounding buildings are particularly noteworthy: no. 15, Lichfield House, was built between 1764 and 1768 by **Athenian Stuart** for Thomas Anson and modelled on the Temple of Minerva in Athens; no. 20, Distillers House, is by **Robert Adam**, who built it from 1771 to 1774 for Sir Watkin Williams. George III was born in no. 31.

Waterloo Place ► Further along Pall Mall, on Waterloo Place, is the entrance to Carlton House Terrace, which has its main façade on The Mall. Several addresses of quality can be found here: no. 5 is the Turf Club, no. 6 the Royal Society, no. 16 the Terrace Club. A short distance away on the right at no. 4 Carlton Gardens was the headquarters of Charles de Gaulle as leader of the Free French from 1940 to 1944. Nos. 7–9 was the German embassy until 1939.

A gentleman's refuge. The 19th century was the golden age of the club.

MEMBERS ONLY

No sign marks the door. At most there is a uniformed doorman, who opens to allow gentlemen to enter. Passers-by on Pall Mall and St James's Street hardly notice that this is the heart of London's clubland. That would be quite unnecessary, as those who belong to this world already know where they will be admitted.

The golden age of the club was the Victorian era, when great numbers of clubs were founded. They were a refuge for gentlemen. Upon payment of fees for joining and for annual membership, the members had the club to themselves. They could dine together in the restaurant, converse or gamble in the lounge and read in the library, obediently attended by servants – all in luxurious surroundings which by no means every member could have afforded himself. The social life of a true gentleman took place in the club. Only when he wanted to sleep was it necessary to go home. Under these circumstances a marriage was nothing but a burden, as the club provided for all the needs of its members. It was only logical that women were not admitted to membership, a rule that applies to this day in many clubs. There was a further inestimable benefit of club membership: not everyone was permitted to join. To be exclusive and different from the others was (and is) the guiding principle of club life. The

consequences of this were long waiting lists; the frequent foundation, on the part of those rejected by certain clubs, of new ones, which of course in turn took great care to ensure that only gentlemen worthy of the honour were admitted; and resulting animosities between some clubs.

Origins: The Coffee House

The story began in 1693 in White's Chocolate House, which under John Arthur had risen to become one of the most expensive coffee houses. Mr Arthur offered »gallantry, pleasure and entertainment« to his customers, which above all meant gambling for large sums and betting on the most far-fetched matters – as in the case of Lord Arlington, who in 1750 wagered £3,000 on the question of which of two rain-drops would be the first to run down the window-pane. An »inner club«, to which not everyone was admitted, had emerged by this time and was to be the basis of London's oldest and most exclusive club, **White's Club**, which was officially

The flag lacks the discretion of a British club. In fact this is not a club but the St James's Club Hotel, founded in 1857, which provides well-to-do guests with all the amenities of a genuine club.

founded several years later at 37-39 St James's Street. George IV, William IV, Edward VII, the Duke of Wellington, Sir Robert Walpole, William Pitt the Elder and of course Beau Brummell, the quintessential dandy, were all members. White's soon had competitors. In 1760 opponents of Pitt's reforming policies led by the Prince of Wales formed **Brook's Club** at 60 St James's Street. These two clubs did not keep their political character for long. Almost 90 years later more important matters demanded members' attention, as a fierce dispute broke out over the issue of whether smoking should be permitted at White's, when up to that time only snuff had been allowed. With great reluctance a smoking lounge was installed, but the pro-smoking faction nevertheless founded the **Marlborough Club**, where they could smoke to their hearts' content in every room.

Victorian Clubs

The Marlborough was founded in a period when clubs were springing up everywhere. Almost every group that had something in common, whether

The armchairs in the Carlton Club are a comfortable retreat.

in social or political terms, founded its own club. For the armed forces there was the **United Services Club** and the **Army and Navy Club**, for fans of horse-racing the **Turf Club**. The **Garrick Club**, founded in 1831 at 15 Garrick Street by the Duke of Sussex, was a meeting place for writers, artists and actors, including Charles Dickens and W.M. Thackeray. Seven years earlier the author and politician John Wilson Croker had founded the **Athenaeum Club** at 107 Pall Mall, which aimed to bring together the intellectual elite of the nation. Croker had the honour of being the first to apply the term »Conservative« to the political party known as the Tories, who suffered a disastrous defeat in the 1832 parliamentary election; at this the remaining Tory members of parliament promptly founded a club for the preservation of Conservative values. It was named the **Carlton Club** after its second location, the Carlton Hotel, and is now at 69 St James's Street. To this day membership is restricted to those who espouse the principles of the Conservative Party; the club is a place of political dealings, where careers are made. All Tory prime ministers from Gladstone (in his Tory days) onwards have been members. In the same year the Tories' political opponents, the Whigs, founded the Reform Club at 104-105 Pall Mall. The **Reform Club** has been celebrated in literature: it was the place where Jules Verne's Phileas Fogg wagered that he could go around the world in 80 days. A gentleman could, of course, be a member of several clubs – but not of every one. The novelist W.M. Thackeray, for example, was a member of the Reform, the Garrick and the Athenaeum, but was never accepted for the Traveller's Club, which was a much more snobbish institution.

The Tradition Lives On

White's, Brook's, the Athenaeum, Carlton, Garrick and Reform are just a few of the most distinguished names from the golden age of the clubs. They all still exist, but the time when they were pre-eminent in society, and when the membership included an entertaining array of eccentrics and elderly military men asleep in the armchairs, is now as good as over. On the other hand, their influence should not be underestimated: to be a member of the right club can be extremely advantageous in career terms. The clubs still enjoy the penumbra of exclusivity, even though some have made truly revolutionary concessions to the modern age: the Reform Club, for example, decided to admit women (!) in 1981. It is, after all, proud of being progressive.

✷ St James's Park · Green Park

E–G 6

Location: The Mall, SW 1 **Tube:** St James's Park, Green Park

London's most beautiful park St James's is London's oldest and above all its most beautiful park. In spring and summer, when the flower-beds are in glorious bloom, the park resembles the Kent, Hampshire or Sussex countryside. The area was originally a marshy field which Henry VIII made into a hunting ground in 1532. James I established a menagerie with exotic animals, including several aviaries to the south, which is why the road on that side is called Birdcage Walk. Charles II, advised by the French landscape gardener **Le Nôtre**, converted the park into a formal Baroque garden. Finally **John Nash** was commissioned by George IV in 1829 to give the park its present appearance as a quintessential informal English garden and to turn Le Nôtre's canal into the lake seen today.

Green Park Green Park was also used for Henry VIII's royal hunt. Charles II opened it to the public as Upper St James's Park without making any substantial alterations. Today Green Park is an expanse of grass and

View across St James's Park to the rooftops of Whitehall

trees, and shows no sign of once having been a popular place for duels. Spencer House, the former residence of the the the earls of that name, Princess Diana's family, stands on the east side of Green Park. It is a fine example of an aristocratic 18th-century London residence (entrance in St James's Street; tours Sun 10.30am–4.45pm; closed Jan, Aug). At the edge of the park facing Buckingham Palace is the memorial for Canadians who died in the two world wars. The memorial for the fallen from Asia, Africa and the Caribbean is at the west end of Constitution Hill, which forms the southern boundary of the park.

◄ Spencer House

✶ St Martin-in-the-Fields

G 6

Location: Trafalgar Square, WC 2   **Tube:** Charing Cross

St Martin-in-the-Fields rises above the bustle in the north-western corner of ►Trafalgar Square. A church stood here as early as 1222. It was completely remodelled in 1544 for Henry VIII and rebuilt in 1726 to designs by **James Gibbs**, a pupil of Wren. Because St Martin's is the Admiralty church the flag of the Royal Navy, the White Ensign, is hoisted on official occasions. It is also the church of the royal family, as ►Buckingham Palace belongs to the parish.

The Admiralty church

Gibbs's new St Martin's was a masterpiece. With its Corinthian portico and slender, 56m/184ft-high tower, it became a model for many churches in the North American colonies. The royal coat of arms appears in the tympanum. The oval ceiling by the Italian artists Bagutti and Arturi, the royal box to the left of the altar and the Admiralty box opposite are among the features to admire inside the church. William Hogarth, Sir Joshua Reynolds and Nell Gwynne, mistress of Charles II, are among those buried in St Martin's.

> ## ! *Baedeker* TIP
>
> **In a good cause**
> The café in the crypt of St Martin-in-the-Fields serves a decent lunch or snack at a reasonable price. Customers here are doing a good deed: the proceeds from the café go to help the needy.

»Pearlies« collect money for a good cause.

St Martin's has a special significance not only for kings and admirals, but also for a quite different group of people: the **»pearlies«**, a society composed of market traders from the East End who have a tradition of collecting for charity. Every October St Martin's is the venue for the **Costermongers' Harvest Festival**, when they wear suits and dresses covered in mother-of-pearl buttons and elect a pearly king and a pearly queen. Since the period when »Dick« Sheppard was vicar here (1914–1927), St Martin's has also been one of London's main places of refuge for the poor and homeless.

St Mary-le-Bow

Location: Cheapside, EC 2   **Tube:** St Paul's, Bank

The Cockney church

St Mary-le-Bow has a special place in Londoners' hearts: only those born within the sound of **Bow Bells** are considered true Cockneys. Since the Middle Ages, the Great Bell of Bow has chimed every morning to wake the citizens of London, and every evening at nine to send them to bed. It marks the acoustic boundaries of the City.

St Mary-le-Bow has Norman origins and was one of the first stone-built churches in London. Following the Great Fire Sir Christopher Wren rebuilt it from 1670 to 1683. The church suffered considerable damage in the Second World War and was not reconsecrated until 1964; the crucifix was donated by Germany. The name St Mary-le-Bow comes from the Norman arches of the crypt, a motif that Wren took up on the 73m/240ft-tall tower with its 3m/10ft-long weather-vane in the shape of a dragon. Roman bricks can be seen next to these arches in the 11th-century crypt.

★ ★ St Paul's Cathedral

Location: Ludgate Hill, EC 4   **Tube:** St Paul's, Mansion House

The second-largest dome in the world

St Paul's Cathedral, seat of the diocese of London and »parish church of the British Commonwealth«, is the largest and most famous place of worship in the City. The present cathedral with a massive dome that dominates its surroundings is the fifth church to stand on the site, which was probably once occupied by a Roman Temple of Diana. **Old St Paul's**, built in the 12th and 13th centuries, was one of the richest churches in the world. This large Gothic cathedral, burial place of the Anglo-Saxon King Ethelred among others, was severely damaged by fire in 1561, partially rebuilt by Inigo Jones (1627–1642) and finally destroyed in the Great Fire of 1666.

The architect of the present building, begun in 1675 and completed in 1711 as a successor to Old St Paul's, was **Christopher Wren**. The design was approved only after conflicts with the church commissioners, who found Wren's first plans too radical. The result was a compromise between Wren's original idea for the cathedral (shown by the model in the crypt) and the commissioners' wish to have a Latin cross as the ground plan. Despite this, St Paul's is undoubtedly Wren's masterpiece, the crowning glory of his life's work. The dome is the second-largest in the world after that of St Peter's in Rome. The wedding of Prince Charles and Princess Diana was held in St Paul's in 1981; the funeral service for the Queen Mother was held here in 2002.

This is one of the largest architectural spaces of any church in the world. All Souls' Chapel on the left has been used since 1925 as a memorial chapel for Field Marshal Lord Kitchener, who died in 1916. St Dunstan's Chapel, with a 17th-century oak screen and a mosaic by Salviati, is in the north aisle. Further along are memorials to the painter John Leighton, General Charles George Gordon and Prime Minister Lord Melbourne. The massive monument to the Duke of Wellington, who died in 1852, is by Alfred Stevens. In 1912 an equestrian statue by John Tweed was added to it. The two large allegorical groups on the monument represent Courage and Cowardice, Truth and Deceit.

Nave

✔ **DON'T MISS**

- Funeral monument of John Donne
- Tombs of Christopher Wren, Admiral Nelson and the Duke of Wellington in the crypt
- Whispering Gallery
- View from the galleries of the dome

◄ Wellington Monument

The baptismal font, statues of Joshua Reynolds and Dr Samuel Johnson, among others, and Holman Hunt's Pre-Raphaelite painting *The Light of the World* are in the north transept. In the south transept the eye is drawn to John Flaxman's Nelson Monument, which has allegories of the North Sea, the Baltic Sea, the Mediterranean Sea and the Nile. The inscription on the base, Copenhagen – Nile – Trafalgar, refers to Nelson's greatest victories.

Transepts

◄ Nelson Monument

The highlight of St Paul's is the view up to the dome. Eight mighty double piers with Corinthian capitals, each of which is supported by four additional piers, bear the weight of the dome. The eight scenes from the life of the apostle Paul are the work of Sir James Thornhill. The mosaics were done by Salviati in the late 19th century.

✶✶ *Dome*

The oak choir stalls, carved in masterly fashion in the atelier of **Grinling Gibbons** in the 17th century, are a veritable kaleidoscope of powerful images. The high altar with its cathedral-like vault was executed in 1958 by Dykes Bower and Godfrey Allan on the basis of drawings by Wren. The wrought-iron gates in the choir and choir aisles are all the work of the Huguenot Jean Tijou. In the American Memorial Chapel behind the high altar a roll of honour records the names of the 28,000 Americans stationed in Britain who lost their lives in the Second World War. The effigy from the tomb of John Donne, poet and dean of St Paul's, is situated in the south choir aisle. This is the only sculpture from Old St Paul's that survived the fire of 1666.

Choir

◄ Effigy of John Donne

Steps lead down to the crypt from both sides of the choir. It occupies the whole area beneath the church. The north part of the crypt houses the treasury and the tombs of many famous persons, including the painters Constable, Turner, Landseer and Reynolds, Sir

Crypt

ST PAUL'S CATHEDRAL

✶ ✶ The second-largest church dome in the world after St Peter's in Rome is the result of a catastrophe: Old St Paul's burned down in the Great Fire of 1666 and had to be replaced. The new cathedral is Sir Christopher Wren's main architectural legacy.

🕐 Opening times:
Mon–Sat 8.30am–4pm, galleries Mon–Sat 9.30am–4pm. On Sundays the cathedral is open only for church services. Visitors should respect this.

① Towers
The two 47m/154ft-high towers house the peal of bells. There are twelve bells in the north tower, while »Great Paul«, cast in 1882 and at almost 17 tons the largest bell in England, hangs in the south tower.

② Nave, choir and transepts
St Paul's is 170m/558ft long and 75m/246ft wide at the transepts. Don't miss the view from the crossing at the centre of the church up into the dome – it is overwhelming!

③ Dome
The dome is 111m/365ft in height from the ground to the cross. Two galleries, the Stone Gallery and the Golden Gallery, provide wonderful views over London.

④ Crypt
Many famous Britons are buried in the crypt: Wellington, Nelson, Lawrence of Arabia and, of course, Wren.

⑤ Pediment
The statue of St Paul at the top of the pediment, and of the apostles James and Peter on each side, are b Francis Bird.

St Paul's Cathedral

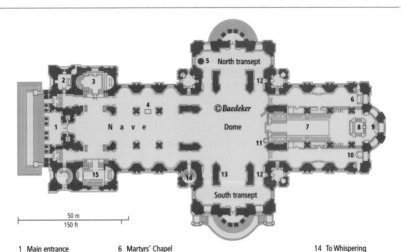

5 North transept

©Baedeker

N a v e   Dome

South transept

50 m
150 ft

1 Main entrance
2 All Souls' Chapel
3 St Dunstan's Chapel
4 Wellington Monument
5 Font
6 Martyrs' Chapel
7 Choir
8 High altar
9 American Memorial Chapel
10 St Mary's Chapel
11 Pulpit
12 Entrance to crypt
13 Nelson Monument
14 To Whispering Gallery, library and dome
15 Chapel of St Michael and St George

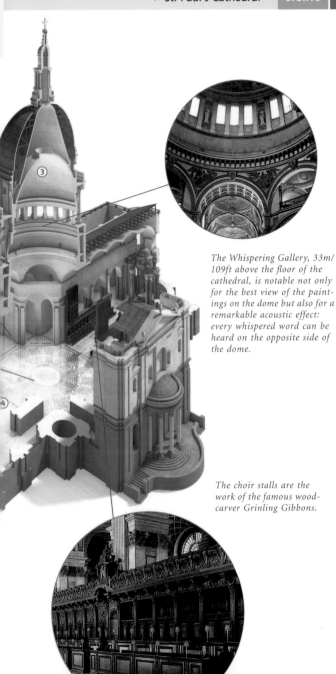

*The Whispering Gallery, 33m/
109ft above the floor of the
cathedral, is notable not only
for the best view of the paintings on the dome but also for a
remarkable acoustic effect:
every whispered word can be
heard on the opposite side of
the dome.*

*The choir stalls are the
work of the famous wood-
carver Grinling Gibbons.*

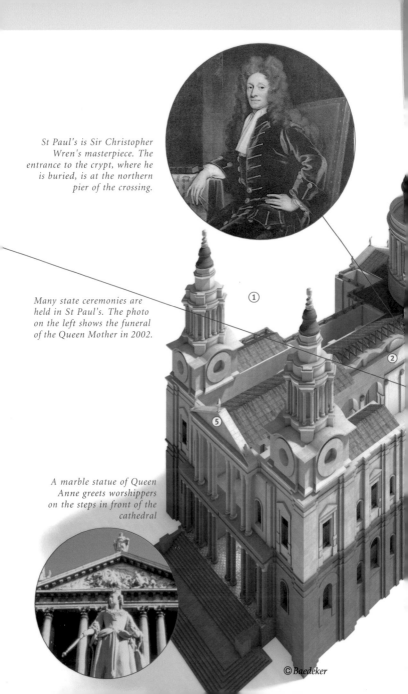

St Paul's is Sir Christopher Wren's masterpiece. The entrance to the crypt, where he is buried, is at the northern pier of the crossing.

Many state ceremonies are held in St Paul's. The photo on the left shows the funeral of the Queen Mother in 2002.

A marble statue of Queen Anne greets worshippers on the steps in front of the cathedral

① ② ⑤

© Baedeker

Tombs of
Wren,
Nelson and
Wellington ►

Alexander Fleming, who discovered penicillin, T.E. Lawrence, better known as **Lawrence of Arabia,** and finally beneath the south aisle the plain tomb of the architect, Sir Christopher Wren. Wren's tomb is inscribed with the words »Lector, si monumentum requiris, circumspice« – »reader, if you require a monument, look around you.« The sarcophaguses of Wellington and Nelson are also in the crypt. Nelson's marble tomb was originally intended as a sarcophagus for Cardinal Wolsey, Henry VIII's chancellor. The coffin containing Nelson's mortal remains was made from the mainmast of the French flagship *L'Orient*, sunk at the Battle of the Nile in 1798.

Galleries and Dome

Triforium Gallery

Trophy Room ►

143 steps lead to the triforium gallery above the south aisle, where plans and models of the earlier churches on the site are displayed. The western part of the gallery gives access to the Trophy Room. Here there is an exhibition of the Wren designs that were rejected by the church commissioners and other drawings.

Whispering
Gallery

The Whispering Gallery is reached from the library at the end of the Triforium Gallery. It takes its name from a peculiarity of the acoustics: every word spoken in a whisper can be heard, even 48m/158ft away at the opposite side of the circle. This gallery provides not only the best place to admire Thornhill's paintings on the dome, but also the most impressive view of the size and proportions of the nave.

Stone Gallery
Golden Gallery

117 more steps remain to be climbed to the Stone Gallery, from where 166 further steps lead to the Golden Gallery at the foot of the lantern. On the way up an opening in the floor affords an awe-inspiring view down to the floor of the cathedral. The ball on top of the lantern is large enough to hold ten people.

★ Science Museum

C/D 7

Location: Exhibition Road,
South Kensington, SW 7
Internet: www.nmsi.ac.uk

Tube: South Kensington

Opening times:
daily 10am–6pm

The theme of the Science Museum is the history and role of the sciences, industry and technology. For children, above all, it is a great experience. They can operate machinery and carry out many experiments, especially on the lower floor, a hands-on area where three- to six-year-olds can examine household machines and find out where things come from. In the Launch Pad Gallery there is a

The Science Museum has nostalgia as well as high-tech.

wide range of activities, including tasks that older children can try for themselves.

The first section of the ground floor is a large hall presenting all kinds of ways to generate energy. The next area, reached by passing a Foucault pendulum, is the Space Hall, where rockets are on display and visitors can build one for themselves on a computer. The department that follows contains 150 of the most important exhibits in the museum, such asStephenson's locomotive *Rocket*, built in 1829, and the Apollo 10 space capsule.

The sections on the first floor are devoted to the making of iron and steel, glass manufacture, telecommunications – with a telephone made by Graham Bell and a telegraph from the year 1846 – plastics, gas exploration, agriculture, meteorology, land surveying, the measurement of time and food, with the world's oldest tinned food (1823).

The themes on the second floor are paper-making and printing (a typewriter from 1875 here has the original positioning of keys, valid to this day), mathematics and data processing – including the calculating machine Engine 1, constructed by Charles Babbage in 1832 – as well as navigation, ship-building and technologies of the future. The exhibitions on the third floor are concerned with optics, the measurement of temperature, oceanography, radio and especially aviation. Visitors can carry out experiments on the physics of flying

Ground floor and first floor

◀ Rocket and Apollo 10

◀ Food tin from 1823

Second and third floor

◀ Engine 1

and admire the originals of aircraft such as the Vickers Vimy, in which Alcock and Brown were the first to cross the Atlantic in 1919, and a Gloster E 28/39, the first British jet aeroplane.

Fourth and fifth floors
The fourth and fifth floors are all about medicine, for both humans and animals. The exhibits include the first working stethoscope (1818) and experimental apparatus used by Louis Pasteur.

Wellcome Wing
The Wellcome Wing, opened in summer 2000, has multi-media presentations of modern science and technology. The attractions include Digitopolis, where users can move around a virtual landscape, and an Imax 3D cinema.

✴ Shri Swaminarayan Mandir

Outer suburb

Location: 105-119 Brentfield Road, Neasden, NW 10

Tube: Neasden (then bus no. 112 or 232), Stonebridge Park (then bus PR 2)

🕐 Opening times: daily 9am–6pm

A visit to the largest Hindu temple outside India involves a trip to Brentfield Road in the north-west of London. British Hindus raised the money for this astonishing, 21m/69ft-high building, for which 2,800 tons of sandstone and 2,000 tons of Carrara marble were used. The building materials were transported to be worked in India, and the construction was then completed in London in a matter of weeks. The result – wonderful sculptures of the Hindu pantheon of gods – is open for visits by non-Hindus, who can find explanations in the exhibition entitled »Understanding Hinduism«.

Wembley Stadium
Wembley Stadium, the mecca of English football, is situated some distance further north-west (tube: Wembley Park). At the inauguration and opening match on 28 April 1923, over 200,000 (!) people crowded into the stadium, which has now been demolished. A spectacular new arena opens in 2007.

Smithfield Market

J 4

Location: Charterhouse Street/ West Smithfield, EC 1

Tube: Barbican, Farringdon

London's principal meat market
More than 1,300 tons of meat are bought and sold each day in the Victorian market hall at Smithfield. Since it opened in 1866 Smithfield Market has been London's main market for meat, and it is still worth a visit, as poultry, cheese and other delicacies are also on sale. Come early to see the action, as the market does business only

between 4.30am and 9am. On the site of the market the monk Rahere established the famous Bartholomew Fair, which came to an end only in 1855, when the festivities were thought to have become excessive. Knightly tournaments and executions also took place on the »Smooth Field«. In 1381 the rebel Wat Tyler was beheaded here.

 Baedeker TIP

The first pint of the day
A trip to Smithfield Market is worthwhile only at a truly uncivilized hour of the day. However, a hearty breakfast afterwards in one of the nearby pubs makes amends for such an early start. The proper drink for market traders is beer, and the pubs around Smithfield have a special licence to serve it from 6.30am. The recommended hostelries are The Fox and Anchor (115 Charterhouse Street) and Hope & Sir Loin (94 Cowcross Street).

Around Smithfield Market

St Bartholomew-the-Great, the oldest parish church in the City, lies hidden behind a half-timbered 16th-century gatehouse to the south of the market halls. The church constitutes the remains of a hospital and monastery founded in 1123 by Rahere, who was also Henry I's court jester. By the time of the dissolution of the monasteries under Henry VIII it had been extended to a considerable size, but the nave was then torn down and the choir converted into a parish church; in the 18th century the buildings were used as a storehouse, shed, inn, smithy and printing-house, in which Benjamin Franklin worked in 1724.

The horseshoe arches in the choir and the billet mouldings are characteristic of Norman church architecture. Rahere, who died in about 1145, lies in a 16th-century tomb which shows him reclining and dressed in the black habit of the Augustinians. A crowned angel at his feet holds a shield with the coat of arms of the monastery. Other points of interest in the church are the alabaster tomb of Sir Walter Mildmay, chancellor of the exchequer to Elizabeth I, the early 15th-century font in which William Hogarth was baptized and the cloister built in 1405, which is entered through a Norman doorway with 15th-century doors. The place where the nave once stood is now the small churchyard; the 13th-century gate that remains here was originally the entrance to the south aisle.

★
St Bartholomew-the-Great

The continuation of Charterhouse Street to the north of Smithfield Market leads to Charterhouse Square, where the courtyard of the Charterhouse, the London branch of the Carthusian order originat-

Charterhouse

ing in the Chartreuse monastery, can be seen through the gatehouse. The London Charterhouse was founded in 1371 by Sir Walter de Manny and dissolved in 1535 by Henry VIII, who had the prior hanged, drawn and quartered at Tyburn and one of his arms nailed to the gatehouse. The estate then came into the possession of, among others, John Dudley, Duke of Northumberland (executed in 1553) and Thomas Howard, Duke of Norfolk (executed in 1572 for conspiring with Mary Queen of Scots). In 1611 Thomas Sutton bought the Charterhouse and converted it into a home for the elderly and a school. Today the Charterhouse is still home to 40 pensioners, who have to be members of the Church of England and either bachelors or widowers, and must have served as army officers or in the clergy.

St John's Gate To the north of the market (via St John Street and St John Lane) is St John's Gate, the former gatehouse of the priory of the Knights of St John. The Order of the Knights of St John was founded in the 11th century in Jerusalem, came to England in the 12th century and settled on this site in Clerkenwell in 1148. In 1381 Wat Tyler burned it down during his rebellion against taxes, and the prior was beheaded on Tower Hill. The priory was rebuilt in 1504, but shortly afterwards in 1537 the order was dissolved. The gatehouse, which dates from 1504, is the only remaining part of the priory. It houses a museum about the history of the English Knights of St John. From 1721 to 1723 St John's Church was built on the site of the priory church using the walls of its choir. The 15th-century altarpiece depicts the victory of the Knights of St John over the Turks at the siege of Rhodes. The Norman crypt (1140–1180) has survived (opening ⏱ times: Mon–Fri 10am–5pm, Sat 10am–4pm).

∗ Soho

Location: between Oxford Street, Charing Cross Road, Leicester Square, Piccadilly Circus and Regent Street	**Tube:** Oxford Circus, Tottenham Court Road

No longer a den of vice Soho, still a synonym for iniquity and vice, was once an aristocratic district. It was one of Henry VIII's hunting grounds – hence the name »so-ho«, an old hunting call. In the 17th century, when the area was no longer used for the chase, nobles built their London residences here. In later decades they moved on to more fashionable areas, making way for immigrants from the continent of Europe and Asia, who gave Soho a more down-to-earth character. Not until the 19th century did Soho acquire its reputation as the red-light district par excellence; in 1958 street prostitution was banned, and since the local authorities' campaign in the 1980s to clean it up, Soho has become almost harmless. It does not take long to realize that the at-

The ballerina Anna Pavlova made her debut in the Palace Theatre. Nowadays dancers perform here in musicals.

mosphere in Soho is no more seedy than that in other, similar districts of London.

For many companies, an address in Soho is a mark of quality: the central location attracts film and record companies, publishers and advertising agencies. The creative people from offices in Wardour Street and elsewhere have set their stamp on the local scene. For food-lovers Soho is one of the best areas for delicatessens and restaurants. It is also a good place to buy ingredients for dishes from all parts of the world – on Berwick Street Market, for example, or in Chinatown. Lovers of exotic food flock to the restaurants in Soho. No part of London is more attractive to theatre-goers, as some of the best-known theatres in the West End are here (▶Practicalities, theatre). The criminal underworld and shady establishments, bars and revues, pornography and prostitution still exist in places such as Great Windmill Street, but Soho is much more than this.

The best way to get to know Soho is to go there twice – once during the day, and again at night. Daylight hours reveal what has happened to **Carnaby Street**, famous for the flower-power scene in the 1960s. Until recently it was just another pedestrian zone with an unexciting range of retailers, but has become a busy shopping street with innovative little stores. In **Wardour Street** it is worth taking a look inside the church of **St Anne's Soho**, where one of the graves is that of Theodore, King of Corsica; after that go along **Dean Street**, where Karl Marx lived at house no. 28 from 1851 to 1856, and stroll over to

Soho Square, a haven of quiet with a statue of Charles II and the re-construction of a Tudor garden shed in the middle of the square. Go back along **Greek Street** past the House of St Barnabas, built on the corner of Soho Square in 1746, which gives an idea of how Soho looked in its upper-class days, and on to the junction with **Old Compton Street**, the heart of Soho. Here the abundance of pubs, bars, cafés and restaurants is an opportunity to choose a place for a second visit in the evening. Frith Street runs parallel to Old Compton Street and is the home of **Ronnie Scott's Club**, London's best-known jazz club; straight ahead is the **Palace Theatre**, built in 1891 and today owned by Andrew Lloyd Webber. In 1910 Anna Pavlova made her London debut in the theatre. The Palace is on Cambridge Circus, from where **Shaftesbury Avenue** leads to Piccadilly Circus past some of London's most famous theatres, such as the Lyric (1888), the Apollo (1901), the Globe (1903) and the Shaftesbury Theatre (1911). The finest of all these theatres is the Victorian Palace Theatre, but it is not always easy to get tickets; one place to try is the Half Price Ticket Booth on Leicester Square.

✳
Chinatown –
a slice of China

An excellent way to round off an evening is a meal is one of the res-taurants in Chinatown, which is concentrated around Gerrard Street, spilling over into Lisle Street and part of Wardour Street. This dis-trict, the centre of the 60,000-strong Chinese community in London,

is a microcosm of China with exotic foodstores, acupuncture practices, bookshops, hair-dressers, countless crowded restaurants, Peking ducks dangling in their windows, and even phone-boxes in the shape of pagodas. The language spoken on all sides is Cantonese. Chinatown developed from the late 1940s; before then most London Chinese lived around the docks in Limehouse.

Leicester Square is the hub of the West End theatre world. This has not always been its role. After the second Earl of Leicester built a house here in 1631, other persons of rank such as Sir Isaac Newton, Sir Joshua Reynolds and William Hogarth followed. In the 19th century, however, a number of music-halls set up here. Today the cinemas, especially the Empire and Odeon, dominate the square.

> **! Baedeker TIP**
>
> **Dim sum**
>
> »Tiny bites to touch the heart«: this is the translation of dim sum, the best way to try authentic south Chinese food in Chinatown. The delicacies, in baskets and pots on a trolley, are wheeled through the restaurant, and guests take what they fancy for a standard price. Good places to eat dim sum are Chuen Cheng Ku (17 Wardour Street, tel. 7 743 2282) and Harbour City (46 Gerrard Street, tel. 7 439 7859). But remember: dim sum is not served after 6pm.

South Bank

G / H 6

Location: south bank of the Thames, western part

Tube: Waterloo

The south bank of the Thames between Waterloo and Westminster Bridge was originally a place of quays and small factories, which made it a prime target for the German bombing raids in the Second World War. Since the completion of the Royal Festival Hall in 1951 it has gradually developed into a cultural quarter, the South Bank Centre. At the start of the millennium it gained further momentum with the giant wheel, the London Eye, and the opening of the IMAX cinema in front of Waterloo Station.

From an industrial area to a cultural centre

The Oxo Tower on Barge House Street is not a youthful building, but it is now more up-to-date than ever: this 1930s block with a tower, formerly a factory for the production of the Oxo beef drink, was converted into a trendy apartment and commercial building. The bar and restaurant on the 8th floor have made it part of a cool scene. The observation platform can be visited without the need to dine in the restaurant.

Oxo Tower

← *In London and all over the world: the residents of Chinatown celebrate Chinese New Year with a parade.*

South Bank Centre The South Bank Centre can hardly be regarded as an architectural triumph. Too much naked concrete gives it a cold atmosphere. The cultural attractions, however, are first class, starting with the **National Theatre**, which has three auditoria: the Lyttelton Theatre, the Olivier Theatre – named after its first director, Sir Laurence Olivier – and the Cottesloe Theatre. To the west of Waterloo Bridge is the **Queen Elizabeth Hall**, a venue for symphony concerts, chamber music and solo concerts since 1967. It stands next to the **Royal Festival Hall**, which was built in 1951 to designs by Robert Matthew and J.M. Martin. The Museum of the Moving Image has closed. Re-opening is planned, but the when and where remain unclear.

◄ Hayward Gallery The outside of the Hayward Gallery, which was built on top of the whole complex, as it were, shows what awaits on the inside: modern art. The building, a work of the New Style from 1968, is divided into two levels, equipped with excellent artificial lighting. The gallery 🕑 stages temporary exhibitions of modern art of extremely high quality (opening times: daily 11am–7pm).

★ ★
British Airways London Eye The Jubilee Gardens were laid out to the west of Hungerford Bridge in 1977 for the 25th anniversary of the queen's accession to the throne. Since the start of the 21st century it has been the site of London's newest landmark, the British Airways London Eye. The London Eye is the world's largest observation wheel, designed by David Marks and Julia Barfield. It is 135m/443ft in height and turns full circle once every half hour, giving the passengers in its 32 glass capsules enough time to enjoy the amazing view – over a distance of 40km/25mi in good weather.

County Hall The massive bulk of County Hall, built from 1912 to 1932 and formerly the seat of the Greater London Council, now houses the **London Aquarium**, which features a shark tank and a »touch pool« for visitors with rolled-up sleeves, and **Dalí Universe** with works of 🕑 the Spanish Surrealist and eccentric Salvador Dalí (both attractions daily 10am–6pm).

Southwark

Location: south bank of the Thames, eastern part   **Tube:** London Bridge

London's first red-light district In Roman times the men of Londinium frequented dubious taverns and visited prostitutes in the area now at the south end of London Bridge. In this respect little changed until the 19th century, except that bull-fights, bear-baiting and theatres added to the range of en-

Trippers with a head for heights take a ride on the London Eye. →

Southwark Cathedral: one of London's oldest Gothic buildings

tertainments in the red-light district. The brothels were pulled down to make way for quays and warehouses, most of which have now been converted into apartment buildings.

✳ Southwark Cathedral   J 6

Fine Gothic architecture

Southwark Cathedral, the seat of the diocese of Southwark, is London's most beautiful Gothic church after ► Westminster Abbey. According to tradition a ferryman's daughter named Mary founded a convent here. It became known as St Mary of the Ferry. In 1106 Gifford, Bishop of Winchester, ordered the building of a large church, now called St Mary Overie, meaning »over the river«. This church burned down and was rebuilt from 1207 by Bishop Peter de Rupibus. The lower part of the 55m/180ft-tall tower, the crossing, and the choir and retro-choir date from this period. The nave, added in the 13th century and remodelled in 1469, was rebuilt between 1890 and 1896 by Sir Arthur Blomfield.

Interior
North side ►

The 12th-century Norman doorway to the cloister has been preserved in the north aisle. To its right the original wooden roof bosses are visible. Look for Judas Iscariot (in a kilt!) being swallowed by the devil. The poet **John Gower** (1330–1408) is buried under the sixth window. The effigy is a reclining figure resting its head on his books *Speculum Meditantis*, *Vox Clamantis* and *Confessio Amantis*. The north transept with its Norman arches is the site of the Lockyer

Monument in memory of the quack Lionel Lockyer († 1672), who claimed to be able to make miraculous pills from the rays of the sun. The Trehearne Monument in the north choir aisle portrays John Trehearne, a favourite of James I, with his family. Trehearne and his wife are shown holding a tablet with the inscription: »Had kings a power to lend their subjects breath, Trehearne thou shouldst not be cast down by death«. The wooden effigy of a knight from the late 13th century in the corner is one of the oldest of its kind in England.

The choir, which was divided to create a retro-choir, dates from about 1273, making it one of the oldest Gothic church buildings in London. The high altar with its 13th-century columns was made in 1520.

◄ Choir

The south choir aisle is the burial place of **Lancelot Andrewes**, Bishop of Winchester, who died in 1626. He translated the New Testament into English. The interesting features of the south transept, built around 1310, include the coat of arms and cardinal's hat of Cardinal Beaufort, half-brother of King Henry IV. Finally, in the south aisle, the Shakespeare window and the memorial to William Shakespeare of 1912 are also worthy of note. Southwark Cathedral is the burial place of Shakespeare's brother Edmund, who died in 1607, and Lawrence Fletcher, who leased the Blackfriars Theatre and the Globe Theatre in partnership with Shakespeare and Burbage. Part of the 13th-century arcade has survived next to the font.

◄ South side

◄ Shakespeare Monument

Around Southwark Cathedral

A few yards away from the cathedral, under the railway arches bearing the tracks to London Bridge Station, is a market hall built in 1851. Borough Market was mentioned as early as 1276; it is now a high-class market for food-lovers with stalls selling much more than the traditional fruit and vegetables.

Borough Market

In today's St Thomas Street opposite the market, a hospital is recorded in the 12th century. It moved to the west of London in 1862. All that remains, now in the roof of St Thomas's Church, is the gynaecological **operating theatre**, which gives an impression of medical practices in the era before antiseptic hygiene (opening times: daily 10.30am–5pm).

> ## ! *Baedeker* TIP
>
> ### The George Inn
> Diagonally opposite the entrance to Borough Market an entry leads from Borough High Street to the George Inn – just the right place for a pint in historic surroundings. This pub dating from 1676 is London's only remaining galleried coaching inn. The creaking floorboards and scrubbed tables go back to the days when waggoners stopped here in Southwark before delivering their goods in the City on the other bank of the Thames. In summer there are tables outside in the courtyard.

The London Dungeon (28–34 Tooley Street) below London Bridge Station claims to portray the cruel and bloody side of British history:

London Dungeon

the murder of Thomas Becket, the plague, burning at the stake, torture chambers and Jack the Ripper. In reality it is no more than a collection of wax figures with gaping wounds, smeared in artificial blood. This »attraction« cannot be recommended for children, even though it is specifically aimed at them (opening times: April–June daily 10am–5.30pm; July–Sept until 7.30pm; Nov–March 10.30am–5pm).

Winston Churchill's Britain at War
This multi-media exhibition shows how Londoners coped with everyday life during the war (64–66 Tooley Street; opening times: Oct–March daily 10am–4.30pm; April–Sept until 5.30pm).

Hays Galleria
Hays Galleria, is on the Thames side of the London Bridge City shopping centre. The rattling, spouting and hissing steel sculpture in the middle is David Kemp's *The Navigator*.

HMS Belfast
HMS Belfast, the Royal Navy's last large cruiser, is anchored at Symons Wharf. The 11,500-ton ship, launched in 1938, was involved in operations including the sinking of the *Scharnhorst* and the D-Day landings in Normandy in June 1944. After the war, *HMS Belfast* was on service in the Far East before being decommissioned in 1963. The cruiser is now a museum ship and part of the ▶Imperial War Museum (opening times: March–Oct daily 10am–6pm; Nov–Feb until 5pm).

> ! **Baedeker TIP**
>
> **Bird's eye view of London**
> … without having to fly. On the ground floor of City Hall an aerial view of Greater London, 16 x 10 metres (53 x 33 ft) in size and made of 200,000 individual images, has been reproduced on the floor.

City Hall
The egg-shaped leaning glass building on the bank of the Thames close to *HMS Belfast* is London's new city hall, designed by Sir Norman Foster and opened in 2002 (opening times: Mo–Fri 8am–8pm).

HMS Belfast, the Royal Navy's last big cruiser

A reconstruction of Sir Francis Drake's legendary **Golden Hind** lies in St Mary Overie Dock to the west of Southwark cathedral. Costumed guides tell the story of the privateers.

St Mary Overie Dock

Clink Street takes its name from the dungeon of the palace of the bishops of London that once stood on this site. The Clink Prison Museum is devoted to the history of this infamous prison and its inmates, many of whom were prostitutes, drunkards and debtors (opening times: daily 10am–6pm).

Clink Prison Museum

🕐

Vinopolis is the world's first interactive wine museum. Visitors are taken on an electronic »wine-odyssey« under the railway arches, finishing up in the tasting and sales room. To enjoy a glass of wine without paying the high admission price, just stop in the Cantina Vinopolis. All those who prefer beer should go to The Anchor pub, which has a pleasant terrace on the Thames. The inn has existed since the 17th century, the present building since the 18th century.

Vinopolis

◄ The Anchor

The Bramah Museum of Tea and Coffee at 40 Southwark Street, a short distance south of Vinopolis, explains how tea and coffee came to London, and where and how they were drunk (opening times: daily 10am–6pm).

◄ Bramah Museum of Tea and Coffee

The headquarters of William Shakespeare's theatre company lay in today's Park Street to the south of The Anchor. It was just one of several Elizabethan theatres in Southwark. The round, thatched theatre was built in 1598 but closed again in 1644, as the plaque in Park Street records. Thanks to years of efforts by the American actor Sam Wanamaker, the world of Shakespeare lives again, though a little further to the west. The plays are performed in the open air, as they were 400 years ago. An exhibition explains the history of the Elizabeth theatre. There are no tours when matinees are staged – as an alternative visit the excavations of the first theatre on Bankside, The Rose, where Shakespeare learned his trade (opening times: May–Sept daily 9am–noon, 1pm–4pm; Oct–April daily 10am–5pm; tours every 15–30 min)

★ ★
Shakespeare's Globe Theatre

The Queen herself came to the opening of the Globe Theatre.

Close by in the old Bankside Power Station, the ► Tate Gallery displays its collection of modern art.

Tate Modern

✳ The Strand

G / H 5 / 6

Location: between Trafalgar Square and Temple Bar

Tube: Charing Cross, Aldwych, Temple

The Strand is the main thoroughfare from the west of London to the City. Its name derives from a long-gone path on the banks of the Thames. Today the street is lined with old-established pubs and hotels, many of which were founded in the 19th century when the Strand was the focus of London's entertainment scene.

Craven Street

Starting from the Trafalgar Square end of the Strand, Craven Street branches off to the right. For almost 29 years house no. 36 (a museum since early 2006) was the home of **Benjamin Franklin**; the German poet **Heinrich Heine** stuck it out for just three months at no. 32 and recorded his impressions of London in his *English Fragments*: *Send a philosopher to London; but a poet on no account! Send a philosopher and place him on a corner of Cheapside, where he will learn more than from all the books at the last Leipzig fair, and as the flood of humanity surges around him, a sea of new thoughts will rise before him, the eternal spirit that hovers above will waft in his face, the best-hidden secrets of human society will suddenly be revealed to him, the pulse of the world will sound in his ears. ...But do not send a poet to London! This naked earnestness in all things, this colossal uniformity, this machine-like activity, this irksomeness of pleasure itself, this excess of London crushes the imagination and tears the heart to pieces ...*

Savoy Hotel

Beyond Bedford Street on the left is the Adelphi Theatre, built in 1881 and refurbished in 1930 in the art deco style. Further along on the other side of the street is the legendary Savoy Hotel, the first hotel to have electric light and an en-suite bathroom for every room when it opened in 1889. The founder of the hotel and the owner of the Savoy Theatre, Richard D'Oyly Carte, employed a certain César Ritz, who later became a competitor, as his first hotel manager. Next door is an old-established restaurant, **Simpson's in the Strand**, a bastion of traditional English roast beef, which may be cheaper elsewhere but is nowhere better. The Savoy Chapel is also close to the hotel. Its official name is the Queen's Chapel of the Savoy, as it is the queen's private property. It was built in the late Perpendicular style in the reigns of Henry VII and Henry VIII on the site of the Savoy Palace, which was destroyed in the Peasants' Revolt of 1381.

Savoy Chapel ►

St Mary-le-Strand

On the right, beyond the approach to Waterloo Bridge, is Somerset House, where the ► Courtauld Institute Galleries and King's College are located. Further along is the church of St Mary-le-Strand, completed in 1724 by James Gibbs, in which Bonnie Prince Charlie secretly converted from Catholicism to the Anglican faith in 1750.

A little way on is St Clement Danes. Sir **Christopher Wren** built the church in 1681 and James Gibbs added a tower in 1719. The name derives from a Danish settlement on the site. The role of St Clement Danes as the central church of the Royal Air Force is shown by the badges of 800 RAF units set into the floor, the rolls of honour with the names of 125,000 members of the Allied air forces who lost their lives in the Second World War, the altar and font of the Dutch and Norwegian air forces in the crypt and, in front of the church, memorials to Lord Dowding and **Air Marshal Arthur Harris**, known as Bomber Harris for his advocacy of air-raids in the Second World War. The third memorial outside the church represents **Samuel Johnson**, who belonged to this parish. This church is well known to London children from the song *Oranges and Lemons*, which the bells chime out each day at 9am, noon, 3pm and 6pm. The song refers to the custom that the traders of Clare Market treated the children of St Clement Danes on every market day. A children's service still takes place in the church annually in March, when every child is given an orange and a lemon.

From here it is not far to the fortress-like **Royal Courts of Justice** or Law Courts, a magnificent Victorian building completed in 1882. This is a court for civil cases – criminal trials are held at the ▶ Old Bailey. The figures of two Chinese and a gilded lion mark the entrance to **Twinings**, an old-established supplier of tea that began in 1708 as Tom's Coffee House. Twinings has a small tea museum. The Strand ends a short distance further on at Temple Bar Memorial, the boundary between Westminster and the City.

St Clement Danes

◀ *Oranges and Lemons*

Not a medieval castle but a court of law: the Royal Courts of Justice

A detour down to the Thames at Waterloo Bridge leads to Cleopatra's Needle, an Egyptian obelisk of pink granite situated on Victoria Embankment below the bridge. It was presented to the British Crown by the viceroy of Egypt, Mohammed Ali. After a stormy voyage that cost the lives of six sailors it was placed here in 1878 and immediately nicknamed Cleopatra's Needle. The hieroglyphs on the obelisk, which was erected in Heliopolis in about 1500 BC, praise the deeds and victories of Thutmosis III and Ramses the Great. The counterpart to this obelisk stands in Central Park in New York.

Embankment

◀ *Cleopatra's Needle*

★★ Tate Gallery

Two houses

Internet
www.tate.org.uk

The Tate Gallery opened in 1897 in a neoclassical building by Sidney R. J. Smith on Millbank by the Thames. The basis for the gallery was a donation by the sugar manufacturer and art collector Sir Henry Tate. Today there are two main parts to the collection, which are on display in two separate places: British art from the 16th to the 20th century in the old gallery on Millbank (Tate Britain), and international modern art in Bankside Power Station on the south bank of the Thames (Tate Modern). The two galleries are connected by a **shuttle boat service** (Tate to Tate).

★★ Tate Britain   G 7/8

Location: Millbank, SW 1   **Tube:** Pimlico

⏰
Opening times:
daily 10am–5.50pm

The rooms in Tate Britain either have a theme or are devoted to a particular artist.
The earliest work is *A Man in a Black Cap*, painted in 1545 by John Bettes. The 17th century is represented by painters such as Anthony van Dyck (*Lady of the Spencer Family*) and William Dobson (*Endymion Porter*, 1643/1645). There are many illustrations by the draughtsman and engraver William Blake (*Newton*, 1795/1805). One of the most famous works in the collection is William Hogarth's *O the Roast Beef of Old England / The Gate of Calais*, 1748). A large part of the gallery presents landscapes, including paintings by Thomas Gainsborough, Joshua Reynolds, George Stubbs, Edwin Landseer and Henry Fuessli, and particularly by John Constable (*Chain Pier, Brighton*, 1826/1827). Among the notable 19th-century artists are John Everett Millais and James Abbot McNeill Whistler (*Nocturne in Blue and Gold: Old Battersea Bridge*, 1872–1875). Representatives of modern British art include Lucian Freud, David Hockney and Gilbert & George.

In the **Clore Gallery**, designed by James Stirling, the best works from the oeuvre of J.M.W. Turner (1775–1851), including his watercolours and such famous works as *Snow Storm – Steam-Boat off a Harbour's Mouth* are on display.

 DON'T MISS

- William Dobson: *Endymion Porter* (Tate Britain)
- William Hogarth: *O' the Roast Beef of Old England / The Gate of Calais* (Tate Britain)
- John Constable: *Chain Pier, Brighton* (Tate Britain)
- James Abbott McNeill Whistler: *Nocturne in Blue and Gold: Old Battersea Bridge* (Tate Britain)
- Works by J.M.W. Turner in the Clore Gallery (Tate Britain)
- Claude Monet: *Water Lilies* (Tate Modern)
- Vassily Kandinsky: *Cossacks* (Tate Modern)
- Andy Warhol: *Marilyn Diptych* (Tate Modern)

Modern art where electricity was once generated: the turbine hall of the Tate Modern

✶ ✶ Tate Modern   J 6

Location: Bankside Power Station   **Tube:** Blackfriars, Southwark

To house the Tate's modern collection the Swiss team of architects, Herzog de Meuron, converted Bankside Power Station, which was built by Giles Gilbert Scott shortly after the Second World War. Here too the works are either arranged by theme or an individual artist is presented. Among the highlights are works of the French Impressionists and Post-Impressionists such as Paul Cézanne, Edgar Degas, Claude Serrain, Claude Monet (*Water Lilies*), Paul Gauguin, Henri Rousseau, Henri de Toulouse-Lautrec and Marc Chagall; Cubism is represented by, for example, Georges Braque (*Mandola*, 1909/1910) and Fernand Léger. *Woman Crying* and other works by Pablo Picasso are on show, as is a key work of abstract art, Vassily Kandinsky's *Cossacks* from 1911. Among the Dadaist and Surrealist artists are Giorgio de Chirico, Max Ernst, Paul Klee, Salvador Dalí and Joan Miró; Expressionism, Pop Art (Andy Warhol: *Marilyn Diptych*; Roy Lichtenstein: *Whaam!*), Minimal Art, Conceptual Art and loans from the Fröhlich Collection in Stuttgart are also well represented in the Tate Modern.

🕓
Opening times:
Sun–Thu
10am–6.50pm;
Fri, Sat until 10pm

London's newest Thames bridge, the intricate Millennium Bridge by Norman Foster and Anthony Caro, connects the Tate Modern with the City, leading to St Paul's.

✶
Millennium Bridge

✴ The Temple

H 5

Location: Fleet Street, EC 4   **Tube:** Temple

Inns of court From the Temple Bar Memorial on ► Fleet Street a small arch leads to the right into the Temple, a charming, almost secret Georgian jumble of buildings and alleys. **Charles Dickens** described the Temple in *Barnaby Rudge*:

There are, still, worse places than the Temple, on a sultry day, for basking in the sun, or resting idly in the shade. There is yet a drowsiness in its courts, and a dreamy dulness in its trees and gardens; those who pace its lanes and squares may yet hear the echoes of their footsteps on the sounding stones, and read upon its gates, in passing from the tumult of the Strand or Fleet Street, »Who enters here leaves noise behind.« There is still the plash of falling water in fair Fountain Court ...

The Temple, a lawyers' enclave

The inns of court, corporations of and schools for barristers, developed in the reign of Edward I, when clerics were replaced by laymen as lawyers and judges. In the 12th and 13th centuries the Temple was the English headquarter of the Order of Knights Templar, founded in 1119 in Jerusalem. After the dissolution of the order in 1312 its property came into the possession of the Crown. It was then granted to the Earl of Pembroke, and passed after his death to the Order of the Knights of St John, who rented it to a corporation of lawyers. Since then the Temple has been the lawyers' district, as it lies only a stone's throw from the Royal Courts of Justice. Barristers have their chambers in one of the four inns of court (Middle Temple, Inner Temple, ► Lincoln's Inn, ► Gray's Inn). In order to become a barrister, students have to become members of an inn and are required to eat dinner in the hall of their inn at least three times each term.

Middle Temple From Fleet Street the entrance to the Middle Temple is through Wren's gatehouse. The former members of this inn include Sir Walter Raleigh, Sir Thomas More, Thomas de Quincey, W. M. Thackeray and Mahatma Gandhi.

Down the slope lies Middle Temple Hall, which was built in 1572 as ◄ Middle
a dining and assembly hall. Most of the original panelling, the carved   Temple Hall
screen, the double hammer-beam roof, the glass decorated with coats
of arms and the table made from the wood of Sir Francis Drake's
Golden Hind survived the bombing in the Second World War. An
equestrian portrait of Charles I by Sir Godfrey Kneller hangs on the
end wall. Shakespeare's **Twelfth Night** was first performed in this hall
on 2 February 1602 (opening times: Mon–Fri 10am–noon and   ☉
3pm–4pm).

On the left beyond the Fountain Court is a passage to the Inner   **Inner Temple**
Temple. Inner Temple Hall contains statues of Knights Templar and
Knights of the Order of St John (opening times: see Middle Temple
Hall). White and red roses grow in
the Inner Temple Gardens in
memory of the houses of York
(white) and Lancaster (red), which
feuded during the 15th-century
Wars of the Roses.
The **Temple Church** consists of the
original Norman round church of
1185, which was modelled on the
Church of the Holy Sepulchre in
Jerusalem, and a chancel added in
1240 in the Early English Style. Sir
Christopher Wren renovated the
church in 1682. It holds a rare treasure, **nine effigies of Knights
Templar** in black marble from the 12th and 13th centuries; one of
them, its slab below the headrest decorated with a foliage relief, is
said to portray William Marshal, Earl of Pembroke (†1219) and
brother-in-law of King John, regent during the minority of Henry II
(opening times Wed–Sun 10am–4pm). The author **Oliver Goldsmith**   ☉
(1728–1774) is buried in the churchyard.

> **? DID YOU KNOW …?**
>
> ■ Lawyers belong to one of two groups in
> England: barristers, who are qualified to plead
> at the bar in the higher-ranking courts of law
> but do not usually have direct contact to their
> clients; and solicitors, who advise the client
> but do not plead in court, but instead brief the
> barrister. Today the distinction is no longer as
> strict as it used to be.

✳ ✳ Tower of London

K 5/6

Location: Tower Hill, EC 3   **Tube:** Tower Hill, Tower Gateway

The Tower, a stronghold and state prison, lies outside the old city   **A historic site**
wall. This irregular conglomeration of buildings, surrounded by a
crenellated wall and a deep ditch, is the most significant historic site
in England. There was probably a fortress here on the Thames as
early as the Roman period. The Tower originated in the reign of William the Conqueror, who began construction of the White Tower in
1078. From the 12th to the 14th century it was continually enlarged
and strengthened. It was often besieged, but never captured. Until

the time of James I it served as a royal palace, but has also been a prison, mint and treasury – the **Crown Jewels** are still kept here. It was the site of an observatory, until a new one was built in ▶Greenwich, and a menagerie until 1834.

🕐
Opening times:
March–Oct
Mon–Sat
9am–6pm,
Sun 10am–6pm;
Nov–Feb
Tue–Sat
9am–5pm,
Sun, Mon
10am–5pm
(last admission
1 hour earlier)

Tours
every half hour

The history of the Tower reflects the history of England. The large number of prisoners held here included David II of Scotland (1346–1357), John the Good of France (1356–1360), James I of Scotland (1406–1407), Charles, Duke of Orléans (1415), Elizabeth I (1554, before she became queen), Walter Raleigh no less than three times (1592, 1603–1616, 1618) and William Penn (1668–1669). Some of those executed or murdered within its walls were Henry VI (1471), the »little princes in the Tower« Edward V and his brother, the Duke of York (1483), Thomas More (1535), Henry VIII's wives Anne Boleyn (1536) and Catherine Howard (1542), Thomas Cromwell (1540) and the nine-day queen Lady Jane Grey (1554). The last death sentence to be carried out in the Tower was the execution of a German spy in 1941.

Ceremony of the Keys

The Tower is guarded by the Yeoman Warders (»Beefeaters«), who wear the traditional uniform from Tudor times. They are responsible for closing the main gate every evening in the Ceremony of the Keys, a ritual which has been performed unchanged for 700 years by the commander of the Tower, the Chief Warder. To witness the ceremony it is necessary to apply for a pass in writing eight weeks in advance by sending a stamped, self-addressed envelope to **The Ceremony of the Keys, HM Tower of London, EC 3N 4AB**. The ceremony starts at 9.40pm; the pass must be shown at 9.30pm at the main entrance.

! *Baedeker* TIP

Jump the queue

The Tower is one of London's most-visited tourist attractions. To save time, buy a ticket beforehand. They can be purchased up to seven days in advance in any tube station. Those in possession of an advance ticket can use a separate entrance.

Overview

The ground plan of the Tower is an irregular pentagon with an area of over 5 hectares (12 acres). The outer courtyard (Outer Ward), probably built in the 14th century under Edward I, is bounded by a wall with six towers and two bastions. The Inner Ward is defended by a wall with 13 towers built in the 13th century in the reign of Henry III. The entrance is in the south-west corner, originally the site of the Lions' Gate, which took its name from the former royal lion enclosure.

Outer Ward

Bell Tower

A stone bridge flanked by the Middle Tower and Byward Tower (password tower), both built in 1307 by Edward I, spans the moat.

Tower

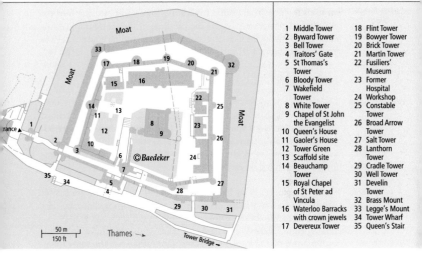

1 Middle Tower	18 Flint Tower
2 Byward Tower	19 Bowyer Tower
3 Bell Tower	20 Brick Tower
4 Traitors' Gate	21 Martin Tower
5 St Thomas's Tower	22 Fusiliers' Museum
6 Bloody Tower	23 Former Hospital
7 Wakefield Tower	24 Workshop
8 White Tower	25 Constable Tower
9 Chapel of St John the Evangelist	26 Broad Arrow Tower
10 Queen's House	27 Salt Tower
11 Gaoler's House	28 Lanthorn Tower
12 Tower Green	29 Cradle Tower
13 Scaffold site	30 Well Tower
14 Beauchamp Tower	31 Develin Tower
15 Royal Chapel of St Peter ad Vincula	32 Brass Mount
16 Waterloo Barracks with crown jewels	33 Legge's Mount
17 Devereux Tower	34 Tower Wharf
	35 Queen's Stair

Opposite the Byward Tower stands the Bell Tower, built in about 1190 during the reign of Richard I, in which **Mary Tudor** imprisoned her half-sister **Elizabeth** for two months.

Traitor's Gate is situated between the walls. In the period when the Thames was the main way of travelling from the Palace of Westminster to the Tower, prisoners who had been condemned in Westminster were brought in through this gate.

Traitor's Gate

St Thomas's Tower was built above Traitor's Gate in 1242 during the reign of Henry III. Wakefield Tower held the Crown Jewels until 1968 and now houses an exhibition about torture. Henry VI, the last king from the house of Lancaster, was killed here while at prayer in 1471. The cage with the eight Tower ravens is at the exit. The hall in which the trial of **Anne Boleyn** was held stood next to this tower.

St Thomas's Tower
Wakefield Tower

The Bloody Tower, which was built under Richard II, stands opposite St Thomas's Tower. Here Richard III imprisoned the sons of his deceased brother, Edward IV, who were ten and twelve years old, and is said to have murdered them in 1483. Two hundred years later their skeletons were found in the White Tower. **Sir Walter Raleigh** was kept prisoner in the same tower, generally in comfortable conditions, for a total of 13 years and used the time to write parts of his History of the World. He was eventually beheaded in 1618 for disobedience to the king.

Bloody Tower

Tower Wharf   Between Cradle Tower and Well Tower is the passage from the Inner Ward to Tower Wharf, built in 1228, where artillery salutes are fired to mark the accession and coronation of monarchs and the birth of princes and princesses. This is the privilege of the Honourable Artillery Company (H.A.C.), the oldest British military unit. It was founded by Henry VIII in 1537 as the Brotherhood of St George.

Inner Ward

Queen's House   The Queen's House, a pretty timber-framed building from the time of Henry VIII, is on the left in the Inner Ward. Here **Anne Boleyn** and **Lady Jane Grey** spent their last days, **Guy Fawkes** was interrogated, and **Rudolf Hess** was imprisoned. Next to it is the house of the Yeoman Gaoler, who still attends ceremonies wearing period uniform and carrying an executioner's axe.

Yeoman Gaoler's House ►

Beauchamp Tower   The three-storey Beauchamp Tower (1199–1216) is named after Thomas Beauchamp, Earl of Warwick, who was imprisoned here by Richard II (1397–1399). Other nobles have left their mark here, including John Dudley, who carved a relief, and Lord Guildford Dudley, husband of Lady Jane Grey, who wrote »Jane« on the wall.

View of the White Tower and Traitors' Gate from the south bank of the Thames

At the place of execution the condemned were beheaded with an axe. Henry VIII made an exception only for Anne Boleyn: she died by the sword. However, most executions took place outside on Tower Hill; to be executed within the Tower was a privilege allowed only to Lord Hastings, **Anne Boleyn**, **Catherine Howard** and **Lady Jane Grey**, the Countess of Salisbury and the Earl of Essex.

Scaffold site

The Chapel Royal of St Peter ad Vincula (»St Peter in Chains«) was built in about 1100 and altered in the 13th century. It is the burial place of many of the executed, including **Thomas More** (executed in 1535), Anne Boleyn (1536), Thomas Cromwell (1540), Catherine Howard (1542), Lord Admiral Seymour of Sudeley (1549), Lord Somerset (1552), John Dudley, Earl of Warwick and Duke of Northumberland (1553), Jane Grey and Guildford Dudley (1554), Robert Devereux, Earl of Essex (1601), James Fitzroy, Duke of Monmouth (1685) and Simon, Lord Fraser of Lovat (1747).

Chapel Royal of St Peter ad Vincula

? DID YOU KNOW ...?

■ ... that the eight ravens bear the responsibility of protecting the kingdom of England? It is said that the monarchy will fall if they should ever leave the Tower. There is little danger of this happening, however, as their wings have been clipped and no pains are spared to keep them safe: in the Second World War they were sheltered from the bombing, and during the outbreak of avian flu in 2006 they were taken indoors.

The **Fusiliers' Museum** on the east side of the Inner Ward displays mementoes and trophies of the old-established regiment of Royal Fusiliers, which is based in the Tower. Next to it is the hospital, behind that the east inner wall with the Constable Tower, the Broad Arrow Tower and the Salt Tower. Hugh Draper, who was confined here in 1561 accused of sorcery, inscribed a horoscope on the wall. From 1605 to 1621 Henry Percy, Earl of Northumberland, was imprisoned in the tower on the north-east corner, the Martin Tower, with a cook, three scientific assistants, a library and his own skittle alley. An exhibition about the history of the Crown Jewels now occupies the tower.

◀ Salt Tower

◀ Martin Tower

The Waterloo Barracks take up the whole north side of the Inner Ward. The Crown Jewels are displayed here (see below). A point of interest behind the barracks is the Bowyer Tower, in which the Duke of Clarence is said to have been drowned in a butt of Malmsey wine.

Waterloo Barracks

✶ ✶ Crown Jewels

The Crown Jewels are the biggest draw for tourists in the Tower. When it is very crowded, visitors glide past on an moving walkway. Most of the jewels date from after 1660, as the ancient regalia and jewels were melted down after the execution of Charles I during Cromwell's government.

No photography

The finest of the Crown Jewels

St Edward's Crown was newly made of pure gold for the coronation of Charles II and is the crown used at coronations. The **Imperial State Crown** was commissioned for the coronation of Queen Victoria in 1837; Elizabeth II still wears it at the opening of parliament. It is set with over 2,800 diamonds and other precious stones, including a large spinel ruby at the front which Pedro the Cruel of Castile donated to the Black Prince in 1369 and Henry V wore on his helmet at the battle of Agincourt. One of the two **Stars of Africa**, which were cut from the largest diamond ever found, the **Cullinan**, is also set into the crown. At the back is the Stuart sapphire, which is said to have been in the possession of Edward the Confessor. **The Imperial Indian Crown**, made in 1911, has an emerald weighing more than 34 carats and over 6,000 diamonds. The most famous diamond in the world was used for **Queen Elizabeth's Crown**. This is the legendary, 108-carat **Koh-i-Noor** (»mountain of light«). It belonged to the Rajah of Lahore, Runjit Singh, but was taken from him by the British in 1849 and presented to Queen Victoria. The crown was made for the consort of George VI, the Queen Mother, who died in 2002. The second **Star of Africa**, at 530 carats the largest cut diamond in the world, is set into the **Royal Sceptre**; the ball of **St Edward's Sceptre**, which weighs 40kg/88lb, is said to contain a piece of the True Cross of Christ.

St. Edward's Crown

Imperial State Crown

Among the other exhibits are the silver font in which children of the royal family are christened, the golden vessel for anointing oil in the shape of an eagle and the Anointing Spoon, the only item remaining from the ancient regalia.

White Tower

Oldest part of the Tower

The White Tower, the most important Norman fortress in England, takes its name from the original building material, white stone from Caen in Normandy. In 1078 William the Conqueror ordered its construction on the site of two bastions built by King Alfred in 885. Gundulf, later Bishop of Rochester, was responsible for the design, and Ranulph Flambard, Bishop of Durham, completed the work in about 1100, after which he took up residence as the very first prisoner. The bones of the little princes murdered in the Bloody Tower were found in 1674 below the stairway leading to the first floor. The four-storey tower is 28m/92ft high, and its walls are three to four metres thick. In the 17th century the cupolas were added to the corner towers and the façade was renewed by Sir Christopher Wren.

Royal Armouries

The White Tower houses the royal collections of weapons and armour, which goes back to the reign of Henry VIII. They include light weapons, hunting weapons, magnificent suits of armour for war and tournaments, European weapons and armour from the Middle Ages to the 19th century, as well as Henry VIII's personal arms and armour.

The Yeoman Warders, guardians of the Tower, are always ready to help.

The Chapel of St John the Evangelist, built in about 1080, is on the first and second floors of the south-east tower. With its robust round columns, cushion capitals and the Norman arches of the apse it is one of the finest buildings in England in the Norman style.

Chapel of St John the Evangelist

✴ ✴ Tower Bridge

Location: Whitechapel, EC 1   **Tube:** Tower Hill

Tower Bridge, a wonderful example of Victorian engineering and architecture, ranks alongside Big Ben as London's best-known landmark. Construction began in 1886 to plans by Horace Jones and

TOWER BRIDGE

✴ ✴ **Tower Bridge competes with Big Ben as London's most famous landmark. It undoubtedly has one advantage over the clock-tower of Parliament: visitors can climb up the towers, see the workings of the bridge and, with a little luck, watch how the bridge is raised. In order not to leave it to chance, look at the website www.towerbridge.org.uk/TowerBridge/English/BridgeLifts/schedule.htm or phone (tel. 7940 3984) to find out when the bridge will be raised and the name of the ship that will be passing through.**

🕐 Opening times:
April–Oct daily 10am–5.30pm, Nov–March daily 9.30am–5pm.

① North tower
Like its opposite number, the north tower is 65m/215ft high and stands on a pier weighing 71,120 tons – the heaviest in the world when they were built. The entrance to the exhibition about the bridge is in the north tower.

② High-level walkway
The walkway between the two towers is 33.5m/110ft above the roadway and 42.4m/139ft above the average water level. This leaves plenty of space below the walkway: in 1912 Frank McLean flew a biplane through the gap between it and the roadway.

③ South tower
The exhibition continues in the south tower with insights into the everyday life of the people who built the bridge.

A world-famous landmark

④ Steel frame
The towers consist of a steel frame clad with masonry. A total of 11,481 tons of iron and steel, 37,477 tons of concrete, 20,320 tons of cement, 29,696 tons of bricks and 30,480 tons of stone were needed to build the bridge.

⑤ Bascules
Each of the bascules weighs 1,220 tons and functions on a see-saw principle, rotating 86° in one minute.

⑥ Passage through the bridge
When the bascules are raised, ships of up to 10,000 tons gross weight can pass through the 61m/202ft-wide opening. In 1952 a full double-decker bus had to make the jump across the gap as the bridge opened. The bus was still on the roadway because the bridge-keepers had misinformed the driver.

The inauguration of Tower Bridge on 30 June 1894 was a great occasion. The Prince and Princess of Wales came by coach from Buckingham Palace. The prince turned a large silver knob, the roadway was raised and the bridge thus officially opened.

③

④

*lge is opened on average
week.*

© Baedeker

Horace Jones produced the basic design: a bridge with a roadway that could be raised.

① ② ⑤ ⑥

Today the br[idge ...]
ten times pe[...]

John Wolfe Barry revised Horace Jones's design.

Each bascule is worked by four hydraulic engines. They are powered by three 300-horsepower steam pumping systems in the engine room below the south approach to the bridge.

John Wolfe Barry and was completed in 1894. The bridge has been painted red, white and blue only since 1977 – before that it was battleship grey. Two 82m/270ft-long suspension bridges connect the banks with the neo-Gothic towers, which stand on foundations sunk 7.5m/25ft into the bed of the Thames. The two moving bascules between the towers are 9m/30ft above the water level at high tide; when the bridge was raised, a high-level walkway was originally open to allow pedestrians to cross the river; today admission is charged for this. It takes only one minute to raise the bascules to let large ships through. This spectacle can nowadays be seen several times a week; it used to take place up to fifteen times each day. Tower Bridge is now a museum about itself: the »Tower Bridge Experience« in the towers tells the story of the bridge; the old steam engines and hydraulic equipment are also open to visitors.

✶ ✶ Trafalgar Square

G 6

Location: Westminster, SW 1   **Tube:** Charing Cross

A majestic square

Trafalgar Square is every bit as busy as ▶ Piccadilly Circus but much more attractive, and above all much more harmonious in appearance. It is also a place to meet for Londoners and tourists, especially in summer. Every year a gigantic Christmas tree from Norway is erected on the square as an expression of gratitude for the liberation of Norway from German occupation in the Second World War. The square takes its name from Admiral Nelson's victory over the Franco-Spanish fleet off the Spanish coast near Cape Trafalgar on 22 October 1805. It was designed by **John Nash**. Work began in 1829 but was not completed until 1851 by **Charles Barry**. Barry was responsible for the terrace on the north side in front of the ▶ National Gallery, from which there is a superb view down ▶ Whitehall to Big Ben and Parliament.

? DID YOU KNOW ...?

■ ... that a yard is defined as the distance from the tip of Henry I's nose to the end of his thumb when his arms were outstretched? This, at any rate, is the traditional explanation. Try it out on the standard yard in Trafalgar Square.

Nelson's Column

Nelson's Column rises to a height of 56m/184ft in the centre of the square. It was erected between 1840 and 1843 to a design by William Railton, who modelled it on a column of the Temple of Mars Ultor in Rome. The statue of Horatio Nelson at the top is over 5m/16ft high; before the admiral was put into position, fourteen stonemasons had dinner on the platform. The bronze reliefs on the base cast from French cannon depict scenes from Nelson's four great victories: the Battle of the Nile (1798) is on the north side, the Battle of Copenhagen (1801) on the east, the Battle of St Vincent (1797) on the west, and on the south, the Battle of Trafalgar with the scene of the dying admiral and his famous signal to the fleet: »England expects that every man will do his duty«. The four monumental lions by Edwin Landseer were added in 1868, the two fountains designed by Sir Edwin Lutyens in 1948.

A number of other monuments have been placed on Trafalgar Square: on the east side is Henry Havelock, who conquered Lucknow in India (the column to the right of it was placed there in the 19th century as a hiding place for a policeman, who could watch the goings-on around the square through a slit and phone for reinforcements), in the north-east corner George IV, between the fountains General Gordon, on the west Charles James Napier, who conquered Sind in India, and on the traffic island facing Whitehall an equestrian statue of Charles I by Le Sueur from 1633. It marks the position of Charing Cross, the site of the last of twelve crosses that Edward I had placed along the route of the funeral procession of his wife Eleanor from Nottinghamshire to Westminster.

A monument to Britain's greatest naval hero, Admiral Horatio Nelson

The old British measures of length (**Imperial Standards of Length**) are set in brass into the balustrade on the north side of the square: one foot, two feet and one imperial yard.

The most noteworthy buildings on Trafalgar Square, apart from the ►National Gallery and ►St Martin-in-the-Fields, are Canada House on the west side and South Africa House on the east side. On the south-west corner Admiralty Arch leads to ►The Mall. To the south is ►Whitehall, to the south-east the ►Strand and to the north Leicester Square and ►Soho.

**Canada House
South Africa
House**

★ ★ Victoria and Albert Museum

D 7

Location: Cromwell Road, SW 7   **Tube:** South Kensington
Internet: www.vam.ac.uk

⏱ **Opening times:**
daily
10am–5.45pm,
Wed and last
Fri of the month
until 10pm

Tours
daily 10.30am,
11.30am, 1.30pm,
3.30pm

Queen Victoria's husband, Prince Consort Albert of Saxe-Coburg-Gotha, conceived the idea of a museum that would collect arts and crafts of the highest quality and inspire would-be craftsmen. Many items from the Great Exhibition of 1851, which were put on show in Marlborough House from 1852, formed the basis for this »Museum of Manufactures«. After five years the collection moved to South Kensington. In 1899 Queen Victoria laid the foundation stone for the present building, designed by **Sir Aston Webb**.

Planning a Visit

The V & A is one of the world's major art museums, and also one of the largest. The problem is that its multitude of departments and exhibits can be confusing. The broad division of the museum into two themes helps visitors to get their bearings: »Art and Design« on the ground floor and part of the first floor contains masterpieces from every area of art, organizing them by style, period or country of origin; »Materials and Techniques« arranges the exhibits according to the materials used.

Europe in the Middle Ages and Renaissance

Gloucester candlestick ▶

This tour of the museum stays on level A. The highlights are at the very beginning: the medieval treasures in room 43 include the ivory Symmachi panel (c. AD 400), the Eltenburg reliquary shrine made in Cologne around 1180, the 12th-century Gloucester candlestick and a rare Flemish silver hand reliquary (13th century). On the right (rooms 25 ff.) is medieval art from countries to the north of the Alps, with such fine items as a kneeling angel by Tilman Riemenschneider (c.1500), stained glass from the Chapel of the Holy Blood in Bruges, a Virgin and Child by Veit Stoss and a remarkable gold cup from Nuremberg in the shape of a castle (1475–1500). The rooms behind the Pirelli Gardens are devoted to the Italian Renaissance, but the absolute highlight of this section is in room 48a:

Raphael cartoons ▶

the cartoons that Raphael produced in 1515/16 as designs for the wall-hangings of the Sistine Chapel.

Modern Europe

The second tour explores level A and some rooms on level B. Rooms 1 to 7 present furniture and furnishings between 1600 and 1800, such as Sèvres porcelain and a cabinet by the French furniture maker Charles Boulle. In rooms 8 and 9 there are similar items from the 19th century, including an armchair and cabinet that belonged to Napoleon and Vienna Secession furniture by Adolf Loos and Otto Wagner. The Cast Courts display plaster casts of masterpieces of sculpture: Michelangelo's David, for example, and Trajan's column. British crafts from 1500 until 1900 are in rooms 5 –58 and 118–125.

Here are Roubiliac's statue of Handel, Henry VIII's writing box, the suit worn by James I for his wedding and the earliest English fork. The largest exhibit is the Great Bed of Ware from the White Hart Inn in Ware, which plays a part in Shakespeare's *Twelfth Night*. It measures 3.6m/12ft in length and breadth.

Plaster casts in the V&A

Adjoining the medieval department on level A is **Asian art**, starting with art from China in the T.T. Tsui Gallery (room 44), where there are large exhibits such as a bronze head of Buddha over 1m in height from the Tang dynasty (700–900) and such smaller treasures as a jade box in the shape of eight geese from the Qing dynasty (1750–1820). In the following section there are objects from Japan, including a collection of netsukes and a 13th-century Buddha sculpture. The most precious piece in the Islamic department is the Ardabil carpet, which was produced in1539/1540 for Safi-al Din, the founder of the Safavid dynasty. The Indian department is the largest collection of Indian art outside the

◄ Ardabil carpet

subcontinent; it contains among other items **Tippoo's Tiger**, a late 18th-century wooden mechanical toy made for the Sultan of Mysore that shows a tiger devouring a British soldier. Its mechanism imitates the roars of the tiger and the cries of the victim.

The finest items from the costume collection are in room 40. Above, in room 40 a, is the collection of musical instruments, with a cembalo made in 1521 in the famous Jerome workshop in Bologna. A notable item from the jewellery collection (rooms 91–93) is a 7th-century golden Irish torque. Not to be missed are the **paintings by John Constable** in the Henry Cole

✔ **DON'T MISS**

- The Gloucester candlestick: 12th-century silver (room 43)
- Raphael cartoons: the designs for the Sistine Chapel (room 48a)
- The Great Bed of Ware: masterpiece of English carpentry that featured in one of Shakespeare's plays (rooms 52-58)
- The Ardabil carpet: a superb 16th-century Persian carpet (room 42)
- Tippoo's Tiger: a macabre mechanical figure (room 41)
- Paintings by John Constable (rooms 87 and 88)
- Morris Room, Gamble Room and Poynter Room: magnificent rooms for the first museum restaurant in England

Victoria and Albert Museum

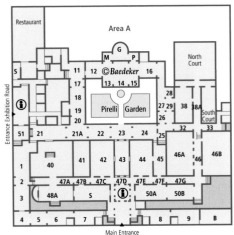

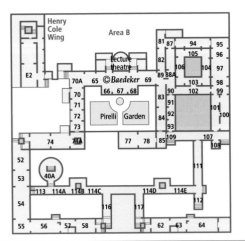

Area A
(levels 0 and 1)

1–7	17th- and 18th-century European furniture
8–9	19th-century European and American art
11–20	Italian Renaissance art
21–22	17th-century European art
23–24	12th- to 15th-century European art
25	15th- and 16th-century Spanish art
27–29	Northern Europe
32–33	Carpets
38	Canon Photo Gallery
40	Dress from 17th century to the present
41	Indian art
42	Islamic art
43	Medieval treasures
44	Chinese art
45	Japanese art
46	Forgeries and copies
46A	Copies of northern European sculpture
46B	Copies of Italian sculpture
47A–E	Indian sculpture
47F–G	Chinese and Korean sculpture
48A	Raphael cartoons
50A–B	Architecture and sculpture
M	Morris Room
G	Gamble Room
P	Poynter Room
S	Museum Shop

Area B
(levels 2 and 3)

40A	Musical instruments
52–58	British crafts 1500–1900
62,63	Best of British
64	European sculpture in stone and wood
65–69	Silver
70A–73	20th-century silver
74	20th-century gallery
77–78	National Art Library
81–82	Metalwork
83–84	Church silver
87–88A	Weapons and armour
89	Copper and brass items

A macabre toy:
Tippoo's Tiger

90 Weapons and armour
91–93 Jewellery and gems
94 Carpets
95–102 Textile collection
103–106 20th-century design
107 Textiles
108 Fans
109 Embroidery
111 Cut and engraved glass
112 Modern glass
113–114E Wrought iron
116–117 Stained glass

Area C
(level 4)

118–126 British crafts
1500–1900
127–128 French ceramics and
enamelwork
129 Temporary exhibitions
131 Glass

Area D
(level 6)

133 Islamic ceramics
134–137 Ceramics and stoneware
138 Temporary exhibitions
139–140 18th- and 19th-century
English porcelain
141 Tiles
142 European porcelain
and enamelwork
143–145 Far Eastern ceramics
and porcelain

Henry Cole Wing

Level 1 Museum Shop
Level 2 Prints, Frank Lloyd
Wright Gallery,
European Ornament Gallery
Level 3 Temporary exhibitions
Level 4 European painting,
Gainsborough, transparencies
and portrait miniatures
Level 5 Prints and drawings
Level 6 Constable watercolours
and paintings

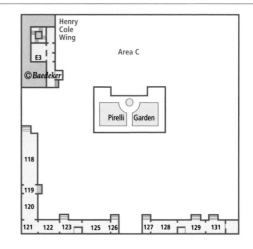

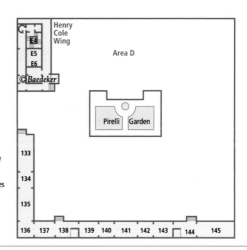

A treasure from the silver department at the V&A: a 13th-century Flemish hand reliquary

Wing (rooms 603–620): the V & A owns the world's largest collection of Constables. In room 406 of this wing wonderful miniatures, mainly from the 16th and 17th centuries, can be seen.

Four further departments are highly recommended: the Glass Gallery, the Ironwork Gallery, which shows the wide range of items that can be made from iron, the 20th Century Gallery (everyday articles) and the Canon Photography Gallery with unique items illustrating the history of photography.

✱ Wallace Collection

E 5

Location: Hertford House, Manchester Square, W 1
Internet: www.wallacecollection.org

Tube: Baker Street, Bond Street

🕐 Opening times:
Mon–Sat
10am–5pm,
Sun noon–5pm

The Wallace Collection has a high-quality and unusually wide range of art and applied art of diverse origins. The fourth Marquis of Hertford, who lived mainly in Paris, built on his forebears' passion for art by developing the family collection into one of the very finest quality; the widow of his son Richard Wallace (1818–1890), who had expanded it further, bequeathed the collection to the nation. Since 1900 the Wallace Collection has been housed in 25 rooms of Hertford House, which was built between 1776 and 1788 for the Duke of Manchester and conveys a good impression of an aristocratic residence of the period. Many rooms contain pieces by the French furniture makers Boulle (1642–1732), Cressent (1685–1768) and Riesener (1734–1806) and are furnished with Sèvres porcelain, bronzes and majolica. Rooms 5 to 8 are devoted to weapons and armour.

Paintings and miniatures

The outstanding items, however, are miniatures, such as a *Portrait of Holbein* by Horenbout in rooms 20 and 21, and above all paintings, including Lawrence's *George IV* and *Countess of Blessington* in room 1, works by Clouet and Foppa in rooms 3 and 4, religious subjects by Murillo in rooms 12 and 19 and views of Venice by Canaletto and Guardi in rooms 13 and 14. 17th-century Dutch and Flemish masters are on show in rooms 15 to 19, including paintings by Rubens (*The Holy Family, Isabella Brandt, The Rainbow Landscape*), Rembrandt (*The Good Samaritan*), Frans Hals (*The Laughing Cavalier*), and van Dyck (*Paris*); as well as Velázquez (*Lady with a Fan*), Titian (*Perseus and Andromeda*), Reynolds (*The Strawberry Girl* and a number of fine society portraits), Gainsborough (*Mrs Robinson*) and Philippe de Champaigne. Apart from works by Sir Joshua Reynolds, the following rooms mainly display French paintings by, for example, Fragonard and Watteau (*The Halt During the Chase*). In the inner courtyard, which has been covered with a glass roof, is an excellent bistro serving French food.

✱
Frans Hals
Laughing
Cavalier ▶

★ ★ Westminster Abbey

Location: Broad Sanctuary, SW 1   **Tube:** Westminster
Internet: www.westminster-abbey.org

Westminster Abbey, officially named The Collegiate Church of St Peter in Westminster and a »Royal Peculiar« subject to the Crown, is not only one of London's greatest tourist attractions but also a church attended by the faithful. For this reason the stream of tourists is channelled along a route beginning at the north door and exiting through the west door.

An Anglo-Saxon church is thought to have occupied this site as early as the 7th century. To distinguish it from the Abbey of St Mary-of-the-Graces further east, known as Eastminster, the church was given the name Westminster. Following destruction by the Danes, **Edward the Confessor** refounded the church in 1065. Starting in the reign of Henry III, Edward the Confessor's building was replaced in its turn by the present church in the French Gothic style. In the year 1388 **Henry Yevele** built part of the abbey, which had been destroyed by

🕐
Opening times:
Mon–Fri
9.30am–16.45pm,
Wed until 6pm,
Sat until 2.45pm
(last admission 1hr
earlier)

Westminster Abbey

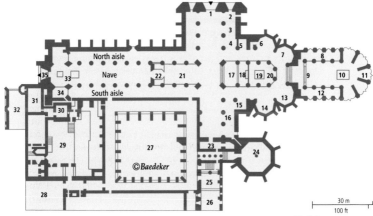

1 North door	10 Tomb of Henry VII	17 Sanctuary
2 Chapel of St Andrew	11 R.A.F. Chapel;	18 High altar
3 Chapel of St Michael	The Battle of Britain	19 St Edward's Chapel
4 Chapel of St John	Memorial Window	20 Henry V's Chantry Chapel
the Evangelist	12 Tomb of Mary,	21 Choir
5 Islip Chapel	Queen of Scots	22 Organ gallery
6 Chapel of St John	13 Chapel of St Nicholas	23 Chapel of St Faith
the Baptist	14 Chapel of St Edmund	24 Chapterhouse
7 Chapel of St. Paul	15 Chapel of St Benedict	25 Chapel of the Pyx
8 Tomb of Elisabeth I	16 Poet's Corner	26 Norman Undercroft
9 Henry VII's Chapel		

27 Cloister	
28 Dean's Yard	
29 Deanery	
30 Jericho Parlour	
31 Jerusalem Chamber	
32 Bookshop	
33 Grave of the unknown	
soldier and monument	
to Sir Winston Churchill	
34 St George's Chapel	
35 West door	

fire in 1298. In 1506 **Abbot Islip** added the roof vaults. The Gothic-style façade with its two 68m/223ft-tall towers was built between 1735 and 1740 by **Nicholas Hawksmoor**, a pupil of Wren. Today Westminster Abbey is 156m/171yd long and 61m/67yd wide at the transepts. The height of the nave, 34m/112ft, makes it the tallest Gothic church interior in England. With the exception of Edward V and Edward VIII, all English kings since William the Conqueror in 1066 have been crowned here, and from the death of Henry III to the funeral of George II in 1760 most English kings were buried here. Persons of national significance are still buried in the abbey or honoured with a memorial tablet.

! **Baedeker** TIP

Organ music
To hear the organ of Westminster Abbey, attend one of the free concerts: every Sunday at 5.45pm.

North Transept

Statesmen's Aisle The north door leads to the north transept, known as Statesmen's Aisle. The memorials to be seen on the right include those for **William Pitt the Elder** († 1778), the statesman and judge Lord Mansfield († 1793) and Warren Hastings († 1818), Governor General of India; on the left are memorials to Lord Norris († 1801) in St Andrew's Chapel, the dramatic tomb of Elizabeth Nightingale († 1734) by Roubiliac in St Michael's Chapel and that of Sir Francis Vere († 1608), a military commander under Elizabeth I, in St John's Chapel. The memorial to Admiral Peter Warren († 1752) is at the ambulatory railing. In front of it is the grave of **William Ewart Gladstone** († 1898) and next to it the memorial to **Sir Robert Peel** († 1850).

Royal Chapels

North ambulatory On the left the way to the royal chapels passes through the north ambulatory, where the two-storey Islip Chapel is situated. The funerary monument to Abbott Islip († 1532), a builder of the church, is in the lower part, a chapel of remembrance for the Medical Corps in the upper part. Adjoining it is the Chapel of St John the Baptist. The graves here include that of Thomas Cecil, Earl of Exeter († 1622), counsellor to James I. The place to Cecil's left was intended for his second wife, who declined to be buried here as the place of honour on the right was occupied by Cecil's first wife. Further on, in the Chapel of St Paul, are the graves of Sir Rowland Hill († 1879; at the front), originator of the penny post system, and **James Watt** († 1819; on the right).

Westminster Abbey is the burial place of many English kings. ➜

★★
Chapel of
Henry VII

Twelve steps of black marble lead to the funeral chapel of Henry VII, built from 1503 to 1519 under the direction of Robert Ertue, Henry's court architect. The nave of the chapel, with its rich decoration and beautiful vault, is a magnificent example of the Perpendicular style. The tombs of Henry VII and his wife are by the Florentine sculptor **Torrigiani**. The marriage of Henry VII († 1509) and Elizabeth of York († 1502), who are portrayed as recumbent figures of gilded bronze, united the houses of Lancaster and York and ended the Wars of the Roses. James I lies in the same vault; George II and Edward VI, among others, have their final resting place in front of the tomb of Henry VII. Above the monument are the banners and wonderfully carved stalls of the Knights of the Order of the Bath.

Innocents'
Corner ▶

Innocents' Corner is in the aisle on the left. Sophie and Mary, daughters of James I who died at the age of just three days and two years respectively, are buried here. Next to these graves is a small sarcophagus with the remains of the sons of Edward IV who were murdered in the ▶ Tower; at the front are the tombs of Queen Elizabeth I († 1603) and Mary Tudor († 1558), Elizabeth's Catholic half-sister (»Bloody Mary«).

Tomb of
Elizabeth I ▶

The small funeral chapels contain the marble tomb of the Duc de Montpensier († 1807), brother of the »citizen king« of France, Louis Philippe; next to it is the Royal Air Force Chapel with the Battle of Britain Memorial Window; to the left of that is the tomb of John Sheffield, Duke of Buckinghamshire († 1723), and in front of it the tomb of **Anne of Denmark** († 1618), the wife of James I. Until 1661 Oliver Cromwell was also buried here.

Tomb of
Mary, Queen of
Scots ▶

The noteworthy features of the aisle on the right are the tomb of Lady Margaret Douglas († 1577), daughter of Queen Margaret of Scotland, surrounded by her seven children, the recumbent effigy of Mary, Queen of Scots, who was beheaded in 1587, and the life-size figure of George Monk, Duke of Albemarle († 1670), who restored the house of Stuart to the throne. Charles II, William III and Queen Mary, and Queen Anne with her consort lie in the vault in front of the right-hand aisle.

Henry V
Chantry Chapel ▶

Following on from Henry VII's Chapel is the Henry V Chantry Chapel. The recumbent figure of Henry V is without its head, which was stolen during the reign of Henry VIII.

★★
St Edward's
Chapel

The wooden shrine of Edward the Confessor († 1066), which lacks its original decoration, stands in the centre of St Edward's Chapel above the apse of the old abbey church. The shrine, erected in 1269 in accordance with the wishes of Henry III, was for a long period a place of pilgrimage and the holiest place in the abbey. The old oak coronation chair of Edward I stands at the back wall of the sanctuary. For 700 years the **Stone of Scone**, the symbol of Scottish royal power made of sandstone from the west coast of Scotland, lay beneath the seat. The heads of the biblical Jacob and of the dying St Columba on the island of Iona are said to have rested on the stone. Edward I

Shrine of Edward
the Confessor and
coronation chair ▶

The Perpendicular style at its most glorious: Henry VII's Chapel

brought the stone to London in 1296 as a sign of the subjugation of the Scots; it was not returned to Scotland until 1996. The sword of state and shield of Edward III are next to the chair. On the side walls it is worth noting (from the right of the chair) the plain tombstone of Edward I († 1308); the magnificent porphyry tomb of Henry III († 1272) with a mosaic; the tomb of Queen Eleanor († 1290), the first wife of Edward I, bearing an inscription in Old French; Philippa of Hainault († 1369), wife of Edward III; Edward III himself († 1377); Margaret Woodville († 1472), a daughter of Edward IV who died at the age of nine months; and finally Richard II, who was murdered in 1399.

In the first chapel of the south ambulatory, the Chapel of St Nicholas, is the marble tomb of Sir George Villiers, first Duke of Buckingham († 1606), and his wife; the wife of Henry V, Catherine of Valois, lay buried under it for 350 years and is now in the Henry V Chantry Chapel. The tomb of Elizabeth, Duchess of Northumberland († 1776) is a masterly work by Robert Adam and Nicholas Read (right).

South ambulatory

Among the finest monuments in the Chapel of St Edmund are those of William de Valence, Earl of Pembroke and half-brother of Henry

III, who died in battle at Bayonne in 1296, with plaques of gilded copper and the recumbent effigy of the earl richly decorated with enamelwork (right); the tomb of Eleanor de Bohun, Duchess of Gloucester († 1399) shown as a nun (centre); the alabaster monuments to John of Eltham († 1334), the second son of Edward II (left), and Edward Talbot, Earl of Shrewsbury († 1617; right).

The highlights of the Chapel of St Benedict are the alabaster tomb of Simon Langham († 1376), Abbot of Westminster and Archbishop of Canterbury, on the left; in the centre the grave of Lionel Cranfield, Earl of Middlesex († 1645), Chancellor of the Exchequer to James I, and that of **Anne of Cleves**, fourth wife of Henry VIII.

South Transept · Choir · Sanctuary

✴
Poets' Corner

After the royal chapels, the route through the abbey goes left into the south transept. Statues and memorials to British poets have been placed on its south wall, and even more on the east wall, giving this part of the church the name »Poets' Corner«. The poets commemorated here include **Sir Walter Scott** († 1832), Oliver Goldsmith († 1774), John Gay († 1732), author of the Beggars' Opera, **William Shakespeare** († 1616), John Dryden († 1700), H.W. Longfellow († 1882), **Geoffrey Chaucer** († 1400), Percy Bysshe Shelley († 1822), Lord Byron († 1824), Robert Burns († 1796), Robert Browning († 1889), **Charles Dickens** († 1870), Lord Tennyson († 1892), Lewis Carroll († 1898), **Rudyard Kipling** († 1936), Dylan Thomas († 1953) and T. S. Eliot († 1965). On the right (the west side): a relief with a group of figures around the actor David Garrick († 1779); the novelist W.M. Thackeray († 1863), **Sir Laurence Olivier** († 1989) and above left a statue of George Frederick Handel by Roubiliac.

Choir and sanctuary

The choir extends beyond the transept into the middle of the nave. The sanctuary, the place where English sovereigns are crowned, faces the altar. Its mosaic floor, brought to London from Rome in 1268, is usually covered. There are three very fine medieval tombs on the left: they belong to the founder of the house of Lancaster, Edmund Crouchback († 1296); Aymer de Valence, Earl of Pembroke († 1324); and Crouchback's wife, Aveline († 1273). The clergy sit on the right on the so-called sedilia, seats of oak that are probably situated above the grave of the 7th-century Saxon king Saebert. An eye-catching feature of the high altar, which Gilbert Scott designed in 1867, is Salviati's glass mosaic depicting *The Last Supper*.

Cloister

In its present form the cloister dates from the 13th and 14th centuries, but it was first built in the 11th century. Here too there are

The choir and main altar of Westminster Abbey →

many graves, as well as a café. The Deanery, Jericho Parlour and Jerusalem Chamber (not open to the public), where Henry IV died, are on the west side of the cloister.

◄ Jerusalem Chamber

Nave

From the cloister the tour enters the south aisle, where a memorial tablet to **Lord Baden Powell** († 1914), founder of the Scout movement, is set into the floor. On the right are the Abbot's Pew, a small oak gallery built in the 16th century by Abbot Islip, and memorials to the Methodist John Wesley († 1791) and **Sir Godfrey Kneller** († 1723), the last-named designed by the artist himself, the only painter commemorated in Westminster Abbey. The monuments on the left include a bust of **Pasquale Paoli** († 1807), a Corsican national hero, and the memorial to William Thynne († 1584), a translator of the Bible.

South aisle

Stone slabs in the nave cover the graves of, among others, the architects Sir Charles Barry († 1860) and Sir Gilbert Scott († 1878), the explorer of Africa **David Livingstone** († 1873), the inventor **Robert Stephenson** († 1859), and the prime ministers Andrew Bonar Law († 1923) and **Neville Chamberlain** († 1940). A short distance from

Nave

the west doorway is the grave of the unknown soldier, who is buried in soil from Flanders, and the memorial stone to **Sir Winston Churchill** († 1965).

North aisle

Above the door to the north aisle is the allegorical monument to **William Pitt the Younger** († 1806). Pitt is portrayed as an orator, with History listening on the right while Anarchy on the left is in chains. Further notable monuments in this aisle commemorate William Wilberforce († 1833), one of the leading opponents of slavery; the statesman Charles James Fox († 1806); the poet **Ben Jonson** († 1637); the composers Orlando Gibbons († 1625) and **Henry Purcell** († 1695); William Croft († 1727), who like Purcell was abbey organist; and **Charles Darwin** († 1882). There is a window in honour of the engineer Isambard Kingdom Brunel († 1859) and on the left at the end of the choir the black sarcophagus of **Sir Isaac Newton** († 1726).

St George's Chapel

Before leaving the abbey it is worth taking a look inside St George's Chapel, which is dedicated to those who fell in the First World War. In addition to the memorial to Franklin D. Roosevelt, a 14th-century portrait of Richard II is particularly worthy of note.

Chapter House · Pyx Chamber · Abbey Museum

🕐
Opening times:
April–Oct daily
10.30am–5.30pm;
Nov–March
until 4pm

The Chapter House can be reached from the cloister or from outside the church through the entrance in Dean's Yard. A single column, a copy of the original made in 1866, supports the vault of the octagonal room (1245–1255), which has a diameter of 20m/66ft. The architect was probably Henry of Reims. Remarkable features of the Chapter House are the Roman sarcophagus in the vestibule and, in the octagon, the 13th-century plasterwork, the ribs around the six windows and the circular 13th-century tympanum above the doorway. The Chapter House was the meeting-place of the Great Council in 1257 and the House of Commons from 1282 to 1547; after that it was an official archive until 1865.

Pyx Chamber

The Pyx Chamber (Chapel of the Pyx), part of Edward the Confessor's church, is the site of the oldest altar in the abbey. The name comes from the pyx, a wooden box that was kept here and held the samples of gold and silver coins used in the annual trial of the coinage of the realm.

The Abbey Museum in the Norman undercroft, a survival from the time of Edward the Confessor, displays **Abbey Museum** seals, documents, Mary II's coronation chair and the saddle, helm and shield of Henry V from the Battle

! *Baedeker* TIP

A wooden head

It is worth taking a close look at the figure of Edward II in the Abbey Museum: it is the oldest wooden image of a monarch in Europe.

of Agincourt. The curiosity of the museum is a collection of life-size wax funeral effigies of prominent persons that were shown in the abbey at their funerals. The figures include those of Charles II, Elizabeth I, Mary II, William III, the Duke of Buckingham and Admiral Lord Nelson.

The College Garden, today used by Westminster School, is thought to be the oldest garden in England (opening times: only Tue–Thu; access from the Little Cloister).   **College Garden**

Around Westminster Abbey

The Tudor gatehouse diagonally opposite the west door of the abbey is approximately on the site where the abbey bell-tower and sanctuary once stood. This was a place of asylum for refugees, including the mother of Edward V, who gave birth to her son in the sanctuary.   **Sanctuary**

Westminster School, one of the leading schools in London, lies to the south of the abbey buildings. It was first mentioned as a monastery school in 1339, but was refounded in 1560 by Elizabeth I. Former pupils include Dryden, Locke, Ben Jonson, Wren, Churchill, Peter Ustinov and Andrew Lloyd Webber. Shrove Tuesday is the occasion for »**tossing the pancake**«, when the school cook throws a pancake to the pupils. The one who grabs the largest piece receives a coin from the dean.   **Westminster School**

Middlesex Guildhall, built in 1913. faces Parliament Square. During the Second World War the Allied military courts sat here. Memorial tablets in the entrance hall with the signatures of George of Greece, Wilhelmina of Holland and Haakon of Norway commemorate this.   **Middlesex Guildhall**

St Margaret's Church to the north of Westminster Abbey, founded by Edward the Confessor in the 11th century and altered between 1488 and 1523 by Robert Stowell on the commission of the wool merchants of Westminster, has been the official church of the House of Commons since Palm Sunday 1614, when a service was held for the members of the house, mostly Puritans, for the first time. The church is also popular for the weddings of the English aristocracy. Winston Churchill, for example, married here. The main attraction of the church is the Flemish stained glass of the east window, a gift from the Spanish monarchs Ferdinand and Isabella for the marriage of Prince Arthur, the older brother of Henry VIII, to Catherine of Aragon. When the window arrived in London, Arthur had already died and Catherine was married to Henry. Then glass was then sent to Waltham Abbey and bought back by Parliament in 1758. The most notable of the funerary monuments is that of **Sir Walter Raleigh**, founder of the state of Virginia, who is thought to have been buried here after his execution.   **St Margaret's Church**

★ Westminster Cathedral

F 7

Location: Ashley Place, SW 1   **Tube:** Victoria

⊙ Opening times: Tower viewing gallery April–Oct daily 9am–5pm, Nov–March Thu–Sun

Westminster Cathedral is the seat of the Cardinal Archbishop of Westminster and, along with Liverpool Metropolitan Cathedral, the most important Catholic church in England. The 120m/132yd-long church was built between 1895 and 1903 in a Romanesque-Byzantine style to designs by John Francis Bentley. Its ground plan is that of a four-domed basilica. Next to the north-west door is the lift to the top of the 94m/308ft-tall St Edward's Tower with a view over much of London. Two columns of red Norwegian granite in the vestibule symbolize the precious blood of Christ, to which the cathedral is dedicated. Next to the left-hand column is a bronze image of St Peter, a copy of the famous seated St Peter from St Peter's Cathedral in Rome. The nave, the widest in England at 52m/170ft, has two aisles. The decoration work is still in progress; the mosaics of the chapels have been completed. The most interesting chapels are St George's Chapel, with the tomb of John Southwark, who died in 1654; the Chapel of St Thomas of Canterbury in the north transept, in which Cardinal Herbert Vaughan, who initiated the construction of the cathedral, is buried; and the Chapel of St Patrick and the Saints of Ireland, where the colours of Irish regiments from the First World War are kept. The crypt chapel, dedicated to St Peter, houses a collection of holy relics, including Thomas Becket's bishop's mitre and fragments of the holy cross.

★ ★ Whitehall

G 6

Location: Westminster, SW 1   **Tube:** Westminster, Embankment, Charing Cross

Government quarter

The street Whitehall has become a synonym for the district from which Britain is governed. The name comes from Whitehall Palace, which stretched for over half a mile from ▶Trafalgar Square to Westminster Bridge on one side, and from the Thames to ▶ St James's Park on the other side. It originated in the 13th century as York Palace, the residence of the Archbishop of York. Cardinal Wolsey extended this palace, and after his fall from favour Henry VIII moved in and made it into a royal palace. He commissioned a great hall for festivities, a jousting ground and the Holbein Gate, a large Renaissance building close to the present site of the Cenotaph. James I had even more ambitious plans, which he entrusted to Inigo Jones and John Webb, but only the Banqueting House was actually built and is the only part of the palace to have survived the fire of 1698.

Winston Churchill and the flags of the Commonwealth on Parliament Square

From Parliament Square to Trafalgar Square

A walk along Whitehall begins at the ►Houses of Parliament on Parliament Square. Around the lawn here are the flags of the Commonwealth states and monuments to British and American statesmen, of which the statue of Sir Winston Churchill is undoubtedly the most impressive. From here walk along Parliament Street towards Trafalgar Square.

Parliament Square

The first street on the left, King Charles Street, divides the Public Offices, a large complex of buildings erected between 1868 and 1873. The northern part houses the Foreign Office, Commonwealth Office, the Home Office and the India Office Library, while the southern part is occupied by the Treasury.

Public Offices

Steps at the end of King Charles Street lead down to the Cabinet War Rooms. The war cabinet directed British operations in the Second World War from these 19 bunker rooms. They have been kept as they were in 1945 with all sorts of interesting items, such as the telephone that Churchill used for conversations with Roosevelt. Even Churchill's simple bedroom has been preserved just as it was – although he preferred to watch the bombing raids from the roof or slept in the Savoy. Some of the rooms have been converted into a Churchill museum(opening times: May–Sept daily 9.30am–6pm, Oct to April from 10am).

✷ Cabinet War Rooms

🕐

Cenotaph Opposite the Foreign Office in the middle of the road is the national monument for the fallen of the two world wars, the Cenotaph (from the Greek, meaning »empty grave«). It was designed by Sir Edward Lutyens and unveiled in 1920 on the second anniversary of the armistice of 11 November 1918 as a memorial to those who died in the »Great War«, as the First World War was known. After the Second World War the dedication was changed and now reads »To the Glorious Dead«. There are no religious symbols on the Cenotaph, just the emblems of the army, air force, royal navy and merchant navy. On Remembrance Day, the second Sunday in November, representatives of the Commonwealth states gather at the Cenotaph at 11am to honour the fallen.

Downing Street On the left is a massive iron gate, guarded by police and besieged by tourists eager to see what lies behind. This is Downing Street, a modest but famous cul-de-sac. Since 1735, when George II put the house at the disposal of the first prime minister, Sir Robert Walpole, number ten has been the prime minister's official residence. Number eleven is the residence of the chancellor of the exchequer, and number twelve is also a government building. All three houses were built in the 1680s for the diplomat Sir George Downing. From outside they are plain-looking, but behind the façades the houses are surprisingly spacious. However, the tourists do not get a good look at the façades, as Downing Street has been closed to the public since the gates were installed in Margaret Thatcher's time.

A famous door: no. 10 Downing Street

Adjoining Downing Street are **Dover House**, headquarters of the Scottish Office and the former **Treasury Building**, the offices of the First Lord of the Treasury, the Chancellor of the Exchequer and the Privy Council.

Horse Guards For most visitors Horse Guards is the highlight of Whitehall. This building, designed by William Kent and completed in 1753, symmetrically arranged around a small courtyard with an arched gateway and two sentry-boxes, occupies the site of the former Whitehall guardhouse. The great attraction, however, is not the building, but

The Queen's Life Guards during the changing of the guard on Horse Guards Parade

the soldiers on guard in front of it: a foot guard and two mounted soldiers of the Household Cavalry who keep to their posts regardless of the tourists scurrying around them. The Household Cavalry consists of the Queen's Life Guards with their scarlet coats and helmets with white plumes, and the Blues and Royals, who have a blue coat and a red plume. The Life Guards began as the personal bodyguard of Charles I, while the Blues and Royals originated as a regiment under Cromwell. The Changing of the Guard, which takes place every day (Mon–Sat 11am, Sun 10am) in almost every weather, is an extremely popular tourist attraction. To get a good view it is advisable to arrive early. The Horse Guards are based in Hyde Park Barracks in Knightsbridge, and the long ride back to the barracks is timed so that they ride past ▶Buckingham Palace at about the moment when the Foot Guards parade there.

✶ ✶
◀ Changing of the Guard

Behind the Horse Guards building and facing ▶St James's Park is the parade ground Horse Guards Parade. In June the official birthday of Queen Elizabeth II is celebrated here with the colourful pageantry of **Trooping the Colour**. However, normal tourists and Londoners can only glimpse this spectacle from a distance.

◀ Horse Guards Parade

On the opposite side of the road is the Banqueting House, the only part of Whitehall Palace to have been preserved in its entirety. It is the third building on this site but the first in London to be designed in the Palladian style, a task entrusted by Charles I to **Inigo Jones**. It was built between 1619 and 1622. It is a clear expression of Palladian

Banqueting House

London policemen are, of course, friendly at all times.

THE LONDON POLICE AND THEIR FOREBEARS

»Wanted: one hundred thousand men to serve as watchmen in London. The following need not apply for this lucrative position: all those who are under the age of sixty, seventy, eighty or ninety and who are not blind in one eye and scarcely able to make out anything with the other; deaf as a doorpost; possessed of a racking asthmatic cough; fast as a snail and so sturdy that they are not able to lock away a stout old washerwoman for her rascally doings.«

This job advertisement published in 1821 in a London newspaper satirized the pathetic condition of the London police – or what purported to be a police force. There was, to be precise, **no police force for the whole of London**, but only unreliable bands of watchmen in the boroughs, especially the City. The reason for this state of affairs was that the most recent law on policing with general validity was the statute of Winchester of 1285, which in principle still applied. It required that every male subject of the Crown between the ages of 15 and 60 »shall have in his house arms for keeping the peace«. A special statute for London stipulated that every free citizen and taxpayer should serve on the night-watch. Many of the smarter »free

Londoners« avoided this duty by hiring substitutes, usually old, lame or unemployed persons whose idea of devotion to duty was such that they became notorious for their idleness, stupidity, brutality and drunkenness. This was hardly surprising, as officially they earned not a single penny.

The Poacher as Gamekeeper

The aldermen of London did at least give some thought to the safety of their fellow-citizens. In 1603 the office of City Marshal, the head of the watchmen, was created. However, this did little to improve the quality of the force, and the only effect of a further law, designed to regulate the watch precisely and passed in 1663 shortly after the restoration of

Two landmarks that tourists love: Big Ben and a policeman's helmet.

Charles II, was to give the watchmen the **nickname »Charley«**. The results were the opposite of what was intended: the security force attracted dubious characters. The most sinister of them was Jonathan Wild, first a marshalman and later »Thieftaker General of Great Britain and Ireland«. He took full advantage of the fact that rewards were paid for stolen goods restored to the owner, and earned a fortune by controlling a small army of burglars, pickpockets and footpads – though only until 1725, when he was hanged at Tyburn.

Serious Efforts

The first attempt to form a true police force was made in 1742 by the author Henry Fielding in his capacity as alderman of the City, and later by his brother John. The first of »Mr Fielding's people« were seven fearless men who pursued thieves and burglars, and went down in the history of London as the **»Bow Street runners«**, as their headquarters was in Bow Street near Covent Garden. It may have been this that prompted the City of London to create a police force that kept watch during daylight hours as

well as after dark. These men were dressed in capacious blue coats, as blue was regarded as the most suitable colour for lending dignity to an execution. In 1798 the Thames Police was founded to counteract river pirates, and in 1805 the Bow Street Runners were reinforced by a mounted unit as a measure against highwaymen on country roads. They patrolled an area of 20 miles around London and were known as »Robin Redbreasts« due to their red waistcoats.

Scotland Yard

London still lacked a police force that was responsible for the whole city and, above all, competent. The man who took up the cause was **Sir Robert Peel** (1788–1850), who made a first attempt in 1821 when he was home secretary. The main opposition to his plan came from the City of London, and Peel was not able to get his Metropolitan Police Bill (1829) through Parliament until he conceded the right of the City to retain its own police force. This law created a new force directly responsible to the home secretary: the **London Metropolitan**

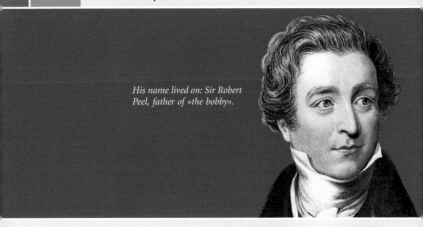

His name lived on: Sir Robert Peel, father of »the bobby«.

Police, who quickly set up their headquarters in a building at the back of No. 4, Whitehall Place. Access to the building was through a yard with a now-famous name: Scotland Yard, the best-known police force in the world, was born. It originally consisted of 3,000 men clothed in blue uniforms and top hats, which they were also required to wear when off duty. This soon changed, as the new force was not at all popular, and there were cases of people being murdered or, if they were lucky, only beaten by Peel's »blue devils«. The requirement to wear uniform in private was rescinded. In its early years the role of the Metropolitan Police was purely to maintain public order. Moreover, it had competitors. In 1839 the Bow Street Runners and the Thames Police were merged with it, but the same year saw the foundation of the City of London Police, which still exists today. It was not until 1842, following two spectacular murders, that the first criminal investigation department was founded in Scotland Yard. By the time the force acquired a new uniform – a cloak and the famous helmet – in 1864, it already had a considerable reputation, expressed in the nickname »Bobby«, which perpetuated the memory of Sir Robert Peel. The criminal investigation department was greatly expanded in the early 1870s. Its successes lie behind the fame of Scotland Yard, in spite of setbacks such as the Jack the Ripper murders, which remain unsolved to this day, and it tends to be forgotten that detectives constitute only a part of the Metropolitan Police.

Although they are not universally loved by local citizens, the London police have an international reputation for helpfulness. This, too, is rooted in tradition: from the very beginning they were unarmed. It is also noticeable that Scotland Yard detectives are seldom portrayed as heroes in crime fiction. They are generally represented as, at best, honest triers lacking in imagination,, and sometimes even appear as buffoons, as in the Sherlock Holmes, Miss Marple and Hercule Poirot stories. Perhaps this should be seen as an indication that the Metropolitan Police operate collectively, with each officer doing his job in an inconspicuous way.

principles: the horizontal lines marked by rows of windows on two storeys and alternating segmental and triangular pediments, the verticals by Ionic columns and pilasters on the ground floor and Corinthian columns and pilasters on the first floor. The Banqueting House served as a hall for royal banquets and receptions and is still used by the royal family and government. History was made here: in 1533 the marriage of Anne Boleyn and Henry VIII took place in the previous building, in which Henry also died; Princess (later Queen) Elizabeth was conducted from here to the Tower. Charles I had to pass through a window to the scaffold erected on Whitehall – a bust of him by Le Sueur above the entrance marks the spot; Charles's successor Oliver Cromwell lived and died (1658) within the walls of the palace, and at the restoration of the Stuarts this was the place where Parliament swore fealty to the new monarch Charles II. William of Orange received the offer of royal sovereignty after the Glorious Revolution in the Banqueting House.

✸ ✸
◀ Rubens ceiling

Inside the Banqueting House is a single room in the shape of a double cube, 38m/125ft in length, 18m/60ft in width and 18m/60ft in height. The glory of the room are the nine allegorical ceiling paintings which Charles I commissioned Peter Paul Rubens to carry out in 1635. The apotheosis of Charles I is at the centre, and a further motif is the union of the crowns of England and Scotland. Rubens received £3,000 and a knighthood for the work (opening times: Mon–Sat 10am – 5pm).

🕐

Ministry of Defence

To the right of the Banqueting House is the massive headquarters of the Ministry of Defence. The standards of the British armed forces fly from the roof of the building, which stands on part of the remains of Whitehall Palace: Henry VIII's wine cellar. In front are monuments to Sir Walter Raleigh and Field Marshal Montgomery.

Old War Office

Beyond Horse Guards Avenue and next to the Banqueting House is the Old War Office. At the end of Horse Guards Avenue, overlooking the Thames, is a further remnant of Whitehall Palace: Queen Mary's Terrace. Sir Christopher Wren designed the steps and quay in 1691.

Scotland Yard

Back on Whitehall there is a street on the right with the name Great Scotland Yard. Until the 16th century the Scottish kings had a palace here. However, Scotland Yard became a legendary address as the first headquarters of the London Metropolitan Police, founded in 1829 by Sir Robert Peel. In 1890 the police moved out, and since 1967 have been based in New Scotland Yard in Victoria Street close to ►Westminster Abbey.

Old Admiralty

On the opposite side of the road is the Old Admiralty building. The older part is a work of Thomas Ripley dating from 1723–1726, while the domed extension at the back was added between 1895 and 1907. From here ►Trafalgar Square is only a few steps away.

Wimbledon

Outer suburb

Location: south London **Tube:** Southfields
Internet: www.wimbledon.org

Mecca for tennis fans Every summer Wimbledon, a desirable residential area with well-tended gardens, extensive parks and sports grounds about 10km/6mi south of the city centre, is the venue for the world-famous tennis tournament. The tournament has a strange history. The organizer, the All England Lawn Tennis and Croquet Club, originally existed only for the game of croquet. In 1877, when the club needed money to buy a roller for the lawn, the members hit upon the idea of staging a tennis tournament. Tennis was then coming into fashion, and the contestants' starting fees were used to buy the roller, which is displayed in a prominent position.

Wimbledon Lawn Tennis Museum Visitors to Wimbledon Lawn Tennis Museum in Church Road (gate 4) can find out everything they wanted to know about the »white sport«, admire tennis equipment, see the famous trophies and even take a look at the hallowed turf of Centre Court (opening times: daily 10.30am–5pm).

Holy ground for tennis players: Wimbledon Centre Court

Southside House , part of Wimbledon King's College School built in 1687, is undeservedly often overlooked. It is not just the home of the Pennington family, who live here as in the old days with candlelight and open fires, but a store of hidden treasures: paintings by Anthony van Dyck and Hogarth, Romney's portrait of Lady Hamilton, the necklace that Marie-Antoinette wore on the scaffold ... (tours Easter to Sept, Wed–Sun 2pm, 3pm, 4pm).

? DID YOU KNOW ...?

■ ... that the most successful Wimbledon contestant of all time was neither Pete Sampras nor Björn Borg, neither Steffi Graf nor Martina Navratilova, but Hugh Lawrence »Laurie« Doherty? Doherty won no less than 14 titles between 1897 and 1906: the singles from 1902 to 1906 and the men's doubles with his brother Frank »Reggie« Doherty from 1897 to 1905. To keep things in the family, Reggie held the singles title from 1897 to 1900.

★ ★ Windsor Castle

Excursion

Location: Windsor, Berkshire, 35km/ 22mi west of London
Bus: Green Line 700, 701, 702 from Victoria Station and Hyde Park Corner

Train: Windsor & Eton Riverside from Waterloo; Windsor & Eton Centre from Paddington, change in Slough

Everyone who stays in London for longer than just a few days should go to Windsor. The world's largest inhabited castle is well worth the trip. Windsor Castle rises above the Thames on a chalk rock. Edward the Confessor was responsible for the construction of the first, wooden castle. In about 1110 Henry I had the first stone structures built. In the reign of Henry II the wooden palisade was replaced by a stone wall with square towers, and Henry III extended the defences. In 1189 the English barons laid siege to the castle and defeated the Welsh troops of Prince John, later to be King John Lackland, who was forced to sign **Magna Carta** a short distance away in Runnymede. Edward III, born in 1312 in Windsor, tore down the old wooden castle and had William of Wykeham, Bishop of Winchester, build further fortifications, including the Round Tower. The north terrace was added under Elizabeth I. In the reign of Charles II the castle was converted into a comfortable palace, but was little used and extended only when George III took up residence in 1800. George IV ordered thorough restoration work, which continued into the reign of Queen Victoria.

Windsor has been the summer residence of the royal family for 900 years. When the queen is at home, her standard flies from the Round Tower; but her rest is surely disturbed by the aircraft that take off from Heathrow and roar over the castle at low altitude. The buildings are grouped around two courtyards, the Lower Ward and Upper Ward, between which the Round Tower stands. The Lower Ward is

🕐
Opening times:
March–Oct daily
10am–5.15pm,
Nov–Feb daily
10am–4.15pm,
last admission
1 1/4 hrs earlier

Changing of the
guard April–June
Mon–Sat 11am;
July–March
every other day

Windsor Castle, the residence of English monarchs, rises majestically above the Thames.

bordered on the north by St George's Chapel; the apartments of state are situated on the north side of the Upper Ward.

Lower Ward · Middle Ward

The entrance to the Lower Ward is the monumental Henry VIII Gateway, built in the reign of that king. The south side of the court, between the Salisbury Tower and the Henry III Tower, was once accommodation for members of the Order of Military Knights of Windsor, founded by Edward III.

Horseshoe Cloisters

Curfew Tower ▶

Horseshoe Cloisters, opposite the entrance gate, was built in the time of Henry IV and takes its name from the ground plan. In the northwest corner lies the entrance to the Curfew Tower, which was built in 1227 under Henry II and is the oldest surviving part of the castle; it includes part of the dungeon and an escape tunnel.

Canons' Residence

A small courtyard situated towards the Thames houses the canons of St George's Chapel and the chapter library, both of which are part of Canons' Cloister, dating from 1333. In 1390 **Geoffrey Chaucer** spent time in the Winchester Tower in the north-east corner.

Deanery

A walk along the north side of St George's Chapel leads to the pretty Dean's Cloisters, built in 1356, and the Deanery.

Windsor Castle

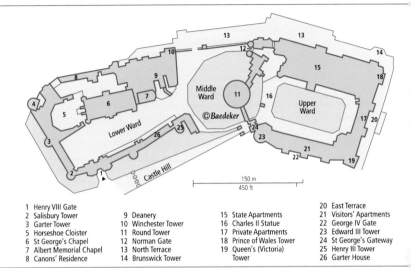

1 Henry VIII Gate
2 Salisbury Tower
3 Garter Tower
5 Horseshoe Cloister
6 St George's Chapel
7 Albert Memorial Chapel
8 Canons' Residence
9 Deanery
10 Winchester Tower
11 Round Tower
12 Norman Gate
13 North Terrace
14 Brunswick Tower
15 State Apartments
16 Charles II Statue
17 Private Apartments
18 Prince of Wales Tower
19 Queen's (Victoria) Tower
20 East Terrace
21 Visitors' Apartments
22 George IV Gate
23 Edward III Tower
24 St George's Gateway
25 Henry III Tower
26 Garter House

St George's Chapel is the **chapel of the Order of Knights of the Garter**. This remarkable example of late Perpendicular architecture was begun in 1474 by Edward IV on the site of a chapel of Henry I and completed in the reign of Henry VIII (opening times: Mon–Sat 10.30am–3pm). The enormous window above the main entrance contains 75 stained-glass windows from the 16th century. They portray popes, kings, princes, military commanders, bishops and saints. Since 1882 the north and south façades have been adorned with the coats of arms and heraldic beasts of the houses of York and Lancaster: falcon, stag, bull, black dragon, hind and greyhound for York; lion, unicorn, swan, antelope, panther and red dragon for Lancaster.

In the bright interior, the eye is drawn to the wonderful fan vault of the nave. The 15th-century choir with its choir stalls carved from Windsor oak is especially magnificent. The rich detail of the carvings depicts scenes from the lives of St George, Edward III and the Knights of the Garter. The coats of arms, swords and standards of 700 Knights of the Garter are behind and above the choir stalls. The graves of **Henry VIII**, Jane Seymour and **Charles I** are in the centre of the choir. Below it is the Royal Tomb House, built in 1240, in which **George III**, **George IV** and **William IV** are buried. Further notable features are the Bray Chapel, now the bookshop, with the funerary monument of Sir Reginald Bray († 1503) in the south aisle; in the south-west corner the Beaufort Chapel with the tombs of the Earl of Worcester († 1526) and the Duke of Kent, father of Queen Victoria; in the north-west corner the Urswick Chapel with a marble monu-

★ ★
St George's Chapel

ment to Charlotte, a daughter of George IV, and diagonally opposite the tomb of **George V** and Queen Mary; among those buried in the north ambulatory are **George VI** (left) and **Edward IV** (right); in the south ambulatory **Edward VII** and **Henry VI**; in the south-east corner is the Lincoln Chapel with the tomb of the Earl of Lincoln († 1585) and his countess, and on the wall of the choir the Oxenbridge Chantry, with the sword of Edward III attached to its south wall.

✱
Albert
Memorial
Chapel

The Albert Memorial Chapel is next to St George's Chapel. It was built by Henry VII as his funeral vault, but remained empty, as he was buried in ► Westminster Abbey. James II used it as a Catholic chapel, and Queen Victoria ordered alterations to make it into a place of memorial for her consort, **Prince Albert** after his death in 1861. It is lavishly decorated with marble, mosaics, sculpture and stained glass showing scenes from the Bible, members of the royal dynasty and relatives of Prince Albert, whose remains lie in a sarcophagus. To the right of it is the porphyry sarcophagus of the Duke of Clarence († 1892), the eldest son of Edward VII. The marble figure in Scottish dress by the west door represents the Duke of Albany († 1884).

St George's Chapel is the place of worship of the Order of Knights of the Garter.

The Round Tower rises majestically between the Lower Ward and the Upper Ward. It was built in the reign of Edward III on an artificial mound on which William the Conqueror had erected a keep. A wonderful panorama of the castle and Thames valley is the reward for climbing to the viewing terrace 24m/80ft above the ground.

Round Tower

Upper Ward

The Upper Ward or Quadrangle is bounded by the State Apartments in the north, the Visitors' Apartments in the south and the Private Apartments of the royal family in the east. A statue of Charles II made in 1679 stands on the west side of the courtyard.

The State Apartments are open to visitors when the court is not in residence (same opening times as the castle). In their present form they are largely the result of alterations by Geoffrey Wyattville in the first half of the 19th century. A tour of the apartments leads from the terrace to the room in which **Queen Mary's Doll House**, produced by Edward Lutyens in 1923, is displayed.

✷ ✷ State Apartments

This is followed by the collection of porcelain in the China Museum and the Grand Staircase, which is dominated by Chantrey's statue of George IV and decorated with weapons and armour, including a suit of armour that belonged to Henry VIII.

◀ Grand Staircase

The Grand Vestibule is equipped with armour, standards and military mementoes such as a cloak that Napoleon wore. An exhibit which almost has the status of a holy relic is the bullet that killed Nelson at the battle of Trafalgar.

◀ Grand Vestibule

The walls of the 30m/98ft-long Waterloo Chamber, decorated with carvings by Grinling Gibbons and an enormous Indian carpet, are hung with portraits of men connected with the events of the years 1813 to 1815, including Wellington, Blücher, Castlereagh, Metternich, Pope Pius VII, Tsar Alexander I, Friedrich Wilhelm III of Prussia and the English kings George III and George IV.

◀ Waterloo Chamber

From here turn left into the Garter Throne Room, where the Order of the Garter has been awarded since the reign of George IV. The large reception room adjoining is decorated in opulent Rococo style. Tapestries depicting the story of Jason and Medea and a large malachite vase, a present from Tsar Nicolas I, can be seen here.

◀ Garter Throne Room Grand Reception Room

The queen's banqueting hall, the 14th-century St George's Hall, was destroyed by fire in 1992 but has now been restored. The paintings include works by van Dyck, Kneller and Lely.

◀ St George's Hall

The next rooms were the state chambers of the queen. In the Queen's Guard Chamber armour, Indian cannon and a golden shield presented to Henry VIII by François I of France are displayed. The ceiling in the Queen's Presence Chamber with a portrait of Catherine of Braganza was painted by **Antonio Verrio**. The tapestries, which tell the story of Esther and Mordechai, continue in the Queen's Audience Chamber, which also has a ceiling painted by Verrio. The Queen's

◀ Queen's Rooms

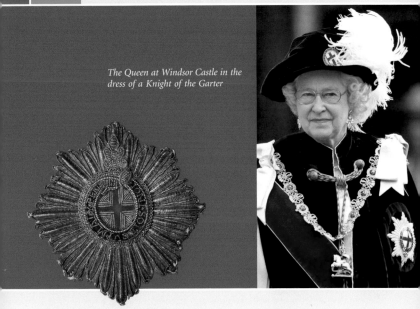

The Queen at Windsor Castle in the dress of a Knight of the Garter

HONI SOIT QUI MAL Y PENSE

In 1348 at Windsor Castle King Edward III founded the Most Noble Order of the Garter, the highest decoration that the kingdom of England can bestow.

The occasion for the foundation of the order is said to have been a feast at which a lady lost her garter. The king picked up the garter and put it round his own leg, which aroused much laughter among the courtiers. Edward retorted that his knights would soon be honoured to receive such a garter. The Order of the Garter, modelled on Arthur's Round Table, was an attempt to establish a select band of men who would maintain knightly virtues in an era, the late Middle Ages, when it was apparent that chivalry was on the wane. Membership was confined to 26 knights or – in modern times – ladies, though this number can be exceeded through nomination of supernumerary knights by the monarch, who is the sovereign of the order. The order is awarded in a splendid ceremony in the Garter Throne Room at Windsor Castle. On ceremonial occasions the insignia of the order, which are on view in room 46 of the British Museum, consist of a heavy gold collar bearing a figure known as »The George«, on less important occasions a riband over the left shoulder with a badge called »The Lesser George«, in addition to the famous garter of dark blue velvet with the motto »Honi soit qui mal y pense«, meaning »dishonour to those who think it dishonourable«, which the knights wear below their left knee and the ladies on their upper left arm. The knights wear their regalia on the Monday of Royal Ascot week in June for a service in St George's Chapel.

Ballroom, built under Charles II for Catherine of Braganza, was hung in George IV's reign with paintings by **Anthony van Dyck**, including *Charles I and his Family, The Children of Charles I, Charles I on Horseback* and a self portrait of the artist. The last room in the suite was the queen's private chamber and is now known as the Queen's Drawing Room. The works of art here include van Dyck's painting of Charles I's five children.

The highlights of the King's Closet and the King's Wardrobe are paintings by Holbein, Rubens, Rembrandt and van Dyck's famous *Triple Portrait of Charles I*. Works by Canaletto and Gainsborough are hung in the next room, the King's State Bed Chamber; the King's Drawing Room has Rubens's *Holy Family*, and van Dyck's *Saint Martin*. The final room is the King's Dining Room with wood carvings by Grinling Gibbons, a fine ceiling painted by Verrio (1678–1680) and a portrait of Catherine of Braganza by Jacob Huysmans.

◄ King's Rooms

Frogmore House and Mausoleum, the burial place of Queen Victoria, are in Home Park. It is open to visitors only for a few days in May and August (information tel. 7 766 7305).

Home Park
Great Park

Windsor · Eton

The town of Windsor with its half-timbered houses and inns dating from the 17th and 18th centuries, its narrow, crooked alleys and cobblestones presents an essentially medieval appearance. The Guildhall was designed by Sir Christopher Wren.

Windsor

Legoland is a short distance out of town on the B 3022 towards Ascot. The attractions of the 60ha/150-acre site are rides, a medieval castle, pirate ships, a miniature town and all manner of technical wonders made with the famous coloured bricks. A shuttle bus starts from Windsor parish church and opposite the Theatre Royal (opening times: mid-March–Oct daily 10am–6pm, Aug until 8pm).

✱
Legoland
Windsor

🕑

Eton is just across the Thames bridge. The world-famous Eton College, founded in 1440 by Henry VI, is one of England's elite schools. Former pupils include Henry Fielding, William Pitt, Percy Bysshe Shelley, William Ewart Gladstone and the Duke of Wellington. The Lower School, for the younger boys, was built between 1624 and 1639, the Upper School from 1689 to 1692. The most remarkable feature of the buildings is the school chapel, built in 1441 in the Perpendicular style. Its late 15th-century wall paintings depict scenes from the life of the Virgin. There is a small museum about the history of the college.

Eton

INDEX

LIST OF MAPS AND ILLUSTRATIONS

PHOTO CREDITS

AKG p. 29 (above), 31, 50, 233
Baedeker-Archiv p. 3 (below), 4 (left), 26, 28, 38 (2 x), 51, 68, 71, 98, 126, 143 (above), 226 (below), 241 (above left, below right)
Corporation of London p. 268 (right), 269 (below 2x, above left)
Courtauld Institute Galleries p. 161
Eisenschmid p. 1, 4 (right), 21, 55, 94, 117, 128, 137 (right), 146, 149, 164, 165, 177, 181, 195, 199, 201, 211, 230, 254, 260, 287
HB Verlag/Kiedrowski p. 2 (2 x), 5, 7 (above) 12, 13 (above left, below left), 14 (above left), 16, 36, 52/53, 63, 66, 75, 100, 104, 112, 119, 125, 130/131, 145, 150, 152, 155, 156, 159, 172, 174, 196, 205, 210, 219, 221, 227, 234, 248, 251, 266, 270, 273, 283,

inside back cover (2 x)
Heathrow Express p. 59
Hemispheres/laif p. 169
IFA p. 14 (right), 137 (left), 180, 288, 294
Interfoto p. 24, 29 (below), 32, 47, 48, 226 (above), 292, 300 (left)
laif p. 7 (below), 4, 13 (centre), 22, 42, 127, 142/143, 235, 250
London Transport p. 106, 108, 124
look p. 8 (above), 10/11, 53, 78, 81, 78, 134, 192
Maier p. 6 (below), 4 (left), 8 (right), 9 (centre and below), 11, 14 (below left), 18, 56, 76, 102, 106, 107, 179, 184, 191 (above left), 237, 243, 245, 258, 290
Mauritius p. 206
Müller front cover inside, 232, 264, 278
National Gallery p. 3 (above left), 216

National Portr. Gallery p. 217
picture alliance/dpa p. 19, 34, 43, 44, 46, 69, 70, 115, 190, 191 (below left and above centre), 240, 255, 269 (above right), 291, 300 (right)
picture alliance/photoshot p. 208
Scala p. 241 (far right)
Stetter p. 5 (center), 9 (above), 136, 178, 190, 191 (far right)
Thomas p. 23, 113, 118, 139, 163, 185, 186, 193, 198, 203, 223, 229, 236, 242, 247, 252, 271, 289, 298
University of Bristol p. 268 (left)
Victoria & Albert Museum p. 274, 275
Wrba p. 3 (above right), 281
ZEFA p. 74, 296
Zegers p. 15

cover photo: laif/Jänicke

PUBLISHER'S INFORMATION

Illustrations etc: 218 illustrations, 22 maps and diagrams, one large city plan
Text: Rainer Eisenschmid, with contributions by Dr. Eva-Maria Blattner, Martina Johnson, Reinhard Strüber, John Sykes and Werner Voran
Editing: Baedeker editorial team (Rainer Eisenschmid, John Sykes)
Translation: John Sykes
Cartography: Christoph Gallus, Hohberg; Franz Huber, Munich; MAIRDUMONT/Falk Verlag, Ostfildern (city plan)
3D illustrations: jangled nerves, Stuttgart
Design: independent Medien-Design, Munich; Kathrin Schemel

Editor-in-chief: Rainer Eisenschmid, Baedeker Ostfildern

1st edition 2008

Copyright: Karl Baedeker Verlag, Ostfildern
Publication rights: MAIRDUMONT GmbH & Co; Ostfildern

Printed in China

DEAR READER,

We would like to thank you for choosing this Baedeker travel guide. It will be a reliable companion on your travels and will not disappoint you.
This book describes the major sights, of course, but it also recommends the best pubs, as well as hotels in the luxury and budget categories, and includes tips about where to eat or go shopping and much more, helping to make your trip an enjoyable experience. Our author Rainer Eisenschmid ensures the quality of this information by making regular journeys to London and putting all his know-how into this book.

Nevertheless, experience shows us that it is impossible to rule out errors and changes made after the book goes to press, for which Baedeker accepts no liability. Please send us your criticisms, corrections and suggestions for improvement: we appreciate your contribution. Contact us by post or e-mail, or phone us:

▶ **Verlag Karl Baedeker GmbH**
Editorial department
Postfach 3162
73751 Ostfildern
Germany
Tel. 49-711-4502-262, fax -343
www.baedeker.com
E-Mail: baedeker@mairdumont.com

Baedeker Travel Guides in English at a glance:

▶ Andalusia

▶ Dubai · Emirates

▶ Egypt

▶ Ireland

▶ London

▶ Mexico

▶ New York

▶ Portugal

▶ Rome

▶ Thailand

▶ Tuscany

▶ Venice